THE MEMOIRS OF BABUR

THE
MEMOIRS OF BABUR

ANNETTE S. BEVERIDGE

GYAN

Published by

Gyan Publishing House
5, Ansari Road
Daryaganj, New Delhi-110002
Phone: 011-47034999, 9811692060
E-mail: books@gyanbooks.com

Distribution Network
gyanbooks.com
India, USA, Canada, UK, Australia

ISBN: 978-93-7014-114-8 (PB)

First Published, 1908

2nd Impression 2025

Printed at: Gyan Press, Delhi.

THE MEMOIRS OF BABUR
Author: ANNETTE S. BEVERIDGE

The Memoirs of Bābur

A New Translation of the Bābur-nāma, incorporating Leyden and Erskine's of 1826 A.D.

BY

ANNETTE S. BEVERIDGE, M.R.A.S.

Fasciculus I. Farghāna

To follow :

„ II. Kābul

„ III. Hindūstān

„ IV. Preface, Index, Maps, etc.

LONDON : LUZAC & CO., 46 Great Russell Street, W.C.

(Opposite the British Museum)

THE MEMOIRS OF BABUR

SECTION I. FARGHĀNA.

In the name of God, the Merciful, the Compassionate.

In[1] the month of Ramẓān of the year 899 (June 1494) and in the twelfth year of my age,[2] I became ruler[3] in the country of Farghāna. Haidarābād MS. fol. 1b.

(a. Description of Farghāna.)

Farghāna is situated in the fifth climate[4] and at the limit of settled habitation. On the east it has Kāshghar; on the west, Samarkand; on the south, the mountains of the Badakhshān border; on the north, though in former times there must have been towns such as Almālīgh, Almātū and

[1] The manuscripts relied on for revising the first section of the Memoirs, (*i.e.* 899 to 908 AH.—1494 to 1502 AD.) are the Elphinstone and the Ḥaidarābād Codices. To variants from them occurring in Dr. Kehr's own transcript no authority can be allowed because throughout this section, his text appears to be a compilation and in parts a retranslation from one or other of the two Persian translations (*Wāqi'āt-i-bāburi*) of the *Bābur-nāma*. Moreover Dr. Ilminsky's imprint of Kehr's text has the further defect in authority that it was helped out from the Memoirs, itself not a direct issue from the Turkī original.

Information about the manuscripts of the *Bābur-nāma* can be found in the JRAS for 1900, 1902, 1905, 1906, 1907 and 1908.

The foliation marked in the margin of this book is that of the Ḥaidarābād Codex and of its facsimile, published in 1905 by the Gibb Memorial Trust.

[2] Bābur, born on Friday, Feb. 14th. 1483 (Muḥarram 6, 888 AH.), succeeded his father, 'Umar Shaikh who died on June 8th. 1494 (Ramẓān 4, 899 AH.).

[3] *pād-shāh*, protecting lord, supreme. It would be an anachronism to translate *pādshāh* by King or Emperor, previous to 913 AH. (1507 AD.) because until that date it was not part of the style of any Tīmūrid, even ruling members of the house being styled Mīrzā. Up to 1507 therefore Bābur's correct style is Bābur Mīrzā. (*Cf.* f. 215 and note.)

[4] See *Āyīn-i-akbarī*, Jarrett, p. 44.

Yāngī which in books they write Tarāz,[1] at the present time all is desolate, no settled population whatever remaining, because of the Mughūls and the Aūzbegs.[2]

Farghāna is a small country,[3] abounding in grain and fruits. It is girt round by mountains except on the west, *i.e.* towards Khujand and Samarkand, and in winter[4] an enemy can enter only on that side.

Fol. 2. The Saiḥūn River (*daryā*) commonly known as the Water of Khujand, comes into the country from the north-east, flows westward through it and after passing along the north of Khujand and the south of Fanākat,[5] now known as Shāhrukhiya, turns directly north and goes to Turkistān. It does not

[1] The Ḥai. MS. and a good many of the W.-i-B. MSS. here write Aūtrār. [Aūtrār like Tarāz was at some time of its existence known as Yāngī (New).] Tarāz seems to have stood near the modern Auliya-ātā; Ālmālīgh,—a Metropolitan see of the Nestorian Church in the 14th. century,—to have been the old capital of Kuldja, and Ālmātū (var. Ālmātī) to have been where Vernoe (Vierny) now is. Ālmālīgh and Ālmātū owed their names to the apple (*ālmā*). *Cf.* Bretschneider's Mediæval Geography p. 140 and T.R. (Elias and Ross) *s.nn.*

[2] *Mughūl u Aūzbeg jihatdīn.* I take this, the first offered opportunity of mentioning (1) that in transliterating Turkī words I follow Turkī lettering because I am not competent to choose amongst systems which *e.g.* here, reproduce Aūzbeg as Ūzbeg, Özbeg and Euzbeg; and (2) that style being part of an autobiography, I am compelled, in pressing back the Memoirs on Bābur's Turkī mould, to retract from the wording of the western scholars, Erskine and de Courteille. Of this compulsion Bābur's bald phrase *Mughūl u Aūzbeg jihatdīn* provides an illustration. Each earlier translator has expressed his meaning with more finish than he himself; 'Abdu'r-raḥīm, by *az jihat 'ubūr-i (Mughūl u) Aūzbeg,* improves on Bābur, since the three towns lay in the tide-way of nomad passage (*'ubūr*) east and west; Erskine writes "in consequence of the incursions" etc. and de C. "*grace aux ravages commis*" etc.

[3] Schuyler (ii, 54) gives the extreme length of the valley as about 160 miles and its width, at its widest, as 65 miles.

[4] Following a manifestly clerical error in the Second W.-i-B. the *Akbar-nāma* and the Mems. are without the seasonal limitation, "in winter." Babūr here excludes from winter routes one he knew well, the Kīndīrlīk Pass; on the other hand Kostenko says that this is open all the year round. Does this contradiction indicate climatic change? (*Cf.* f. 54*b* and note; A.N. Bib. Ind. ed. i, 85 (H. Beveridge i, 221) and, for an account of the passes round Farghāna, Kostenko's *Turkistān Region*, Tables of Contents.)

[5] Var. Banākat, Banākaṣ, Fīākat, Fanākand. Of this place Dr. Rieu writes (Pers. cat. i, 79) that it was also called Shāsh and, in modern times, Tāshkīnt. Bābur does not identify Fanākat with the Tāshkīnt of his day but he identifies it with Shāhrukhiya (*cf.* Index *s.nn.*) and distinguishes between Tāshkīnt-Shāsh and Fanākat-Shāhrukhiya. It may be therefore that Dr. Rieu's Tāshkīnt-Fanākat was Old Tāshkīnt,—(Does Fanā-kīnt mean Old Village?) some 14 miles nearer to the Saiḥūn than the Tāshkīnt of Bābur's day or our own.

join any sea[1] but sinks into the sands, a considerable distance below [the town of] Turkistān.

Farghāna has seven separate townships,[2] five on the south and two on the north of the Saiḥūn.

Of those on the south, one is Andijān. It has a central position and is the capital of the Farghāna country. It produces much grain, fruits in abundance, excellent grapes and melons. In the melon season, it is not customary to sell them out at the beds.[3] Better than the Andijān *nāshpāti*,[4] there is none. After Samarkand and Kesh, the fort[5] of Andijān is the largest in Mawārā'u'n-nahr (Transoxiana). It has three gates. Its citadel (*ark*) is on its south side. Into it water goes by nine channels; out of it, it is strange that none comes at even a single place.[6] Round the outer edge of the ditch[7] runs a gravelled highway; the width of this highway divides the fort from the suburbs surrounding it.

Andijān has good hunting and fowling; its pheasants grow Fol. 2*b*.

[1] *hech daryā qātilmās.* A gloss of *digar* (other) in the Second W.-i-B. has led Mr. Erskine to understand "meeting with no other river in its course." I understand Bābur to contrast the destination of the Saiḥūn which he [erroneously] says sinks into the sands, with the outfall of *e.g.* the Amū into the Sea of Aral.

Cf. First W.-i-B. I.O. MS. 215 f. 2; Second W.-i-B. I.O. MS. 217 f. 1*b* and Ouseley's Ibn Haukal p. 232-244; also Schuyler and Kostenko *l.c.*

[2] Bābur's geographical unit in Central Asia is the township or, with more verbal accuracy, the village *i.e.* the fortified, inhabited and cultivated oasis. Of frontiers he says nothing.

[3] *i.e.* they are given away or taken. Bābur's interest in fruits was not a matter of taste or amusement but of food. Melons, for instance, fresh or stored, form during some months the staple food of Turkistānis. *Cf.* T.R. p. 303 and (in Kāshmīr) 425; Timkowski's *Travels of the Russian Mission* i, 419 and Th. Radloff's *Réceuils d'Itinéraires* p. 343.

N.B. At this point two folios of the Elphinstone Codex are missing.

[4] Either a kind of melon or the pear. For local abundance of pears *see* *Āyīn-i-akbarī*, Blochmann p. 6; Kostenko and Von Schwarz.

[5] *qūrghān, i.e.* the walled town within which was the citadel (*ark*).

[6] *Tūqūz tarnau sū kīrār, bū 'ajab tūr kim bīr yirdīn ham chiqmās.* Second W.-i-B. I.O. 217 f. 2, *nuh jū'ī āb dar qila' dar mī āyid u īn 'ajab ast kah hama az yak jā ham na mī bar āyid.* (*Cf.* Mems. p. 2 and *Méms.* i, 2.) I understand Bābur to mean that all the water entering was consumed in the town. The supply of Andijān, in the present day, is taken both from the Āq Būrā (*i.e.* the Aūsh Water) and, by canal, from the Qarā Daryā.

[7] *khandaqning tāsh yānī.* Second W.-i-B. I.O. 217 f. 2 *dar kinār sang bast khandaq.* Here as in several other places, this Persian translation has rendered Turkī *tāsh*, outside, as if it were Turkī *tāsh*, stone. Bābur's adjective *stone* is *sangīn* (f. 45*b* l. 8). His point here is the unusual circumstance of a high-road running round the outer edge of the ditch Moreover Andijān is built on and

so surprisingly fat that rumour has it four people could not finish one they were eating with its stew.[1]

Andijānīs are all Turks, not a man in town or bāzār but knows Turkī. The speech of the people is correct for the pen; hence the writings of Mīr 'Alī-shīr *Nawā'ī*,[2] though he was bred and grew up in Hīrī (Harāt), are one with their dialect. Good looks are common amongst them. The famous musician, Khwāja Yūsuf, was an Andijānī.[3] The climate is malarious; in autumn people generally get fever.[4]

Again, there is Aūsh (Ūsh), to the south-east, inclining to east, of Andijān and distant from it four *yīghāch* by road.[5] It has a fine climate, an abundance of running waters[6] and a most beautiful spring season. Many traditions have their rise

---

of loess. Here, obeying his Persian source, Mr. Erskine writes "stone-faced ditch"; M. de C. obeying his Turkī one, "*bord extérieur*."

1 *qīrghāwal āsh-kīnasī bila*. *Āsh-kīna*, a diminutive of *āsh*, food, is the rice and vegetables commonly served with the bird. Kostenko i, 287 gives a recipe for what seems *āsh-kīna*.

2 b. 1440; d. 1500 AD.

3 Yūsuf was in the service of Bāī-sunghar Mīrzā *Shāhrukhī* (d. 837 AH.-1434 AD.). *Cf.* Daulat Shāh's *Memoirs of the Poets* (Browne) pp. 340 and 350-1. (H.B.)

4 *gūzlār aīl bīzkāh hūb būlūr*. Second W.-i-B. (I.O. 217 f. 2) here and on f. 4 has read Turkī *gūz*, eye, for Turkī *gūz* or *goz*, autumn. It has here a gloss not in the Ḥaidarābād or Kehr's MSS. (*Cf.* Mems. p. 4 note.) This gloss may be one of Humāyūn's numerous notes and may have been preserved in the Elphinstone Codex, but the fact cannot now be known because of the loss of the two folios already noted. (*See* Von Schwarz and Kostenko concerning the autumn fever of Transoxiana.)

5 The Pers. trss. render *yīghāch* by *farsang*; Ujfalvy also takes the *yīghāch* and the *farsang* as having a common equivalent of about 6 *kilomètres*. Bābur's statements in *yīghāch* however, when tested by ascertained distances, do not work out into the *farsang* of four miles or the *kilomètre* of 8 *kil.* to 5 miles. The *yīghāch* appears to be a variable estimate of distance, sometimes indicating the time occupied on a given journey, at others the distance to which a man's voice will carry. (*Cf.* Ujfalvy *Expédition scientifique* ii, 179; Von Schwarz p. 124 and de C.'s Dict. *s.n. yīghāch*. In the present instance, if Bābur's 4 y. equalled 4 f. the distance from Aūsh to Andijān should be about 16 m.; but it is 33 m. 1¾ fur. *i.e.* 50 *versts*. (Kostenko ii, 33.) I find Bābur's *yīghāch* to vary from about 4 m. to nearly 8 m.

6 *āqār sū*, the irrigation channels on which in Turkistān all cultivation depends. Major-General Gérard writes, (Report of the Pamir Boundary Commission, p. 6,) "Osh is a charming little town, resembling Islāmābād in Kāshmīr,—everywhere the same mass of running water, in small canals, bordered with willow, poplar and mulberry." He saw the Āq Būrā, the *White wolf*, mother of all these running waters, as a "bright, stony, trout-stream;" Dr. Stein saw it as a "broad, tossing river." (Buried Cities of Khotan, p. 45.) *Cf.* Réclus vi, cap. Farghāna; Kostenko i, 104; Von Schwarz *s.nn.*

in its excellencies.[1] To the south-east of the walled town (*qūrghān*) lies a symmetrical mountain, known as the Barā Koh;[2] on the top of this, Sl. Maḥmūd Khān built a retreat (*ḥajra*) and lower down, on its shoulder, I, in 902AH. (1496AD.) built another, having a porch. Though his lies the higher, mine is the better placed, the whole of the town and the suburbs being at its foot.

The Andijān torrent[3] goes to Andijān after having traversed the suburbs of Aūsh. Orchards (*bāghāt*)[4] lie along both its banks; all the Aūsh gardens (*bāghlār*) overlook it; their violets are very fine; they have running waters and in spring are most beautiful with the blossoming of many tulips and roses. Fol. 3.

On the skirt of the Barā-koh is a mosque called the Jauza

[1] *Aūshning faẓilatidā khaili aḥādis wārid dūr.* Second W.-i-B. (I.O. 217 f. 2) *Faẓilat-i-Aūsh aḥadis wārid ast.* Mems. (p. 3) "The excellencies of Usb are celebrated even in the sacred traditions." *Mêms.* (i, 2) "*On cite beaucoup de traditions qui célèbrent l'excellence de ce climat.*" Aūsh may be mentioned in the traditions on account of places of pilgrimage near it; Bābur's meaning may be merely that its excellencies are traditional. *Cf.* Ujfalvy ii, 172.

[2] Most travellers into Farghāna comment on Bābur's account of it. One much discussed point is the position of the Barā Koh. The personal observations of Ujfalvy and Schuyler led them to accept its identification with the rocky ridge known as the Takht-i-sulaimān. I venture to supplement this by the suggestion that Bābur, by Barā Koh, did not mean the whole of the rocky ridge, the name of which, Takht-i-sulaimān, an ancient name, must have been known to him, but one only of its four marked summits. Writing of the ridge Madame Ujfalvy says, "*Il y a quatre sommets dont le plus élevé est le troisième comptant par le nord.*" Which summit in her sketch (p. 327) is the third and highest is not certain, but one is so shewn that it may be the third, may be the highest and, as being a peak, can be described as symmetrical *i.e.* Bābur's *mauzūn*. For this peak an appropriate name would be Barā Koh.

If the name Barā Koh could be restricted to a single peak of the Takht-i-sula'mān ridge, a good deal of earlier confusion would be cleared away, concerning which have written, amongst others, Ritter (v, 432 and 732); Réclus (vi. 54); Schuyler (ii, 43) and those to whom these three refer. For an excellent account, graphic with pen and pencil, of Farghāna and of Aūsh *see* Madame Ujfalvy's *De Paris à Samarcande* cap. v.

[3] *rūd.* This is a precise word since the Āq Būrā (the White Wolf), in a relatively short distance, falls from the Kūrdūn Pass, 13,400 ft. to Aūsh, 3040 ft. and thence to Andijān, 1380 ft. *Cf.* Kostenko i, 104; Huntingdon in Pumpelly's *Explorations in Turkistān* p. 179 and the French military map of 1904.

[4] Whether Bābur's words, *bāghāt, bāghlār and bāghcha* had separate significations, such as orchard, vineyard and ordinary garden *i.e.* garden-plots of small size, I am not able to say but what appears fairly clear is that when he writes *bāghāt u bāghlār* he means *all sorts of gardens*, just as when writes *begāt u beglār,* he means *begs of all ranks*.

Masjid (Twin Mosque).[1] Between this mosque and the town, a great main canal flows from the direction of the hill. Below the outer court of the mosque lies a shady and delightful clover-meadow where every passing traveller takes a rest. It is the joke of the ragamuffins of Aūsh to let out water from the canal[2] on anyone happening to fall asleep in the meadow. A very beautiful stone, waved red and white[3] was found in the Barā Koh in 'Umar Shaikh Mīrzā's latter days; of it are made knife handles, and clasps for belts and many other things. For climate and for pleasantness, no township in all Farghāna equals Aūsh.

Again there is Marghīnān; seven *yīghāch*[4] by road to the west of Andijān,—a fine township full of good things. Its apricots (*aūrūk*) and pomegranates are most excellent. One sort of pomegranate, they call the Great Seed (*Dāna-i-kalān*); its sweetness has a little of the pleasant flavour of the small apricot (*zard-alū*) and it may be thought better than the Semnān pome-
Fol. 3*b*. granate. Another kind of apricot (*aūrūk*) they dry after stoning it and putting back the kernel;[5] they then call it *subḥānī*; it is very palatable. The hunting and fowling of Marghīnān are good; *āq kīyīk*[6] are had close by. Its people are Sārts,[7] boxers,

[1] Madame Ujfalvy has sketched a possible successor. Schuyler found two mosques at the foot of Takht-i-sulaimān, perhaps Bābur's Jauza Masjid.

[2] *aūl shāh-jū'īdīn sū qūyārlār.*

[3] Ribbon Jasper, presumably.

[4] Kostenko (ii, 30), 71½ versts *i.e.* 47 m. 4½ fur. by the Postal Road.

[5] Instead of their own kernels, the Second W.-i-B. stuffs the apricots, in a fashion well known in India by *khūbānī*, with almonds (*maghz-i badām*). The Turkī wording however allows the return to the apricots of their own kernels and Mr. Rickmers tells me that apricots so stuffed were often seen by him in the Zar-afshān Valley. My husband has shewn me that Niẓāmī in his Haft Paikar appears to refer to the other fashion, that of inserting almonds:—

> "I gave thee fruits from the garden of my heart,
> Plump and sweet as honey in milk;
> Their substance gave the lusciousness of figs,
> In their hearts were the kernels of almonds."

[6] What this name represents is one of a considerable number of points in the *Bābur-nāma* I am unable to decide. *Kīyīk* is a comprehensive name (*cf.* Shaw's Vocabulary); *āq kīyīk* might mean *white sheep* or *white deer*. It is rendered in the Second W.-i-B., here, by *ahū-i-wāriq* and on f. 4, by *ahū-i-safed*. Both these names Mr. Erskine has translated by "white deer," but he mentions that the first is said to mean *argālī i.e. ovis poli*, and refers to *Voyages de Pallas* iv, 325.

[7] Concerning this much discussed word, Bābur's testimony is of service. It seems to me that he uses it merely of those settled in towns (villages) and

noisy and turbulent. Most of the noted bullies (*jangralār*) of Samarkand and Bukhārā are Marghīnānīs. The author of the Hidāyat[1] was from Rashdān, one of the villages of Marghīnān.

Again there is Asfara, in the hill-country and nine *yīghāch*[2] by road south-west of Marghīnān. It has running waters, beautiful little gardens (*bāghcha*) and many fruit-trees but almonds for the most part in its orchards. Its people are all Persian-speaking[3] Sārts. In the hills some two miles (*bīr shar'ī*) to the south of the town, is a piece of rock, known as the Mirror Stone.[4] It is some 10 arm-lengths (*qārī*) long, as high as a man in parts, up to his waist in others. Everything is reflected by it as by a mirror. The Asfara district (*wilāyat*) is in four sub-divisions (*balūk*) in the hill-country, one Asfara, one Warūkh, one Sūkh and one Hushyār. When Muḥammad *Shaibānī* Khān defeated Sl. Maḥmūd Khān and Alacha Khān and took Tāshkīnt and Shāhrukhiya,[5] I went into the Sūkh and Hushyār Fol. 4. hill-country and from there, after about a year spent in great misery, I set out (*'azīmat*) for Kābul.[6]

Again there is Khujand,[7] twenty-five *yīghāch* by road to the

---

without any reference to tribe or nationality. I am not sure that he uses it always as a noun; he writes of a *Sārt kishi*, a Sārt person. His Asfara Sārts may have been Turkī-speaking settled Turks and his Marghīnānī ones Persian-speaking Tājiks. *Cf.* Shaw's Vocabulary; *s.n.* Sārt; Schuyler i, 104 and note; Nalivkine's *Histoire du Khanat de Khokand* p. 45 n. Von Schwarz *s.n.*; Kostenko i, 287; Petzhold's *Turkistan* p. 32.

[1] Shaikh Burhānu'd-dīn 'Alī *Qilīch*: b. *circa* 530 AH. (1135 AD.) d. 593 AH. (1197 AD.). *See* Hamilton's *Hidāyat*.

[2] The direct distance, measured on the map, appears to be about 65 m. but the road makes *détour* round mountain spurs. Mr. Erskine appended here, to the "*farsang*" of his Persian source, a note concerning the reduction of Tatar and Indian measures to English ones. It is rendered the less applicable by the variability of the *yīghāch*, the equivalent for a *farsang* presumed by the Persian translator.

[3] Hai. MS. *Farsī-gū'ī*. The Elph. MS. and all those examined of the W.-i-B. omit the word *Farsī*; some writing *kohī* (mountaineer) for *gū'ī*. I judge that Bābur at first omitted the word *Farsī*, since it is entered in the Hai. MS. above the word *gū'ī*. It would have been useful to Ritter (vii, 733) and to Ujfalvy (ii, 176). *Cf.* Kostenko i, 287 on the variety of languages spoken by Sārts.

[4] Of the Mirror Stone neither Fedtschenko nor Ujfalvy could get news.

[5] Bābur distinguishes here between Tāshkīnt and Shāhrukhiya. *Cf.* f. 2 and note to Fanākat.

[6] He left the hill-country above Sūkh in Muḥarram 910 AH. (mid-June 1504 AD.).

[7] For a good account of Khujand *see* Kostenko i, 346.

west of Andijān and twenty-five *yīghāch* east of Samarkand.[1] Khujand is one of the ancient towns; of it were Shaikh Maṣlaḥat and Khwāja Kamāl.[2] Fruit grows well there; its pomegranates are renowned for their excellence; people talk of a Khujand pomegranate as they do of a Samarkand apple; just now however, Marghīnān pomegranates are much met with.[3] The walled town (*qūrghān*) of Khujand stands on high ground; the Saiḥūn River flows past it on the north at the distance, may be, of an arrow's flight.[4] To the north of both the town and the river lies a mountain range called Munūghul;[5] people say there are turquoise and other mines in it and there are many snakes. The hunting and fowling-grounds of Khujand are first-rate; *āq kīyīk*,[6] *būghū-marāl*,[7] pheasant and hare are all had in great plenty. The climate is very malarious; in autumn there is much fever;[8] people rumour it about that the very sparrows get fever and say that the cause of the malaria is the mountain range on the north (*i.e.* Munūghul).

Kand-i-badām (Village of the Almond) is a dependency of Khujand; though it is not a township (*qaṣba*) it is rather a good

[1] Khujand to Andijān 187 m. 2 fur. (Kostenko ii, 29-31) and, helped out by the time-table of the Transcaspian Railway, from Khujand to Samarkand appears to be some 154 m. 5½ fur.

[2] Both men are still honoured in Khujand (Kostenko i, 348). For Khwāja Kamāl's Life and *Dīwān*, *see* Rieu ii, 632 and Ouseley's Persian Poets p. 192. *Cf.* f. 83*b* and note.

[3] *kūb artūq dūr*, perhaps brought to Hindūstān where Bābur wrote the statement.

[4] Turkish arrow-flight, London, 1791, 482 yards.

[5] I have found the following forms of this name,—Ḥai. MS., M:nūgh:l; Pers. trans. and Mems., Myoghil; Ilminsky, M:tugh:l; *Mėms.* Mtoughuil; Réclus, Schuyler and Kostenko, Mogul Tau; Nalivkine, "d'apres Fedtschenko," Mont Mogol; Fr. Map of 1904, M. Muzbek. It is the western end of the Kurāma Range (Kīndīr Tau), which comes out to the bed of the Sīr, is 26⅔ miles long and rises to 4000 ft. (Kostenko, i, 101). Von Schwarz describes it as being quite bare; various writers ascribe climatic evil to it.

[6] Pers. trans. *ahū-i-safed*. *Cf.* f. 3*b* note.

[7] These words translate into *Cervus marāl*, the Asiatic Wapiti, and to this Bābur may apply them. Dictionaries explain *marāl* as meaning *hind* or *doe* but numerous books of travel and Natural History show that it has wider application as a generic name, *i.e.* deer. The two words *būghū* and *marāl* appear to me to be used as *e.g.* drake and duck are used. *Marāl* and duck can both imply the female sex, but also both are generic, perhaps primarily so. *Cf.* for further mention of *būghū-marāl* f. 219 and f. 276. For uses of the word *marāl*, *see* the writings *e.g.* of Atkinson, Kostenko (iii, 69), Lyddeker, Littledale, Selous, Ronaldshay, Church (Chinese Turkistan), Biddulph (Forsyth's Mission).

[8] *Cf.* f. 2 and note.

approach to one (*qaṣbacha*). Its almonds are excellent, hence its name; they all go to Hormuz or to Hindūstān. It is five or six *yīghāch*[1] east of Khujand. Fol. 4b.

Between Kand-i-badām and Khujand lies the waste known as Hā Darwesh. In this there is always (*hamesha*) wind; from it wind goes always (*hameshā*) to Marghīnān on its east; from it wind comes continually (*dā'im*) to Khujand on its west.[2] It has violent, whirling winds. People say that some darweshes, encountering a whirlwind in this desert,[3] lost one another and kept crying, "Hāy Darwesh! Hāy Darwesh!" till all had perished, and that the waste has been called Hā Darwesh ever since.

Of the townships on the north of the Saihūn River one is Akhsī. In books they write it Akhsīkīt[4] and for this reason the

[1] Schuyler (ii, 3), 18 m.

[2] Ḥai. MS. *Hamesha bū deshltā yīl bār dūr. Marghīnānghā kīm sharqī dūr, hamesha mündīn yīl bārūr; Khujandghā kīm gharibī dūr, dā'im mündīn yīl kilūr.*

This is a puzzling passage. It seems to say that wind always goes east and west from the steppe as from a generating centre. E. and de C. have given it alternative directions, east or west, but there is little point in saying this of wind in a valley hemmed in on the north and the south. Bābur limits his statement to the steppe lying in the contracted mouth of the Farghāna valley (*pace* Schuyler ii, 51) where special climatic conditions exist such as (*a*) difference in temperature on the two sides of the Khujand narrows and currents resulting from this difference,—(*b*) the heating of the narrows by sun-heat reflected from the Mogol-tau,—and (*c*) the inrush of westerly wind over Mīrzā Rabāṭ. Local knowledge only can guide a translator safely but Bābur's directness of speech compels belief in the significance of his words and this particularly when what he says is unexpected. He calls the Hā Darwesh a whirling wind and this it still is. Thinkable at least it is that a strong westerly current (the prevailing wind of Farghāna) entering over Mīrzā Rabāṭ and becoming, as it does become, the whirlwind of Hā Darwesh on the hemmed-in steppe,—becoming so perhaps by conflict with the hotter indraught through the Gates of Khujand—might force that indraught back into the Khujand Narrows (in the way *e.g.* that one Nile in flood forces back the other), and at Khujand create an easterly current. All the manuscripts agree in writing to (*ghā*) Marghīnān and to (*ghā*) Khujand. It may be observed that, looking at the map, it appears somewhat strange that Bābur should take, for his wind objective, a place so distant from his (defined) Hā Darwesh and seemingly so screened by its near hills as is Marghīnān. But that westerly winds are prevalent in Marghīnān is seen *e.g.* in Middendorff's *Einblikke in den Farghāna Thal* (p. 112). *Cf.* Réclus vi, 547; Schuyler ii, 51; Cahun's *Histoire du Khanat de Khokand* p. 28 and Sven Hedin's *Durch Asien's Wüsten s.n. būrān.*

[3] *bādiya*; a word perhaps selected as punning on *bād*, wind.

[4] *i.e.* Akhsī Village. This word is sometimes spelled Akhsīkiṣ but as the old name of the place was Akhsī-kint, it may be conjectured at least that the *ṣā'ī maṣallaṣa* of Akhsīkiṣ represents the three points due for the *nūn* and *tā* of *kint*. Of those writing Akhsīkīt may be mentioned the Ḥai. and Kehr's

poet Asiru-d-dīn is known as *Akhsīkītī*. After Andijān no township in Farghāna is larger than Akhsī. It is nine *yīghāch*[1] by road to the west of Andijān. 'Umar Shaikh Mīrzā made it his capital.[2] The Saiḥūn River flows below its walled town (*qūrghān*). This stands above a great ravine (*buland jar*) and it has deep ravines (*'umiq jarlār*) in place of a moat. When 'Umar Shaikh Mīrzā made it his capital, he once or twice cut other ravines from the outer ones. In all Farghāna no fort is so strong as Akhsī. *Its suburbs extend some two miles further
Fol. 5. than the walled town.* People seem to have made of Akhsī the saying (*misal*), "Where is the village? Where are the trees?" (*Dih kujā? Dirakhtān kujā?*) Its melons are excellent; they call one kind Mīr Tīmūrī; whether in the world there is another to equal it is not known. The melons of Bukhārā are famous; when I took Samarkand, I had some brought from there and some from Akhsī; they were cut up at an entertainment and nothing from Bukhārā compared with those from Akhsī. The fowling and hunting of Akhsī are very good indeed; *āq kīyīk* abound in the waste on the Akhsī side of the Saiḥūn; in the jungle on the Andijān side *būghū-marāl*,[3] pheasant and hare are had, all in very good condition.

Again there is Kāsān, rather a small township to the north of Akhsī. From Kāsān the Akhsī water comes in the same way as the Andijān water comes from Aūsh. Kāsān has excellent air and beautiful little gardens (*bāghcha*). As these gardens all lie along the bed of the torrent (*sā'ī*) people call them the "fine front of the coat."[4] Between Kāsānīs and Aūshīs there is rivalry about the beauty and climate of their townships.

MSS. (the Elph. MS. here has a lacuna) the *Zafar-nāma* (Bib. Ind. i, 44) and Ibn Haukal (Ouseley p. 270); and of those writing the word with the *sā'ī musallasa* (*i.e.* as Akhsīkis), Yāqūt's Dict. i, 162, Reinaud's Abū'l-feda I. ii, 225-6, Ilminsky (p. 5) departing from his source, and I.O. Cat. (Ethé) No. 1029. It may be observed that Ibn Haukal (Ouseley p. 280) writes Banākas for Banākat. For Asīru'd-dīn *Akhsikiti*, *see* Rieu ii, 563; Daulat Shāh (Browne) p. 121 and Ethé I.O. Cat. No. 1029.

[1] Measured on the French military map of 1904, this may be 80 kil. *i.e.* 50 miles.

[2] Concerning several difficult passages in the rest of Bābur's account of Akhsī, *see* Appendix A.

[3] The W.-i-B. here translates *būghū-marāl* by *gazawn* and the same word is entered, under-line, in the Ḥai. MS. *Cf.* f. 3*b* and note and f. 4 and note.

[4] *postīn pesh b:r:h.* This obscure Persian phrase has been taken in the following ways :—

In the mountains round Farghāna are excellent summer-pastures (*yīlāq*). There, and nowhere else, the *tabalghū*[1] grows, a tree (*yīghāch*) with red bark; they make staves of it; they Fol. 5*b*. make bird-cages of it; they scrape it into arrows;[2] it is an excellent wood (*yīghāch*) and is carried as a rarity[3] to distant places. Some books write that the mandrake[4] is found in these mountains but for this long time past nothing has been heard of it. A plant called *Āyīq aūtī*[5] and having the qualities of the mandrake (*mihr-giyāh*), is heard of in Yītī-kīnt;[6] it seems to be

---

(*a*) W.-i-B. I.O. 215 and 217 (*i.e.* both versions) reproduce the phrase.
(*b*) W.-i-B. MS., quoted by Erskine, p. 6 note, *postīn-i mīsh burra*.
(*c*) Leyden's MS. Trs., a sheepskin mantle of five lambskins.
(*d*) Mems., Erskine, p. 6, a mantle of five lambskins.
(*e*) The Persian annotator of the Elph. MS., underlining *pesh*, writes, *panj*, five.
(*f*) Klaproth (Archives, p. 109), *pustini pisch breh, d.h. gieb den vorderen Pelz.*
(*g*) Kehr, p. 12 (Ilminsky p. 6) *postīn bīsh b:r:h.*
(*h*) De. C., i, 9, *fourrure d'agneau de la première qualité.*

The "lambskins" of L. and E. carry on a notion of comfort started by their having read *sayāh*, shelter, for Turkī *sā'ī*, torrent-bed; de C. also lays stress on fur and warmth, but would not the flowery border of a mountain stream prompt rather a phrase bespeaking ornament and beauty than one expressing warmth and textile softness? If the phrase might be read as *postīn pesh perā*, what adorns the front of a coat, or as *postīn pesh bar rah*, the fine front of the coat, the phrase would recall the gay embroidered front of some leathern postins.

[1] Var. *tabarkhūn*. The explanation best suiting its uses, enumerated here, is Redhouse's second, the Red Willow. My husband thinks it may be the Hyrcanian Willow.

[2] Steingass describes this as "an arrow without wing or point" (barb?) and tapering at both ends; it may be the practising arrow, *t'alīm aūqī*, often headless.

[3] *tabarrakluq*. Cf. f. 48*b* foot, for the same use of the word.

[4] *yabrūju'ṣ-ṣannam*. The books referred to by Bābur may well be the *Rauzatu'ṣ-ṣafā* and the *Habību's-siyār*, as both mention the plant.

[5] The Turkī word *āyīq* is explained by Redhouse as *awake* and *alert*; and by Meninski and de Meynard as *sobered* and as *a return to right senses*. It may be used here as a equivalent of *mihr* in *mihr-giyāh*, the plant of love.

[6] Mr. Ney Elias has discussed the position of this group of seven villages. (*Cf.* T. R. p. 180 n.) Arrowsmith's map places it (as Iti-kint) approximately where Mr. Th. Radloff describes seeing it *i.e.* on the Farghāna slope of the Kurāma range. (*Cf. Réceuil d'Itinéraires* p. 188.) Mr. Th. Radloff came into Yītī-kīnt after crossing the Kindirlīk Pass from Tāshkīnt and he enumerates the seven villages as traversed by him before reaching the Sir. It is hardly necessary to say that the actual villages he names may not be those of Bābur's Yītī-kīnt. Wherever the word is used in the *Bābur-nāma* and the *Tārīkh-i-rashīdī*, it appears from the context allowable to accept Mr. Radloff's location but it should be borne in mind that the name Yītī-kīnt (Seven

the mandrake (*mihr-giyāh*) the people there call by this name (*i.e. āyīq aūtī*). There are turquoise and iron mines in these mountains.

If people do justly, three or four thousand men[1] may be maintained by the revenues of Farghāna.

(*b. Historical narrative resumed.*)[2]

As 'Umar Shaikh Mīrzā was a ruler of high ambition and great pretension, he was always bent on conquest. On several occasions he led an army against Samarkand; sometimes he was beaten, sometimes retired against his will.[3] More than once he asked his father-in-law into the country, that is to say, my grandfather, Yūnas Khān, the then Khān of the Mughūls in the camping ground (*yūrt*) of his ancestor, Chaghatāī Khān, the second son of Chīngīz Khān. Each time the Mīrzā brought The Khān into the Farghāna country he gave him lands, but, partly owing to his misconduct, partly to the thwarting of the
Fol. 6. Mughūls,[4] things did not go as he wished and Yūnas Khān, not being able to remain, went out again into Mughūlistān. When the Mīrzā last brought The Khān in, he was in possession of

---

villages or towns) might be found as an occasional name of Altī-shahr (Six towns). See T.R. *s.n.* Altī-shahr.

[1] *kishī*, person, here manifestly fighting men.

[2] Elph. MS. f. 2*b*; First W.-i-B. I.O. 215 f. 4*b*; Second W.-i-B. I.O. 217 f. 4; Mems. p. 6; Ilminsky p. 7; *Mêms.* i. 10.

The rulers whose affairs are chronicled at length in the Farghāna Section of the B.N. are, (I) of Tīmūrid Turks, (always styled Mīrzā), (*a*) the three Mīrān-shāhī brothers, Aḥmad, Maḥmūd and 'Umar Shaikh with their successors, Bāī-sunghar, 'Alī and Bābur; (*b*) the Bāī-qarā, Ḥusain of Harāt: (II) of Chīngīz Khānids, (always styled Khān.) (*a*) the two Chaghatāī Mughūl brothers, Maḥmūd and Aḥmad; (*b*) the Shaibānid Aūzbeg, Muḥammad *Shaibānī* (Shāh-i-bakht or Shaibāq or Shāhī Beg).

In electing to use the name *Shaibānī*, I follow not only the Ḥai. Codex but also Shaibānī's Boswell, Muḥammad Ṣāliḥ Mīrzā. The Elph. MS. frequently uses *Shaibāq* but its authority down to f. 198 (Ḥai. MS. f. 243*b*) is not so great as it is after that folio, because not till f. 198 is it a direct copy of Bābur's own. It may be more correct to write "the Shaibānī Khān" and perhaps even "the Shaibānī."

[3] *bī murād*, so translated because retirement was caused once by the overruling of Khwāja 'Ubaidu'l-lāh *Aḥrārī*. (T.R. p. 113.)

[4] Once the Mīrzā did not wish Yūnas to winter in Akhsī; once did not expect him to yield to the demand of his Mughūls to be led out of the cultivated country (*wilāyat*). His own misconduct included his attack in Yūnas on account of Akhsī and much falling-out with kinsmen. (T.R. *s.nn.*)

Tāshkīnt, which in books they write Shash, and sometimes Chāch, whence the term, a Chāchī, bow.[1] He gave it to The Khān, and from that date (890AH.-1485AD.) down to 908AH. (1503AD.) it and the Shāhrukhiya country were held by the Chaghatāī Khāns.

At this date (*i.e.*, 899AH.-1494AD.) the Mughūl Khānship was in Sl. Maḥmūd Khān, Yūnas Khān's younger son and a half-brother of my mother. As he and 'Umar Shaikh Mīrzā's elder brother, the then ruler of Samarkand, Sl. Aḥmad Mīrzā were offended by the Mīrzā's behaviour, they came to an agreement together; Sl. Aḥmad Mīrzā had already given a daughter to Sl. Maḥmūd Khān;[2] both now led their armies against 'Umar Shaikh Mīrzā, the first advancing along the south of the Khujand Water, the second along its north.

Meantime a strange event occurred. It has been mentioned that the fort of Akhsī is situated above a deep ravine;[3] along this ravine stand the palace buildings, and from it, on Monday, Ramẓān 4, (June 8th.) 'Umar Shaikh Mīrzā flew, with his pigeons and their house, and became a falcon.[4] Fol. 6*b*.

He was 39 (lunar) years old, having been born in Samarkand, in 860AH. (1456AD.) He was Sl. Abū-sa'īd Mīrzā's fourth son,[5] being younger than Sl. Aḥmad M. and Sl. Muḥammad

[1] *i.e.* one made of non-warping wood (Steingass), perhaps that of the White Poplar. The *Shāh-nāma* (Turner, Maçon ed: i, 71) writes of a Chāchī bow and arrows of *khadang*, *i.e.* white poplar. (H.B.)

[2] *i.e.* Rābi'a-sulṭān, married *circa* 893 AH.-1488 AD. For particulars about her and all women mentioned in the B.N. and the T.R. see Gulbadan Begīm's *Humāyūn-nāma*, Or. Trs. Series.

[3] *jar*, either that of the Kāsān Water or of a deeply-excavated canal. The palace buildings are mentioned again on f. 110*b*. *Cf.* Appendix A.

[4] *i.e.* soared from earth, died. For some details of the accident *see* A.N. (H. Beveridge, i, 220.)

[5] Ḥ.S. ii, 192, Firishta, lith. ed. p. 191 and D'Herbélot, sixth.

It would have accorded with Bābur's custom if here he had mentioned the parentage of his father's mother. Three times (fs. 17*b*, 70*b*, 96*b*) he writes of "Shāh Sulṭān Begīm" in a way allowing her to be taken as 'Umar Shaikh's own mother. Nowhere, however, does he mention her parentage. One even cognate statement only have we discovered, *viz.* Khwānd-amīr's (Ḥ.S. ii, 192) that 'Umar Shaikh was the own younger brother (*barādar khurdtar khūd*) of Aḥmad and Maḥmūd. If his words mean that the three were full-brothers, 'Umar Shaikh's own mother was Ābū-sa'īd's Tarkhān wife. Bābur's omission (f. 21*b*) to mention his father with A. and M. as a nephew of Darwesh Muḥ. Tarkhān would be negative testimony against taking Khwānd-amīr's statement to mean "full-brother," if clerical slips were not easy and if Khwānd-amīr's

M. and Sl. Maḥmūd Mīrzā. His father, Sl. Abū-sa'īd Mīrzā, was the son of Sl. Muḥammad Mīrzā, son of Tīmūr Beg's third son, Mīrān-shāh M. and was younger than 'Umar Shaikh Mīrzā, (the elder) and Jahāngīr M. but older than Shāhrukh Mīrzā.

c. 'Umar Shaikh Mīrzā's country.

His father first gave him Kābul and, with Bābā-i-Kābulī[1] for his guardian, had allowed him to set out, but recalled him from the Tamarisk Valley[2] to Samarkand, on account of the Mīrzās' Circumcision Feast. When the Feast was over, he gave him Andijān with the appropriateness that Tīmūr Beg had given Farghāna (Andijān) to his son, the elder 'Umar Shaikh Mīrzā. This done, he sent him off with Khudāī-bīrdī *Tūghchī Tīmūr-tāsh*[3] for his guardian.

d. His appearance and characteristics.

He was a short and stout, round-bearded and fleshy-faced
Fol. 7. person.[4] He used to wear his tunic so very tight that to fasten the strings he had to draw his belly in and, if he let himself out after tying them, they often tore away. He was not choice in dress or food. He wound his turban in a fold (*dastar-pech*); all turbans were in four folds (*chār-pech*) in those days; people

---

means of information were less good. He however both was the son of Maḥmūd's wāzir (Ḥ.S. ii, 194) and supplemented his book in Bābur's presence.

To a statement made by the writer of the biographies included in Kehr's B.N. volume, that 'U.S.'s family (*aūmāgh*) is not known, no weight can be attached, spite of the co-incidence that the Mongol form of *aūmāgh, i.e. aūmāk* means *Mutter-leib*. The biographies contain too many known mistakes for their compiler to outweigh Khwānd-amīr in authority.

[1] *Cf. Rauzatu'ṣ-ṣafā* vi, 266. (H.B.)

[2] Dara-i-gaz, south of Balkh. This historic feast took place at Merv in 870 AH. (1465 AD.). As 'Umar Shaikh was then under ten, he may have been one of the Mīrzās concerned.

[3] Khudāī-birdī is a Pers.-Turkī hybrid equivalent of Theodore; *tūghchī* implies the right to use or (as hereditary standard-bearer,) to guard the *tūgh*; Tīmūr-tāsh may mean *i.a.* Friend of Tīmūr (a title not excluded here as borne by inheritance. *Cf.* f. 12*b* and note), Sword-friend (*i.e.* Companion-in-arms), and Iron-friend (*i.e.* stanch). *Cf.* Dict. *s.n.* Tīmūr-bāsh, a sobriquet of Charles XII.

[4] Elph. and Ḥai. MSS. *qūbā yūzlūq*; this is under-lined in the Elph. MS. by *ya'nī pur ghosht*. *Cf.* f. 68*b* for the same phrase. The four earlier trss. *viz.* the two W.-i-B., the English and the French, have variants in this passage.

wore them without twisting and let the ends hang down.[1] In the heats and except in his Court, he generally wore the Mughūl cap.

e. His qualities and habits.

He was a true believer (*Ḥanafī mażhablīk*) and pure in the Faith, not neglecting the Five Prayers and, his life through, making up his Omissions.[2] He read the Qur'ān very frequently and was a disciple of his Highness Khwāja 'Ubaidu'l-lāh (*Aḥrārī*) who honoured him by visits and even called him son. His current readings[3] were the two Quintets and the *Maṣnawī*;[4] of histories he read chiefly the *Shāh-nāma*. He had a poetic nature, but no taste for composing verses. He was so just that when he heard of a caravan returning from Khitāī as overwhelmed by snow in the mountains of Eastern Andijān,[5] and that of its thousand heads of houses (*awīlūq*) two only had escaped, he sent his overseers to take charge of all goods and, though no heirs were near and though he was in want himself, summoned the heirs from Khurāsān and Samarkand, and in the course of a year or two had made over to them all their property safe and sound. Fol. 7*b*.

He was very generous; in truth, his character rose altogether to the height of generosity. He was affable, eloquent and sweet-spoken, daring and bold. Twice out-distancing all his

1 The apposition may be between placing the turban-sash round the turban-cap in a single flat fold and winding it four times round after twisting it on itself. *Cf.* f. 18 and Hughes *Dict. of Islām s.n.* turban.

2 *qażālār*, the prayers and fasts omitted when due, through war, travel sickness, etc.

3 *rawān sawādī bār idī*; perhaps, wrote a running hand. De C. i, 13, *ses lectures courantes étaient* . . .

4 The dates of 'Umar Shaikh's limits of perusal allow the Quintets (*Khamsatīn*) here referred to to be those of Niẓāmī and Amīr Khusrau of Dihlī. The *Maṣnawī* must be that of Jalālu'd-dīn *Rūmī*. (H.B.)

5 Probably below the Tīrāk (Poplar) Pass, the caravan route much exposed to avalanches.

Mr. Erskine notes that this anecdote is erroneously told as of Bābur by Firishta and others. Perhaps it has been confused with the episode on f. 207*b*. Firishta makes another mistaken attribution to Bābur, that of Ḥasan of Yaq'ūb's couplet. (H.B.) *Cf.* f. 13*b* and Dow's *Hindustan* ii, 218.

braves,[1] he got to work with his own sword, once at the Gate of Akhsī, once at the Gate of Shāhrukhiya. A middling archer, he was strong in the fist,—not a man but fell to his blow. Through his ambition, peace was exchanged often for war, friendliness for hostility.

In his early days he was a great drinker, later on used to have a party once or twice a week. He was good company, on occasions reciting verses admirably. Towards the last he rather preferred intoxicating confects[2] and, under their sway, used to lose his head. His disposition[3] was amorous, and he bore many a lover's mark.[4] He played draughts a good deal, sometimes even threw the dice.

f. His battles and encounters.

He fought three ranged battles, the first with Yūnas Khān,
Fol. 8. on the Saiḥūn, north of Andijān, at the Goat-leap,[5] a village so-called because near it the foot-hills so narrow the flow of the water that people say goats leap across.[6] There he was beaten and made prisoner. Yūnas Khān for his part did well by him and gave him leave to go to his own district (Andijān). This fight having been at that place, the Battle of the Goat-leap became a date in those parts.

His second battle was fought on the Urūs,[7] in Turkistān, with Aūzbegs returning from a raid near Samarkand. He crossed the river on the ice, gave them a good beating, separated off all their prisoners and booty and, without coveting a single thing for himself, gave everything back to its owners.

[1] *yigītlār*, young men, the modern *jighit*. Bābur uses the word for men on the effective fighting strength. It answers to the "brave" of North American Indian story; here de C. translates it by *braves*.

[2] *ma'jūn*. *Cf.* Von Schwarz p. 286 for a recipe.

[3] *mutaiyam*. This word, not clearly written in all MSS., has been mistaken for *yitīm*. *Cf.* JRAS 1910 p. 882 for a note upon it by my husband to whom I owe the emendation.

[4] *na'l u dāghī bisyār īdī*, that is, he had inflicted on himself many of the brands made by lovers and enthusiasts. *Cf.* Chardin's *Voyages* ii, 253 and Lady M. Montague's *Letters* p. 200.

[5] *tīka sīkrītkū*, lit. likely to make goats leap, from *sīkrīmāk* to jump close-footed (Shaw).

[6] *sīkrīkān dūr*. Both *sīkrītkū* and *sīkrīkān dūr*, appear to dictate translation in general terms and not by reference to a single traditional leap by one goat.

[7] *i.e.* Russian; it is the Arys tributary of the Sīr.

His third battle he fought with (his brother) Sl. Aḥmad Mīrzā at a place between Shāhrukhiya and Aūrā-tīpā, named Khwāṣ.[1] Here he was beaten.

g. His country.

The Farghāna country his father had given him; Tāshkīnt and Sairām, his elder brother, Sl. Aḥmad Mīrzā gave, and they were in his possession for a time; Shāhrukhiya he took by a ruse and held awhile. Later on, Tāshkīnt and Shāhrukhiya passed out of his hands; there then remained the Farghāna country and Khujand,—some do not include Khujand in Farghāna,—and Aūrā-tīpā, of which the original name was Aūrūshnā and which some call Aūrūsh. In Aūrā-tīpā, at the time Sl. Aḥmad Mīrzā went to Tāshkīnt against the Mughūls, and was beaten on the Chīr[2] (893AH.-1488AD.) was Ḥafiẓ Beg *Dūldāī;* he made it over to 'Umar Shaikh M. and the Mīrzā held it from that time forth. Fol. 8*b*.

h. His children.

Three of his sons and five of his daughters grew up. I, Ẓahīru'd-dīn Muḥammad Bābur,[3] was his eldest son; my mother was Qūtlūq-nigār Khānīm. Jahāngīr Mīrzā was his second son, two years younger than I; his mother, Fāṭima-sulṭān by name, was of the Mughūl *tūmān*-begs.[4] Nāṣir Mīrzā was his third son; his mother was an Andijānī, a mistress,[5] named Umīd. He was four years younger than I.

'Umar Shaikh Mīrzā's eldest daughter was Khān-zāda Begīm,[6] my full sister, five years older than I. The second

[1] The Fr. map of 1904 shows Kas, in the elbow of the Sīr, which seems to represent Khwāṣ.

[2] *i.e.* the Chīr-chīk tributary of the Sīr.

[3] Concerning his name, *see* T.R. p. 173.

[4] *i.e.* he was a head-man of a horde sub-division, nominally numbering 10,000, and paying their dues direct to the supreme Khān. (T.R. p. 301.)

[5] *ghūnchachī i.e.* one ranking next to the four legal wives, in Turkī *aūdāliq*, whence odalisque. Bābur and Gul-badan mention the promotion of several to Begīm's rank by virtue of their motherhood.

[6] One of Bābur's quatrains, quoted in the *Abūshqā*, is almost certainly addressed to Khān-zāda. *Cf.* A.Q. Review, Jan. 1911, p. 4; H. Beveridge's *Some verses of Bābur*. For an account of her marriage *see Shaibānī-nāma* (Vambéry) cap. xxxix.

time I took Samarkand (905AH.-1500AD.), spite of defeat at Sar-i-pul,[1] I went back and held it through a five months' siege, but as no sort of help or reinforcement came from any beg or ruler thereabouts, I left it in despair and got away; in that throneless time (*fatrat*) Khān-zāda Begīm fell[2] to Muḥammad *Shaibānī* Khān. She had one child by him, a pleasant boy,[3]
Fol. 9. named Khurram Shāh. The Balkh country was given to him; he went to God's mercy a few years after the death of his father (916AH.-1510AD.). Khān-zāda Begīm was in Merv when Shāh Ismā'īl (*Ṣafawī*) defeated the Aūzbegs near that town (916AH.-1510AD.); for my sake he treated her well, giving her a sufficient escort to Qūndūz where she rejoined me. We had been apart for some ten years; when Muḥammadī *kūkūldāsh* and I went to see her, neither she nor those about her knew us, although I spoke. They recognized us after a time.

Mihr-bānū Begīm was another daughter, Nāṣir Mīrzā's full-sister, two years younger than I. Shahr-bānū Begīm was another, also Nāṣir Mīrzā's full-sister, eight years younger than I. Yādgār-sulṭān Begīm was another, her mother was a mistress, called Āghā-sulṭān. Ruqaiya-sulṭān Begīm was another; her mother, Makhdūm-sulṭān Begīm, people used to call the Dark-eyed Begīm. The last-named two were born after the Mīrzā's death. Yādgār-sulṭān Begīm was brought up by my grandmother, Aīsān-daulat Begīm; she fell to 'Abdu'l-laṭīf Sl., a son of Ḥamza Sl. when Shaibānī Khān took Andijān and Akhsī (908AH.-1503AD.). She rejoined me when (917AH.-1511AD.) in Khutlān I defeated Ḥamza Sl. and other sulṭāns and took Ḥiṣār. Ruqaiya-sulṭān Begīm fell in that
Fol. 9b. same throneless time (*fatrat*) to Jānī Beg Sl. (*Aūzbeg*). By him she had one or two children who did not live. In these days

[1] Kehr's MS. has a passage here not found elsewhere and seeming to be an adaptation of what is at the top of Ilai. MS. f. 88. (Ilminsky, p. 10, *ba wujūd . . . tāpīb.*)

[2] *tūshtī*, which here seems to mean that she fell to his share on division of captives. Muḥ. Ṣāliḥ makes it a love-match and places the marriage before Bābur's departure. *Cf.* f. 95 and notes.

[3] *aūghlān*. Khurram would be about five when given Balkh in *circa* 911 AH. (1505 AD.). He died when about 12. *Cf.* H.S. ii, 364.

of our leisure (*furṣatlār*)[1] has come news that she has gone to God's mercy.

i. His ladies and mistresses.

Qūtlūq-nigār Khānīm was the second daughter of Yūnas Khān and the eldest (half-) sister of Sl. Maḥmūd Khān and Sl. Aḥmad Khān.

(*j. Interpolated account of Bābur's mother's family.*)

Yūnas Khān descended from Chaghatāī Khān, the second son of Chīngīz Khān (as follows,) Yūnas Khān, son of Wais Khān, son of Sher-'alī *Aūghlān*, son of Muḥammad Khān, son of Khiẓr Khwāja Khān, son of Tūghlūq-tīmūr Khān, son of Aīsān-būghā Khān, son of Dāwā Khān, son of Barāq Khān, son of Yīsūntawā Khān, son of Mūātūkān, son of Chaghatāī Khān, son of Chīngīz Khān.

Since such a chance has come, set thou down[2] now a summary of the history of the Khāns.

Yūnas Khān (d. 892 AH.-1487 AD.) and Aīsān-būghā Khān (d. 866 AH.-1462 AD.) were sons of Wais Khān (d. 832 AH.-1428 AD.).[3] Yūnas Khān's mother was either a daughter or a grand-daughter of Shaikh Nūru'd-dīn Beg, a Turkistānī Qīpchāq favoured by Tīmūr Beg. When Wais Khān died, the Mughūl horde split in two, one portion being for Yūnas Khān, the greater for Aīsān-būghā Khān. For help in getting the upper hand in the horde, Aīrzīn (var. Aīrāzān) one of the Bārīn *tūmān*-begs and Beg Mīrik *Turkmān*, one of the Chīrās *tūmān*-begs, took Yūnas Khān (aet. 13) and with him Fol. 10. three or four thousand Mughūl heads of houses (*awīlūq*), to Aūlūgh Beg Mīrzā (*Shāhrukhī*) with the fittingness that Aūlūgh Beg M. had taken Yūnas Khān's elder sister for his son, 'Abdu'l-

[1] This *fatrat* (interregnum) was between Bābur's loss of Farghāna and his gain of Kābul; the *furṣatlār* were his days of ease following success in Hindūstān and allowing his book to be written.

[2] *qilāling*, lit. do thou be (setting down), a verbal form recurring on f. 227*b* l. 2. With the same form (*ait*)*āling*, lit. do thou be saying, the compiler of the *Abūshqā* introduces his quotations. Shaw's paradigm, *qiling* only. *Cf.* A.Q.R. Jan. 1911, p. 2.

[3] Kehr's MS. (Ilminsky p. 12) and its derivatives here interpolate the erroneous statement that the sons of Yūnas were Afāq and Bābā Khāns.

'azīz Mīrzā. Aūlūgh Beg Mīrzā did not do well by them; some he imprisoned, some scattered over the country[1] one by one. The Dispersion of Aīrzīn became a date in the Mughūl horde.

Yūnas Khān himself was made to go towards 'Irāq; one year he spent in Tabrīz where Jahān Shāh *Barānī* of the Black Sheep Turkmāns was ruling. From Tabrīz he went to Shīrāz where was Shāhrukh Mīrzā's second son, Ibrāhīm Sulṭān Mīrzā.[2] He having died five or six months later (Shawwal 4, 838 AH.-May 3rd, 1435 AD.), his son, 'Abdu'l-lāh Mīrzā sat in his place. Of this 'Abdu'l-lāh Mīrzā Yūnas Khān became a retainer and to him used to pay his respects. The Khān was in those parts for 17 or 18 years.

In the disturbances between Aūlūgh Beg Mīrzā and his sons, Aīsān-būghā Khān found a chance to invade Farghāna; he plundered as far as Kand-i-badām, came on and, having plundered Andijān, led all its people into captivity.[3] Sl. Abū-sa'īd Mīrzā, after seizing the throne of Samarkand, led an army out to beyond Yāngī (Tarāz) to Aspara in Mughūlistān,
Fol. 10*b*. there gave Aīsān-būghā a good beating and then, to spare himself further trouble from him and with the fittingness that he had just taken to wife[4] Yūnas Khān's elder sister, the former wife of 'Abdu'l-'azīz Mīrzā (*Shāhrukhī*), he invited Yūnas Khān from Khurāsān and 'Irāq, made a feast, became friends and proclaimed him Khān of the Mughūls. Just when he was speeding him forth, the Sāghārīchī *tūmān*-begs had all come into Mughūlistān, in anger with Aīsān-būghā Khān.[5] Yūnas Khān went amongst them and took to wife Aīsān-daulat Begīm, the daughter of their chief, 'Alī-shīr

[1] *i.e.* broke up the horde. *Cf.* T.R. p. 74.

[2] *See* f. 50*b* for his descent.

[3] Descendants of these captives were in Kāshghar when Ḥaidar was writing the T.R. It was completed in 953 AH. (1547 AD.). *Cf.* T.R. pp. 81 and 149.

[4] An omission from his Persian source misled Mr. Erskine here into making Abū-sa'īd celebrate the Khānīm's marriage, not with himself but with his defeated foe, 'Abdu'l-'azīz who had married her 28 years earlier.

[5] Aīsān-būghā was at Āq Sū in Eastern Turkistān; Yūnas Khān's head-quarters were in Yītī-kīnt. The Sāghārīchī *tūmān* was a subdivision of the Kūnchī Mughūls.

Beg. They then seated him and her on one and the same white felt and raised him to the Khānship.[1]

By this Aīsān-daulat Begīm, Yūnas Khān had three daughters. Mihr-nigār Khānīm was the eldest; Sl. Abū-sa'īd Mīrzā set her aside[2] for his eldest son, Sl. Aḥmad Mīrzā; she had no child. In a throneless time (905 AH.) she fell to Shaibānī Khān; she left Samarkand[3] with Shāh Begīm for Khurāsān (907 AH.) and both came on to me in Kābul (911 AH.). At the time Shaibānī Khān was besieging Nāṣir Mīrzā in Qandahār and I set out for Lamghān[4] (913 AH.) they went to Badakhshān with Khān Mīrzā (Wais).[5] When Mubārak Shāh invited Khān Mīrzā into Fort Victory,[6] they were Fol. 11 captured, together with the wives and families of all their people, by marauders of Ābā-bikr *Kāshgharī* and, as captives to that ill-doing miscreant, bade farewell to this transitory world (*circa* 913 AH.-1507 AD.).

Qūtlūq-nigār Khānīm, my mother, was Yūnas Khān's second daughter. She was with me in most of my guerilla expeditions and throneless times. She went to God's mercy in Muḥarram 911 AH. (June 1505 AD.) five or six months after the capture of Kābul.

Khūb-nigār Khānīm was his third daughter. Her they gave to Muḥammad Ḥusain *Kūrkān Dūghlāt* (899 AH.). She had one son and one daughter by him. 'Ubaid Khān (*Aūzbeg*) took the daughter (Ḥabība).[7] When I captured Samarkand and

[1] *Khān kütärdilär.* The primitive custom was to lift the Khān-designate off the ground; the phrase became metaphorical and would seem to be so here, since there were two upon the felt. *Cf.*, however, Th. Radloff's *Réceuil d'Itinéraires* p. 326.

[2] *qūyūb idī*, probably in childhood.

[3] She was divorced by Shaibānī Khān in 907 AH. in order to allow him to make lawful marriage with her niece, Khān-zāda.

[4] This was a prudential retreat before Shaibānī Khān. *Cf.* f. 213.

[5] The "Khān" of his title bespeaks his Chaghatāī-Mughūl descent through his mother, the "Mīrzā," his Tīmūrid-Turkī, through his father. The capture of the women was facilitated by the weakening of their travelling escort through his departure. *Cf.* T.R. p. 203.

[6] Qila'-i-zafar. Its ruins are still to be seen on the left bank of the Kukcha. *Cf.* T.R. p. 220 and Kostenko i, 140. For Mubārak Shāh *Muẓaffarī* *see* f. 213 and T.R. *s.n.*

[7] Ḥabība, a child when captured, was reared by Shaibānī and by him given in marriage to his nephew. *Cf.* T.R. p. 207 for an account of this marriage as saving Ḥaidar's life.

Bukhārā (917 AH.-1511 AD.), she stayed behind,[1] and when her paternal uncle, Sayyid Muḥammad *Dūghlāt* came as Sl. Sa'īd Khān's envoy to me in Samarkand, she joined him and with him went to Kāshghar where (her cousin), Sl. Sa'īd Khān took her. Khūb-nigār's son was Ḥaidar Mīrzā.[2] He was in my service for three or four years after the Aūzbegs slew his father, then (918 AH.-1512 AD.) asked leave to go to Kāshghar to the presence of Sl. Sa'īd Khān.

> "Everything goes back to its source,
> Pure gold, or silver or tin."[3]

People say he now lives lawfully (*tā'ib*) and has found the right way (*ṭarīqā*).[4] He has a hand deft in every thing, penmanship and painting, and in making arrows and arrow-
Fol. 11*b*. barbs and string-grips; moreover he is a born poet and in a petition written to me, even his style is not bad.[5]

Shāh Begīm was another of Yūnas Khān's ladies. Though he had more, she and Aīsān-daulat Begīm were the mothers of his children. She was one of the (six) daughters of Shāh Sulṭān Muḥammad, Shāh of Badakhshān.[6] His line, they say, runs back to Iskandar Fīlkūs.[7] Sl. Abū-sa'īd Mīrzā took another daughter and by her had Ābā-bikr Mīrzā.[8] By this

[1] *i.e.* she did not take to flight with her husband's defeated force, but, relying on the victor, her cousin Bābur, remained in the town. *Cf.* T.R. p. 268. Her case receives light from Shahr-bānū's (f. 169).

[2] Muḥammad Ḥaidar Mīrzā *Kūrkān Dūghlāt Chaghatāī Mūghūl*, the author of the *Tārīkh-i-rashīdī*; b. 905 AH. d. 958 AH. (b. 1499 d. 1551 AD.). Of his clan, the "Oghlāt" (Dūghlāt) Muḥ. Ṣāliḥ says that it was called "Oghlāt" by Mughūls but Qūngūr-āt (Brown Horse) by Aūzbegs.

[3] *Baz garadad ba aṣl-i-khūd hama chīz,*
Zar-i-ṣāfī u naqra u airzīn.

These lines are in Arabic in the introduction to the *Anwār-i-suhailī*. (H.B.) The first is quoted by Ḥaidar (T.R. p. 354) and in Field's *Dict. of Oriental Quotations* (p. 160). I understand them to refer here to Ḥaidar's return to his ancestral home and nearest kin as being a natural act.

[4] *tā'ib* and *ṭarīqa* suggest that Ḥaidar had become an orthodox Musalmān in or about 933 AH. (1527 AD.).

[5] Abū'l-faẓl adds music to Ḥaidar's accomplishments and Ḥaidar's own Prologue mentions yet others.

[6] *Cf.* T.R. *s.n.* and Gul-badan's H.N. *s.n.* Ḥaram Begīm.

[7] *i.e.* Alexander of Macedon. For modern mention of Central Asian claims to Greek descent *see i.a.* Kostenko, Von Schwarz, Holdich and A. Durand. *Cf.* Burnes' *Kābul* p. 203 for an illustration of a silver *patera* (now in the V. and A. Museum), once owned by ancestors of this Shāh Sulṭān Muḥammad.

[8] *Cf.* f. 6*b* note

Shāh Begīm Yūnas Khān had two sons and two daughters. Her first-born but younger than all Aīsān-daulat Begīm's daughters, was Sl. Maḥmūd Khān, called Khānika Khān[1] by many in and about Samarkand. Next younger than he was Sl. Aḥmad Khān, known as Alacha Khān. People say he was called this because he killed many Qālmāqs on the several occasions he beat them. In the Mughūl and Qālmāq tongues, one who will kill (*aūltūrgūchī*) is called *ālāchī*; Alāchī they called him therefore and this by repetition, became Alacha.[2] As occasion arises, the acts and circumstances of these two Khāns will find mention in this history (*tārīkh*).

Sulṭān-nigār Khānīm was the youngest but one of Yūnas Khān's children. Her they made go forth (*chīqārīb īdīlār*) Fol. 12.
to Sl. Maḥmūd Mīrzā; by him she had one child, Sl. Wais (Khān Mīrzā), mention of whom will come into this history. When Sl. Maḥmūd Mīrzā died (900 AH.-1495 AD.), she took her son off to her brothers in Tāshkīnt without a word to any single person. They, a few years later, gave her to Adik (Aūng) Sulṭan,[3] a Qāzāq sulṭān of the line of Jūjī Khān, Chīngīz Khān's eldest son. When Shaibānī Khān defeated the Khāns (her brothers), and took Tāshkīnt and Shāhrukhiya (908 AH.), she got away with 10 or 12 of her Mughūl servants, to (her husband), Adik Sulṭān. She had two daughters by Adik Sulṭān; one she gave to a Shaibān sulṭān, the other to Rashīd Sulṭān, the son of (her cousin) Sl. Sa'īd Khān. After Adik Sulṭān's death, (his brother), Qāsim Khān, Khān of the Qāzāq horde, took her.[4] Of all the Qāzaq khāns and sulṭāns, no one, they say, ever kept the horde in such good order as he;

[1] *i.e.* Khān's child.

[2] The careful pointing of the Ḥai. MS. clears up earlier confusion by showing the narrowing of the vowels from *ālāchī* to *alacha*.

[3] The Elph. MS. (f. 7) writes *Aūng*, Khān's son, Prester John's title, where other MSS. have Adik. Bābur's brevity has confused his account of Sulṭān-nigār. Widowed of Maḥmūd in 900 AH. she married Adik; Adik, later, joined Shaibānī Khān but left him in 908 AH. perhaps secretly, to join his own Qāzāq horde. He was followed by his wife, apparently also making a private departure. As Adik died shortly after 908 AH. his daughters were born before that date and not after it as has been understood. *Cf.* T.R. and G.B.'s H.N. *s.nn.*; also Mems. p. 14 and *Mêms.* i, 24.

[4] Presumably by tribal custom, *yīnkālik*, marriage with a brother's widow. Such marriages seem to have been made frequently for the protection of women left defenceless.

his army was reckoned at 300,000 men. On his death the Khānīm went to Sl. Sa'īd Khān's presence in Kāshghar. Daulat-sulṯān Khānīm was Yūnas Khān's youngest child.
Fol. 12b. In the Tāshkīnt disaster (908 AH.) she fell to Tīmūr Sulṯān, the son of Shaibānī Khān. By him she had one daughter; they got out of Samarkand with me (918 AH.-1512 AD.), spent three or four years in the Badakhshān country, then went (923 AH.-1420 AD.) to Sl. Sa'īd Khān's presence in Kāshghar.[1]

(*k. Account resumed of Bābur's father's family.*)

In 'Umar Shaikh Mīrzā's *ḥaram* was also Aūlūs Āghā, a daughter of Khwāja Ḥusain Beg; her one daughter died in infancy and they sent her out of the *ḥaram* a year or eighteen months later. Fāṯima-sulṯān Āghā was another; she was of the Mughūl *tūmān*-begs and the first taken of his wives. Qarā-gūz (Makhdūm sulṯān) Begīm was another; the Mīrzā took her towards the end of his life; she was much beloved, so to please him, they made her out descended from (his uncle) Minūchihr Mīrzā, the elder brother of Sl. Abū-sa'īd Mīrzā. He had many mistresses and concubines; one, Umīd Āghāchā died before him. Latterly there were also Tūn-sulṯān (var. Yun) of the Mughūls and Āghā Sulṯān.

l. 'Umar Shaikh Mīrzā's Amīrs.

There was Khudāī-bīrdī *Tūghchī Tīmūr-tāsh*, a descendant of the brother of Āq-būghā Beg, the Governor of Hīrī (Herāt, for Tīmūr Beg.) When Sl. Abū-sa'īd Mīrzā, after besieging Jūkī Mīrzā (*Shāhrukhī*) in Shāhrukhiya (868AH.-1464AD.) gave the Farghāna country to 'Umar Shaikh Mīrzā, he put this Khudāī-
Fol. 13. bīrdī Beg at the head of the Mīrzā's Gate.[2] Khudāī-bīrdī was

[1] Sa'īd's power to protect made him the refuge of several kinswomen mentioned in the B.N. and the T.R. This mother and child reached Kāshghar in 932 AH. (1526 AD.).

Here Bābur ends his [interpolated] account of his mother's family and resumes that of his father's.

[2] Bābur uses a variety of phrases to express Lordship in the Gate. Here he writes *aīshiknī bāshlātib*; elsewhere, *aīshīk ikhtiyārī qilmāq* and *mining aīshīkimdā ṣāḥib ikhtiyārī qīlmāq*. Von Schwarz (p. 159) throws light on the duties of the Lord of the Gate (*Aīshīk Āghāsī*). "Das Thür . . . führt in eine

then 25 but youth notwithstanding, his rules and management were very good indeed. A few years later when Ibrāhīm *Begchīk* was plundering near Aūsh, he followed him up, fought him, was beaten and became a martyr. At the time, Sl. Aḥmad Mīrzā was in the summer pastures of Āq Qāchghāī, in Aūrā-tīpā, 18 *yīghāch* east of Samarkand, and Sl. Abū-sa'īd Mīrzā was at Bābā Khākī, 12 *yīghāch* east of Hirī. People sent the news post-haste to the Mīrzā(s),[1] having humbly represented it through 'Abdu'l-wahhāb *Shaghāwal*. In four days it was carried those 120 *yīghāch* of road.[2]

Ḥāfiẓ Muḥammad Beg *Dūldāī* was another, Sl. Malik *Kāshgharī's* son and a younger brother of Aḥmad Ḥājī Beg. After the death of Khudāī-bīrdī Beg, they sent him to control 'Umar Shaikh Mīrzā's Gate, but he did not get on well with the Andijān begs and therefore, when Sl. Abū-sa'īd Mirza died, went to Samarkand and took service with Sl. Aḥmad Mīrzā. At the time of the disaster on the Chīr, he was in Aūrā-tīpā and made it over to 'Umar Shaikh Mīrzā when the Mīrzā passed through on his way to Samarkand, himself taking service with him. The Mīrzā, for his part, gave him the Andijān Command. Later on he went to Sl. Maḥmūd Khān Fol. 13*b*.

---

grosse, vier-eckige, höhe Halle, deren Boden etwa 2 m. über den Weg erhoben ist. In dieser Halle, welche alle passiren muss, der durch das Thor eingeht, reitet oder fahrt, ist die Thorwache placiert. Tagsüber sind die Thore beständig öffen, nach Eintritt der Dunkelheit aber werden dieselben geschlossen und die Schlüssel dem zuständigen Polizeichef abgeliefert. . . . In den erwähnten Thorhallen nehmen in den hoch unabhängigen Gebieten an Bazartagen haufig die Richter Platz, um jedem der irgend ein Anliegen hat, so fort Recht zu sprechen. Die zudiktierten Strafen werden auch gleich in diesem selben locale vollzogen und eventuell die zum Hangen verurteilten Verbrecher an den Deckbalken aufgehängt, so dass die Besucher des Bazars unter den gehenkten durchpassieren müssen."

[1] *bu khabarnī 'Abdu'l-wahhāb shaghāwaldīn 'arẓa-dāsht qīlib Mīrzāghā chāptūrdīlār.* This passage has been taken to mean that the *shaghāwal, i.e.* chief scribe, was the courier, but I think Bābur's words shew that the *shaghāwal's* act preceded the despatch of the news. Moreover the only accusative of the participle and of the verb is *khabarnī*. 'Abdu'l-wahhāb had been 'Umar Shaikh's and was now Aḥmad's officer in Khujand, on the main road for Aūrā-tīpā whence the courier started on the rapid ride. The news may have gone verbally to 'Abdu'l-wahhāb and he have written it on to Aḥmad and Abū-sa'īd.

[2] Measured from point to point even, the distance appears to be over 500 miles. Concerning Bābā Khākī *see* H.S. ii. 224; for rapid riding *i.a.* Kostenko iii, cap. Studs.

in Tāshkīnt and was there entrusted with the guardianship of Khān Mīrzā (Wais) and given Dīzak. He had started for Makka by way of Hind before I took Kābul (910AH. Oct. 1504AD.), but he went to God's mercy on the road. He was a simple person, of few words and not clever.

Khwāja Ḥusain Beg was another, a good-natured and simple person. It is said that, after the fashion of those days, he used to improvise very well at drinking parties.[1]

Shaikh Mazīd Beg was another, my first guardian, excellent in rule and method. He must have served (*khidmat qīlghān dūr*) under Bābur Mīrzā (*Shāhrukhī*). There was no greater beg in 'Umar Shaikh Mīrzā's presence. He was a vicious person and kept catamites.

'Alī-mazīd *Qūchīn* was another;[2] he rebelled twice, once at Akhsī, once at Tāshkīnt. He was disloyal, untrue to his salt, vicious and good-for-nothing.

Ḥasan (son of) Yaq'ūb was another, a small-minded, good-tempered, smart and active man. This verse is his:—

> "Return, O Huma, for without the parrot-down of thy lip,
> The crow will assuredly soon carry off my bones." [3]

Fol. 14. He was brave, a good archer, played polo (*chaughān*) well and leapt well at leap-frog.[4] He had the control of my Gate after 'Umar Shaikh Mīrzā's accident. He had not much sense, was narrow-minded and somewhat of a strife-stirrer.

Qāsim Beg *Qūchīn*, of the ancient army-begs of Andijān, was another. He had the control of my Gate after Ḥasan Yaq'ūb Beg. His life through, his authority and consequence waxed without decline. He was a brave man; once he gave some Aūzbegs a good beating when he overtook them raiding near Kāsān; his sword hewed away in 'Umar Shaikh Mīrzā's

[1] *qūshūqlārnī yakhshī aītūrā īkān dūr.* Elph. MS. for *qūshūq*, *tūyūk*. *Qūshūq* is allowed, both by its root and by usage, to describe improvisations of combined dance and song. I understand from Bābur's tense, that his information was hearsay only.

[2] *i.e.* of the military class. *Cf.* Vullers *s.n.* and T.R. p. 301.

[3] The Hūma is a fabulous bird, overshadowing by whose wings brings good-fortune. The couplet appears to be addressed to some man, under the name Hūma, from whom Ḥasan of Yaq'ūb hoped for benefit.

[4] *khāk-bila*; the *Sanglākh*, (quoting this passage) gives *khāk-p:l:k* as the correct form of the word.

presence; and in the fight at the Broad Ford (Yāsī-kījit *circa* 904AH.-July, 1499AD.) he hewed away with the rest. In the guerilla days he went to Khusrau Shāh (907AH.) at the time I was planning to go from the Macha hill-country[1] to Sl. Maḥmūd Khān, but he came back to me in 910AH. (1504AD.) and I shewed him all my old favour and affection. When I attacked the Turkmān Hazāra raiders in Dara-i-khwush (911AH.) he made better advance, spite of his age, than the younger men; I gave him Bangash as a reward and later on, after returning to Kābul, made him Humāyūn's guardian. He went to God's mercy about the time Zamīn-dāwar was taken (*circa* 928AH.-1522AD.). He was a pious, God-fearing Musalmān, an abstainer from doubtful aliments; excellent in judgment and counsel, very facetious and, though he could neither read nor write (*ummiy*), used to make entertaining jokes. Fol. 14*b*.

Bābā Beg's Bābā Qulī ('Alī) was another, a descendant of Shaikh 'Alī *Bahādur*.[2] They made him my guardian when Shaikh Mazīd Beg died. He went over to Sl. Aḥmad Mīrzā when the Mīrzā led his army against Andijān (899AH.), and gave him Aūrā-tīpā. After Sl. Maḥmūd Mīrzā's death, he left Samarkand and was on his way to join me (900AH.) when Sl. 'Alī Mīrzā, issuing out of Aūrā-tīpā, fought, defeated and slew him. His management and equipment were excellent and he took good care of his men. He prayed not; he kept no fasts; he was like a heathen and he was a tyrant.

'Alī-dost Ṭaghāī[3] was another, one of the Sāghārīchī *tumān*-begs and a relation of my mother's mother, Aīsān-daulat Begīm. I favoured him more than he had been favoured in 'Umar Shaikh Mīrzā's time. People said, "Work will come from his hand." But in the many years he was in my presence, no work to speak of[4] came to sight. He must have served Sl. Abū-sa'īd Mīrzā. He claimed to have power to bring on rain with the jade-stone. He was the Falconer (*qūshchī*), worthless Fol. 15.

1 *Cf*. f. 99*b*.

2 One of Tīmūr's begs.

3 *i.e.* uncle on the mother's side, of any degree, here a grandmother's brother. The title appears to have been given for life to men related to the ruling House. Parallel with it are Madame Mère, Royal Uncle, Sulṭān Wālida.

4 *kīm dīsā būlghāī*, perhaps meaning, "Nothing of service to me."

by nature and habit, a stingy, severe, strife-stirring person, false, self-pleasing, rough of tongue and cold-of-face.

Wais *Lāgharī*,[1] one of the Samarkand *Tūghchī* people, was another. Latterly he was much in 'Umar Shaikh Mīrzā's confidence; in the guerilla times he was with me. Though somewhat factious, he was a man of good judgment and counsel.

Mīr Ghiyāṣ Ṭaghāi was another, a younger brother of 'Ali-dost Ṭaghāī. No man amongst the leaders in Sl. Abū-sa'īd Mīrzā's Gate was more to the front than he; he had charge of the Mīrzā's square seal[2] and was much in his confidence latterly. He was a friend of Wais *Lāgharī*. When Kāsān had been given to Sl. Maḥmūd Khān (899AH.-1494AD.), he was continuously in The Khān's service and was in high favour. He was a laugher, a joker and fearless in vice.

'Ali-darwesh *Khurāsānī* was another. He had served in the Khurāsān Cadet Corps, one of two special corps of serviceable young men formed by Sl. Abū-sa'īd Mīrzā when he first began
Fol. 15*b*. to arrange the government of Khurāsān and Samarkand, and, presumably, called by him the Khurāsān Corps and the Samarkand Corps. 'Alī-darwesh was a brave man; he did well in my presence at the Gate of Bīshkārān.[3] He wrote the *naskh ta'līq* hand clearly.[4] His was the flatterer's tongue and in his character avarice was supreme.

Qambar-'alī *Mughūl* of the Equerries (*akhtachī*) was another. People called him The Skinner because his father, on first coming into the (Farghāna) country, worked as a skinner. Qambar-'alī had been Yūnas Khān's water-bottle bearer,[5] later on he became a beg. Till he was a made man, his conduct was excellent; once arrived, he was slack. He was full of talk and of foolish talk,—a great talker is sure to be a foolish one,—his capacity was limited and his brain muddy.

[1] Wais the Thin.

[2] *Cf.* Chardin ed. Langlès v, 461 and ed. 1723 AD. v, 183.

[3] n.e. of Kāsān. *Cf.* f. 74. Hai MS., erroneously, Samarkand.

[4] An occasional doubt arises as to whether a *ṭaurī* of the text is Arabic and dispraises or Turkī and laudatory. *Cf.* Mems. p. 17 and *Mêms.* i, 3.

[5] Elph. and Ḥai. MSS. *aftābachī*, water-bottle bearer on journeys; Kehr (p. 82) *aftābchī*, ewer-bearer; Ilminsky (p. 19) *akhtachi*, squire or groom. Circumstances support *aftābachī*. Yūnas was town-bred, his ewer-bearer would hardly be the rough Mughūl, Qambar-'alī, useful as an *aftābachī*.

(*l. Historical narrative.*)

At the time of 'Umar Shaikh Mīrzā's accident, I was in the Four Gardens (*Chār-bāgh*) of Andijān.[1] The news reached Andijān on Tuesday, Ramẓan 5 (June 9th); I mcunted at once, with my followers and retainers, intending to go into the fort but, on our getting near the Mīrzā's Gate, Shīrīm Ṭaghāī[2] took hold of my bridle and moved off towards the Praying Place.[3] It had crossed his mind that if a great ruler like Sl. Aḥmad Mīrzā came in force, the Andijān begs would make over to him me and the country,[4] but that if he took me to Aūzkīnt and the foothills thereabouts, I, at any rate, should not be made over and could go to one of my mother's (half-) brothers, Sl. Maḥmūd Khān or Sl. Aḥmad Khān.[5] When Khwāja Maulānā-i-qāẓī[6] Fol. 16.

(*Author's note on Khwāja Maulānā-i-qāẓī.*) He was the son of Sl. Aḥmad Qāẓī, of the line of Burhānu'd-dīn 'Alī *Qīlīch*[7] and through his mother, traced back to Sl. Aīlīk *Māẓī*.[8] By hereditary right

---

[1] Bābur was Governor of Andijān and the month being June, would be living out-of-doors. *Cf.* H.S. ii. 272 and Schuyler ii, 37.

[2] To the word Sherīm applies Abū'l-ghāzī's explanation of Nurūm and Ḥājīm, namely, that they are abbreviations of Nūr and Ḥājī Muḥammad. It explains Sultānīm also when used (f. 72) of Sl. Muḥammad Khānika but of Sulṭānīm as the name is common with Bābur, Ḥaidar and Gul-badan, *i.e.* as a woman's, Busbecq's explanation is the better, namely, that it means My Sulṭān and is applied to a person of rank and means. This explains other women's titles *e.g.* Khānīm, my Khān and Ākām (Ākīm), My Lady. A third group of names formed like the last by enclitic *'m* (my), may be called names of affection, *e.g.* Māhīm, My Moon, Jānīm, My Life. (*Cf.* Persian equivalents.) *Cf.* Abū'l-ghāzī's *Shajarat-i-Turkī* (Désmaisons p. 272); and Ogier Ghiselin de Busbecq's *Life and Letters* (Forster and Daniel i, 38.)

[3] *Namāz-gāh*; generally an open terrace, with a wall towards the Qibla and outside the town, whither on festival days the people go out in crowds to pray. (Erskine.)

[4] *Bēglār (nīng) mīnī u wilāyatnī tāpshūrghūlārī dūr*; a noticeably idiomatic sentence. *Cf.* f. 16*b* l. 6 and l. 7 for a repetition.

[5] Maḥmūd was in Tāshkīnt, Aḥmad in Kāshghār or on the Āq-sū.

[6] The B.N. contains a considerable number of what are virtually footnotes. They are sometimes, as here, entered in the middle of a sentence and confuse the narrative; they are introduced by *kīm*, a mere sign of parenthetical matter to follow, and some certainly, known not to be Bābur's own, must have stood first on the margin of his text. It seems best to enter them as Author's notes.

[7] *i.e.* the author of the Hidāyat. *Cf.* f. 3*b* and note; Blochmann *Āyīn-i-akbarī s.n. qulij* and note; Bellew's *Afghan Tribes* p. 100, *Khilich*.

[8] Ar. dead, gone. The precision of Bābur's words *khānwādalār* and *yūsūnlūq* is illustrated by the existence in the days of Tīmūr, in Marghīnān, (Burhānu'd-dīn's township) of a ruler named Aīlīk Khān, apparently a

(*yūsūnlūq*) his high family (*khānwādalār*) must have come to be the Refuge (*marji'*) and Pontiffs (*Shaikhu'l-islām*) of the (Farghāna) country.

and the begs in the fort heard of (the intended departure), they sent after us Khwāja Muḥammad, the tailor,[1] an old servant (*bāyrī*) of my father and the foster-father of one of his daughters. Fol. 16*b*. He dispelled our fears and, turning back from near the Praying Place, took me with him into the citadel (*ark*) where I dismounted. Khwāja Maulānā-i-qāẓī and the begs came to my presence there and after bringing their counsels to a head,[2] busied themselves in making good the towers and ramparts of the fort.[3] A few days later, Ḥasan, son of Yaq'ūb, and Qāsim *Qūchīn*, arrived, together with other begs who had been sent to reconnoitre in Marghīnān and those parts.[4] They also, after waiting on me, set themselves with one heart and mind and with zeal and energy, to hold the fort.

Meantime Sl. Aḥmad Mīrzā took Aūrā-tīpā, Khujand and Marghīnān, came on to Qabā,[5] 4 *yīghāch* from Andijān and there made halt. At this crisis, Darwesh Gau, one of the Andijān notables, was put to death on account of his improper proposals; his punishment crushed the rest.

Khwāja Qāẓī and Aūzūn (Long) Ḥasan,[6] (brother) of Khwāja Ḥusain, were then sent to Sl. Aḥmad Mīrzā to say in effect that, as he himself would place one of his servants in the country and as I was myself both a servant and (as) a son, he would attain his end most readily and easily if he entrusted the service to me. He was a mild, weak man, of few words who, without his begs, decided no opinion or compact (*aun*), action

---

descendant of Sātūq-būghrā Khān (b. 384 AH.-994 AD.) so that in Khwāja Qāẓī were united two dynasties, (*khānwādalār*), one priestly, perhaps also regal, the other of bye-gone ruling Khāns. *Cf.* D'Herbélot p. 433; *Yarkand Mission*, Bellew p. 121; *Tazkirat-i Sulṭān Sātūq-būghrā Khān Ghāzī Pādshāh* and *Tārīkh-i-nāṣirī* (Raverty *s.n.*)

[1] *darzī*; H.S. *khaiyāṭ*.

[2] *bīr yīrgā* (*qūyūb*), lit. to one place.

[3] *i.e.* reconstructed the earthern defences. *Cf.* Von Schwarz *s.n.* loess.

[4] They had been sent, presumably, before 'Umar Shaikh's death, to observe Sl. Aḥmad M.'s advance. *Cf.* f. 6.

[5] The time-table of the Andijān Railway has a station, Kouwa (Qabā).

[6] Bābur, always I think, calls this man Long Ḥasan; Khwānd-amīr styles him Khwāja Ḥasan; he seems to be the brother of one of 'Umar Shaikh's fathers-in-law, Khwāja Ḥusain.

or move; they paid attention to our proposal, gave it a harsh answer and moved forward.

But the Almighty God, who, of His perfect power and without mortal aid, has ever brought my affairs to their right issue, made such things happen here that they became disgusted at having advanced (*i.e.* from Qabā), repented indeed that they had ever set out on this expedition and turned back with nothing done.

One of those things was this: Qabā has a stagnant, morass-like Water,[1] passable only by the bridge. As they were many, there was crowding on the bridge and numbers of horses and Fol. 17. camels were pushed off to perish in the water. This disaster recalling the one they had had three or four years earlier when they were badly beaten at the passage of the Chīr, they gave way to fear. Another thing was that such a murrain broke out amongst their horses that, massed together, they began to die off in bands.[2] Another was that they found in our soldiers and peasants a resolution and single-mindedness such as would not let them flinch from making offering of their lives[3] so long as there was breath and power in their bodies. Need being therefore, when one *yīghāch* from Andijān, they sent Darwesh Muḥammad Tarkhān[4] to us; Ḥasan of Yaq'ūb went out from those in the fort; the two had an interview near the Praying Place and a sort of peace was made. This done, Sl. Aḥmad Mīrzā's force retired.

Meantime Sl. Maḥmūd Khān had come along the north of the Khujand Water and laid siege to Akhsī.[5] In Akhsī was

[1] *bātqāq*. This word is underlined in the Elph. MS. by *dil-dil* and in the Ḥai. MS. by *jam-jama*. It is translated in the W.-i-B. by *āb pur hila*, water full of deceit; it is our Slough of Despond. It may be remarked that neither Zenker nor Steingass gives to *dil-dil* or *jam-jama* the meaning of morass; the *Akbar-nāma* does so. (H.B. ii, 112.)

[2] *ṭawila ṭawila ātlār yīghilib aūlā kīrīshti*. I understand the word *yīghilib* to convey that the massing led to the spread of the murrian.

[3] *jān tārātmāqlār i.e.* as a gift to their over-lord.

[4] Perhaps, Bābur's maternal great-uncle. It would suit the privileges bestowed on Tarkhāns if their title meant *Khān of the Gifts* (Turkī *tar*, gift). In the *Bāburnāma*, it excludes all others. Most of Aḥmad's begs were Tarkhāns, Arghūns and Chingiz Khānids, some of them ancestors of later rulers in Tatta and Sind. Concerning the Tarkhāns *see* T.R. p. 55 and note; A.N. (H.B. *s.n.*) Elliot and Dowson's *History of India*, 498.

[5] *Cf.* f. 6.

Jahāngīr Mīrzā (aet. 9) and of begs, 'Alī-darwesh Beg, Mīrzā Qulī *Kūkūldāsh*, Muḥ. Bāqir Beg and Shaikh 'Abdu'l-lāh, Lord of the Gate. Wais *Lāgharī* and Mīr Ghiyāṣ Ṭaghāī had been there too, but being afraid of the (Akhsī) begs had gone off to Kāsān, Wais *Lāgharī's* district, where, he being Nāṣir Mīrzā's guardian, the Mīrzā was.[1] They went over to Sl. Maḥmūd
Fol. 17b. Khān when he got near Akhsī; Mīr Ghiyāṣ entered his service; Wais *Lāgharī* took Nāṣir Mīrzā to Sl. Aḥmad Mīrzā, who entrusted him to Muh. Mazīd Tarkhān's charge. The Khān, though he fought several times near Akhsī, could not effect anything because the Akhsī begs and braves made such splendid offering of their lives. Falling sick, being tired of fighting too, he returned to his own country (*i.e.* Tāshkīnt).

For some years, Ābā-bikr *Kāshgharī Dūghlāt*,[2] bowing the head to none, had been supreme in Kāshgar and Khutan. He now, moved like the rest by desire for my country, came to the neighbourhood of Aūzkīnt, built a fort and began to lay the land waste. Khwāja Qāzī and several begs were appointed to drive him out. When they came near, he saw himself no match for such a force, made the Khwāja his mediator and, by a hundred wiles and tricks, got himself safely free.

Throughout these great events, 'Umar Shaikh Mīrzā's former begs and braves had held resolutely together and made daring offer of their lives. The Mīrzā's mother, Shāh Sulṭān Begīm,[3] and Jaḥāngīr Mīrzā and the *ḥaram* household and the begs came from Akhsī to Andijān; the customary mourning was fulfilled and food and victuals spread for the poor and destitute.[4]

Fol. 18. In the leisure from these important matters, attention was given to the administration of the country and the ordering of the army. The Andijān Government and control of my Gate were settled (*mukarrar*) for Ḥasan (son) of Yaq'ūb; Aūsh was decided on (*qarār*) for Qāsim *Qūchīn*; Akhsī and Marghīnān assigned (*ta'īn*) to Aūzun Ḥasan and 'Alī-dost Ṭaghāī. For the rest of 'Umar Shaikh Mīrzā's begs and braves, to each accord-

[1] *beg ātākā*, lit. beg for father.
[2] T.R. *s.n.* Ābā-bikr.
[3] *Cf.* f. 6*b* and note.
[4] *faqra u masākin*, *i.e.* those who have food for one day and those who have none in hand. (Steingass.)

ing to his circumstances, were settled and assigned district (*wilāyat*) or land (*yīr*) or office (*mauja*) or charge (*jīrga*) or stipend (*wajh*).

When Sl. Aḥmad Mīrzā had gone two or three stages on his return-march, his health changed for the worse and high fever appeared. On his reaching the Āq Sū near Aūrā-tīpā, he bade farewell to this transitory world, in the middle of Shawwāl of the date 899 (mid July 1494 AD.) being then 44 (lunar) years old.

m. Sl. Aḥmad Mīrzā's birth and descent.

He was born in 855 AH. (1451 AD.) the year in which his father took the throne (*i.e.* Samarkand). He was Sl. Abū-sa'īd Mīrzā's eldest son; his mother was a daughter of Aūrdū-būghā Tarkhān (*Arghūn*), the elder sister of Darwesh Muḥammad Tarkhān, and the most honoured of the Mīrzā's wives.

n. His appearance and habits.

He was a tall, stout, brown-bearded and red-faced man. He had beard on his chin but none on his cheeks. He had very Fol. 18*b*.
pleasing manners. As was the fashion in those days, he wound his turban in four folds and brought the end forward over his brows.

o. His characteristics and manners.

He was a True Believer, pure in the Faith; five times daily, without fail, he recited the Prayers, not omitting them even on drinking-days. He was a disciple of his Highness Khwāja 'Ubaidu'l-lāh (*Aḥrārī*), his instructor in religion and the strengthener of his Faith. He was very ceremonious, particularly when sitting with the Khwāja. People say he never drew one knee over the other[1] at any entertainment of the Khwāja. On one occasion contrary to his custom, he sat with his feet together. When he had risen, the Khwāja ordered the place he had sat in to be searched; there they found, it may have been, a bone.[2] He had read nothing whatever and was ignorant

[1] For fashions of sitting, *see Tawārikh-i-guzīda Naṣrat-nāma* B.M. Or. 3222. Aḥmad would appear to have maintained the deferential attitude by kneeling and sitting back upon his heels.

[2] *bīr sūnkāk bār ikān dūr.* I understand that something defiling must have been there, perhaps a bone.

(*'amī*), and though town-bred, unmannered and homely. Of genius he had no share. He was just and as his Highness the Khwāja was there, accompanying him step by step,[1] most of his affairs found lawful settlement. He was true and faithful to his vow and word; nothing was ever seen to the contrary. He had courage, and though he never happened to get in his own hand to work, gave sign of it, they say, in some of his en-
Fol. 19. counters. He drew a good bow, generally hitting the duck[2] both with his arrows (*aūq*) and his forked-arrows (*tīr-giz*), and, as a rule, hit the gourd[3] in riding across the lists (*maidān*). Latterly, when he had grown stout, he used to take quail and pheasant with the goshawks,[4] rarely failing. A sportsman he was, hawking mostly and hawking well; since Aūlūgh Beg Mīrzā, such a sporting *pādshāh* had not been seen. He was extremely decorous; people say he used to hide his feet even in the privacy of his family and amongst his intimates. Once settled down to drink, he would drink for 20 or 30 days at a stretch; once risen, would not drink again for another 20 or 30 days. He was a good drinker;[5] on non-drinking days he ate without conviviality (*basīṭ*). Avarice was dominant in his character. He was kindly, a man of few words whose will was in the hands of his begs.

p. His battles.

He fought four battles. The first was with Ni'mat *Arghūn*, Shaikh Jamāl *Arghūn's* younger brother, at Āqār-tūzī, near Zamīn. This he won. The second was with 'Umar Shaikh Mīrzā at Khwaṣ; this also he won. The third affair was when he encountered Sl. Maḥmūd Khān on the Chīr, near Tāshkīnt
Fol. 19*b*. (895 AH.-1469 AD.). There was no real fighting, but some Mughūl plunderers coming up, by ones and twos, in his rear and laying hands on his baggage, his great army, spite of its numbers,

[1] *Khwājaning ham āyāghlārī ārādā idī.*
[2] *ilbāsūn*, a kind of mallard (*Abūshqā*), here perhaps a popinjay. *Cf.* Ḥ.S. ii. 193 for Aḥmad's skill as an archer, and Payne-Gallwey's *Cross-bow* p. 225.
[3] *qabāq*, an archer's mark. Abū'l-ghāzī (Kāsān ed. p. 181. 5) mentions a hen (*tūqūq*) as a mark. *Cf.* Payne-Gallwey *l.c.* p. 231.
[4] *qīrghīcha, astar palumbarius.* (Shaw's Voc. Scully.)
[5] Perhaps, not quarrelsome.

broke up without a blow struck, without an effort made, without a coming face to face, and its main body was drowned in the Chīr.[1] His fourth affair was with Ḥaidar *Kūkūldāsh* (*Mughūl*), near Yār-yīlāq; here he won.

q. His country.

Samarkand and Bukhārā his father gave him; Tāshkīnt and Sairām he took and held for a time but gave them to his younger brother, 'Umar Shaikh Mīrzā, after 'Abdu'l-qadūs (*Dūghlāt*) slew Shaikh Jamāl (*Arghūn*); Khujand and Aūrā-tīpā were also for a time in his possession.

r. His children.

His two sons did not live beyond infancy. He had five daughters, four by Qātāq Begīm.[2]

Rābi'a-sulṭān Begīm, known as the Dark-eyed Begīm, was his eldest. The Mīrzā himself made her go forth to Sl. Maḥmūd Khān;[3] she had one child, a nice little boy, called Bābā Khān. The Aūzbegs killed him and several others of age as unripe as his when they martyred (his father) The Khān, in Khujand, (914 AH.-1508 AD.). At that time she fell to Jānī Beg Sulṭān (*Aūzbeg*). Fol. 20.

Ṣāliḥa-sulṭān (Ṣalīqa) Begīm was his second daughter; people called her the Fair Begīm. Sl. Maḥmūd Mīrzā, after her father's death, took her for his eldest son, Sl. Mas'ūd Mīrzā and made the wedding feast (900 AH.). Later on she fell to the Kāshgharī with Shāh Begīm and Mihr-nigār Khānim.

'Āyisha-sulṭān Begīm was the third. When I was five and went to Samarkand, they set her aside for me; in the guerilla times[4] she came to Khujand and I took her (905 AH.); her one little daughter, born after the second taking of Samarkand,

[1] The T.R. (p. 116) attributes the rout to Shaibānī's defection. The Ḥ.S. (ii. 192) has a varied and confused account. An error in the T.R. trs. making Shaibānī plunder the Mughūls, is manifestly clerical.

[2] *i.e.* condiment, *ce qu'on ajoute au pain.*

[3] *Cf.* f. 6.

[4] *qāzāqlār*; here, if Bābur's, meaning his conflicts with Tambal, but as the Begīm may have been some time in Khujand, the *qāzāqlār* may be of Samarkand.

went in a few days to God's mercy and she herself left me at the instigation of an older sister.

Sulṭānīm Begīm was the fourth daughter; Sl. 'Alī Mīrzā took her; then Tīmūr Sulṭān (*Aūzbeg*) took her and after him, Mahdī Sulṭān (*Aūzbeg*).

Ma'sūma-sulṭān Begīm was the youngest of Sl. Aḥmad Mīrzā's daughters. Her mother, Ḥabība-sulṭān Begīm, was of the Arghūns, a daughter of Sl. Ḥusain *Arghūn's* brother. I saw her when I went to Khurāsān (912 AH.-1506 AD.), liked her, asked for her, had her brought to Kābul and took her (913 AH.-1507 AD.). She had one daughter and there and then, went to God's mercy, through the pains of the birth. Her name was at once given to her child.

s. *His ladies and mistresses.*

Mihr-nigār Khānīm was his first wife, set aside for him by his father, Sl. Abū-sa'īd Mīrzā. She was Yūnas Khān's eldest

Fol. 20*b*. daughter and my mother's full-sister.

Tarkhān Begīm of the Tarkhāns was another of his wives.

Qātāq Begīm was another, the foster-sister of the Tarkhān Begīm just mentioned. Sl. Aḥmad Mīrzā took her *par amours* (*'āshiqlār bīlā*) : she was loved with passion and was very dominant. She drank wine. During the days of her ascendancy (*tīrīklīk*), he went to no other of his *ḥaram*; at last he took up a proper position (*aūlnūrdī*) and freed himself from his reproach.[1]

[1] All the (Turkī) Bābur-nāma MSS. and those examined of the W.-i-B. by writing *aūltūrdī* (killed) where I suggest to read *aūlnūrdī* (*devenir comme il faut*) state that Aḥmad killed Qātāq. I hesitate to accept this (1) because the only evidence of the murder is one diacritical point, the removal of which lifts Aḥmad's reproach from him by his return to the accepted rules of a polygamous household ; (2) because no murder of Qātāq is chronicled by Khwānd-amīr or other writers ; and (3) because it is incredible that a mild, weak man living in a family atmosphere such as Bābur, Ḥaidar and Gul-badan reproduce for us, should, while possessing facility for divorce, kill the mother of four out of his five children.

Reprieve must wait however until the word *tīrīklīk* is considered. This Erskine and de C. have read, with consistency, to mean *life-time*, but if *aūlnūrdī* be read in place of *aūltūrdī* (killed), *tīrīklīk* may be read, especially in conjunction with Bābur's *'āshiqlīklār*, as meaning *living power* or *ascendancy*. Again, if read as from *tīrik*, a small arrow and a consuming pain, *tīrīklīk* may represent Cupid's darts and wounds. Again it might be taken as from *tīrāmāk*, to hinder, or forbid.

Under these considerations, it is legitimate to reserve judgment on Aḥmad.

Khān-zāda Begīm, of the Tīrmīẕ Khāns, was another. He had just taken her when I went, at five years old, to Samarkand; her face was still veiled and, as is the Turkī custom, they told me to uncover it.[1]

Laṯīf Begīm was another, a daughter's child of Aḥmad Ḥājī Beg *Dūldāī* (*Barlās*). After the Mīrzā's death, Ḥamza Sl. took her and she had three sons by him. They with other sulṯāns' children, fell into my hands when I took Ḥiṣār (916 AH.-1510 AD.) after defeating Ḥamza Sulṯān and Tīmūr Sulṯān. I set all free.

Ḥabība-sulṯān Begīm was another, a daughter of the brother of Sl. Ḥusain *Arghūn*.

t. His amīrs.

Jānī Beg *Dūldāī* (*Barlās*) was a younger brother of Sl. Malik *Kāshgharī*. Sl. Abū-sa'īd Mīrzā gave him the Government of Samarkand and Sl. Aḥmad Mīrzā gave him the control of his own Gate.[2] He must have had singular habits and manners;[3] many strange stories are told about him. One is this:—While he was Governor in Samarkand, an envoy came to him from the Aūzbegs renowned, as it would seem, for his strength. An Aūzbeg, is said to call a strong man a bull (*būkuh*). "Are you a *būkuh?*" said Jānī Beg to the envoy, "If you are, come, let's have a friendly wrestle together (*kūrāshālīng*)." Whatever objections the envoy raised, he refused to accept. They wrestled and Jānī Beg gave the fall. He was a brave man. Fol. 21.

Aḥmad Ḥājī (*Dūldāī Barlās*) was another, a son of Sl. Malik *Kāshgharī*. Sl. Abū-sa'īd Mīrzā gave him the Government of Hīrī (Harāt) for a time but sent him when his uncle, Jānī Beg

[1] It is customary amongst Turks for a bride, even amongst her own family, to remain veiled for some time after marriage; a child is then told to pluck off the veil and run away, this tending, it is fancied, to the child's own success in marriage. (Erskine.)

[2] Bābur's anecdote about Jānī Beg well illustrates his caution as a narrator. He appears to tell it as one who knowing the point of a story, leads up to it. He does not affirm that Jānī Beg's habits were strange or that the envoy was an athlete but that both things must have been (*īkān dūr*) from what he had heard or to suit the point of the anecdote. Nor does he affirm as of his own knowledge that Aūzbegs calls a strong man (his *zor kīshī*) a *būkuh* (bull) but says it is so understood (*dīr īmish*).

[3] *Cf.* f. 170.

died, to Samarkand with his uncle's appointments. He was pleasant-natured and brave. Wafā'ī was his pen-name and he put together a dīwān in verse not bad. This couplet is his:

"I am drunk, Inspector, to-day keep your hand off me,
"Inspect me on the day you catch me sober."

Mīr 'Alī-sher Nawā'ī when he went from Hirī to Samarkand, was with Aḥmad Ḥājī Beg but he went back to Hirī when Sl. Ḥusain Mīrzā (Bāī-qarā) became supreme (873 AH.-1460 AD.) and he there received exceeding favour.

Fol. 21*b*. Aḥmad Ḥājī Beg kept and rode excellent *tīpūchāqs*,[1] mostly of his own breeding. Brave he was but his power to command did not match his courage; he was careless and what was necessary in his affairs, his retainers and followers put through. He fell into Sl. 'Alī Mīrzā's hands when the Mīrzā defeated Bāī-sunghar Mīrzā in Bukhārā (901 AH.), and was then put to a dishonourable death on the charge of the blood of Darwesh Muḥammad Tarkhān.[2]

Darwesh Muḥammad Tarkhān (*Arghūn*) was another, the son of Aūrdū-būghā Tarkhān and full-brother of the mother of Sl. Aḥmad Mīrzā and Sl. Maḥmūd Mīrzā.[3] Of all begs in Sl. Aḥmad Mīrzā's presence, he was the greatest and most honoured. He was an orthodox Believer, kindly and darwesh-like, and was a constant transcriber of the Qu'rān.[4] He played chess often and well, thoroughly understood the science of fowling and flew his birds admirably. He died in the height of his greatness, with a bad name, during the troubles between Sl. 'Alī Mīrzā and Bāī-sunghar Mīrzā.[5]

'Abdu'l-'alī Tarkhān was another, a near relation of Darwesh Muḥammad Tarkhān, possessor also of his younger sister,[6] that is to say, Bāqī Tarkhān's mother. Though both by the Mughūl rule (*tūrā*) and by his rank, Darwesh Muḥammad

[1] The points of a *tipūchāq* are variously stated. If the root notion of the name be movement (*tip*), Erskine's observation, that these horses are taught special paces, is to the point. To the verb *tiprāmāq* dictionaries assign the meaning of *movement with agitation of mind*, an explanation fully illustrated in the B.N. The verb describes fittingly the dainty, nervous action of some trained horses. Other meanings assigned to *tūpūchāq* are roadster, round-bodied and swift.

[2] *Cf.* f. 37*b*.

[3] *Cf.* f. 6*b* and note.

[4] *mashaf kitābat qilūr īdī*.

[5] *Cf.* f. 36 and H.S. ii. 271.

[6] *sinkilisi ham mūndā idī*.

Tarkhān was the superior of 'Abdu'l-'alī Tarkhān, this Pharoah regarded him not at all. For some years he had the Government of Bukhārā. His retainers were reckoned at 3,000 and he kept them well and handsomely. His gifts (*bakhshīsh*), his visits of enquiry (*purshīsh*), his public audience (*dīwān*), his work-shops (*dast-gāh*), his open-table (*shīlan*) and his assemblies (*majlis*) were all like a king's. He was a strict disciplinarian, a tyrannical, vicious, self-infatuated person. Shaibānī Khān, though not his retainer, was with him for a time; most of the lesser (Shaibān) sulṭāns did themselves take service with him. This same 'Abdu'l-'alī Tarkhān was the cause of Shaibānī Khān's rise to such a height and of the downfall of such ancient dynasties.[1] Fol. 22.

Sayyid Yūsuf, the Grey Wolfer[2] was another; his grandfather will have come from the Mughūl horde; his father was favoured by Aūlūgh Beg Mīrzā (*Shāhrukhī*). His judgment and counsel were excellent; he had courage too. He played well on the guitar (*qūbuz*). He was with me when I first went to Kābul; I shewed him great favour and in truth he was worthy of favour. I left him in Kābul the first year the army rode out for Hindūstān; at that time he went to God's mercy.[3]

Darwesh Beg was another; he was of the line of Aīku-tīmūr Beg,[4] a favourite of Tīmūr Beg. He was a disciple of his Highness Khwāja 'Ubaidu'l-lāh (*Aḥrārī*), had knowledge of the science of music, played several instruments and was naturally disposed to poetry. He was drowned in the Chīr at the time of Sl. Aḥmad Mīrzā's discomfiture. Fol. 22b.

Muḥammad Mazīd Tarkhān was another, a younger full-brother of Darwesh Muḥ. Tarkhān. He was Governor in Turkistān for some years till Shaibānī Khān took it from him. His judgment and counsel were excellent; he was an unscrupulous and vicious person. The second and third times

[1] *khāna-wādalār*, *viz.* the Chaghatāī, the Tīmūrid in two Mīrān-shāhī branches, 'Alī's and Bābur's and the Bāī-qarā in Harāt.

[2] *aūghlāqchī i.e.* player at *kūk-būrā*. Concerning the game, *see* Shaw's Vocabulary; Schuyler i, 268; Kostenko iii, 82; Von Schwarz *s.n. baiga*.

[3] Ẕū'l-ḥijja 910 AH.-May 1505 AD. *Cf.* f. 154. This statement helps to define what Bābur reckoned his expeditions into Hindūstān.

[4] Aīkū (Ayāgū)-tīmūr *Tarkhān Arghūn* d. *circa* 793 AH.-1391 AD. He was a friend of Tīmūr. *See* Ẓ.N. i, 525 etc.

I took Samarkand, he came to my presence and each time I shewed him very great favour. He died in the fight at Kūl-i-malik (918 AH.-1512 AD.).

Bāqī Tarkhān was another, the son of 'Abdu'l-'alī Tarkhān and Sl. Aḥmad Mīrzā's aunt. When his father died, they gave him Bukhārā. He grew in greatness under Sl. 'Alī Mīrzā, his retainers numbering 5 or 6,000. He was neither obedient nor very submissive to Sl. 'Alī Mīrzā. He fought Shaibānī Khān at Dabūsī (905AH.) and was crushed; by the help of this defeat, Shaibānī Khān went and took Bukhārā. He was very fond of hawking; they say he kept 700 birds. His manners and habits were not such as may be told;[1] he grew up with a Mīrzā's state and splendour. Because his father had shewn favour to Shaibānī Khān, he went to the Khān's presence, but that inhuman ingrate made him no sort of return in favour and kind-
Fol. 23. ness. He left the world at Akhsī, in misery and wretchedness.

Sl. Ḥusain *Arghūn* was another. He was known as Qarā-kūlī because he had held the Qarā-kūl government for a time. His judgment and counsel were excellent; he was long in my presence also.

Qulī Muḥammad *Būghdā*[2] was another, a *qūchīn*; he must have been a brave man.

'Abdu'l-karīm *Ishrit*[3] was another; he was an Aūīghūr, Sl. Aḥmad Mīrzā's Lord of the Gate, a brave and generous man.

(*u. Historical narrative resumed.*)

After Sl. Aḥmad Mīrzā's death, his begs in agreement, sent a courier by the mountain-road to invite Sl. Maḥmūd Mīrzā.[4]

Malik-i-Muḥammad Mīrzā, the son of Minūchihr Mīrzā, Sl.

[1] *āndāq ikhlāq u aṭawārī yūq idī kim dīsā būlghāī.* The *Shāh-nāma* cap. xviii, describes him as a spoiled child and man of pleasure, caring only for eating, drinking and hunting. The *Shaibānī-nāma* narrates his various affairs.

[2] *i.e., cutlass*, a parallel sobriquet to *qilīch*, sword. If it be correct to translate by "cutlass," the nickname may have prompted Bābur's brief following comment, *mardāna ikān dūr, i.e.* Qulī Muḥ. must have been brave because known as the Cutlass. A common variant in MSS. from *Būghdā* is Bāghdād; Bāghdād was first written in the Ḥai. MS. but is corrected by the scribe to *būghdā*.

[3] So pointed in the Ḥai. MS. I surmise it a clan-name.

[4] *i.e.* to offer him the succession. The mountain road taken from Aūrā-tīpā would be by Āb-burdan, Sara-tāq and the Kām Rūd defile.

Abū-sa'īd Mīrzā's eldest brother, aspired for his own part to rule. Having drawn a few adventurers and desperadoes to himself, they dribbled away[1] from (Sl. Aḥmad Mīrzā's) camp and went to Samarkand. He was not able to effect anything, but he brought about his own death and that of several innocent persons of the ruling House.

At once on hearing of his brother's death, Sl. Maḥmūd Mīrzā went off to Samarkand and there seated himself on the throne, without difficulty. Some of his doings soon disgusted and alienated high and low, soldier and peasant. The first of these was that he sent the above-named Malik-i-Muḥammad to the Fol. 23*b*.
Kūk-sarāī,[2] although he was his father's brother's son and his own son-in-law.[3] With him he sent others, four Mīrzās in all. Two of these he set aside; Malik-i-Muḥammad and one other he martyred. Some of the four were not even of ruling rank and had not the smallest aspiration to rule; though Malik-i-Muḥammad Mīrzā was a little in fault, in the rest there was no blame whatever. A second thing was that though his methods and regulations were excellent, and though he was expert in revenue matters and in the art of administration, his nature inclined to tyranny and vice. Directly he reached Samarkand, he began to make new regulations and arrangements and to rate and tax on a new basis. Moreover the dependants of his (late) Highness Khwāja 'Ubaid'l-lāh, under whose protection formerly many poor and destitute persons had lived free from the burden of dues and imposts, were now themselves treated with harshness and oppression. On what ground should hardship have touched them? Nevertheless oppressive exactions were made from them, indeed from the Khwāja's very children. Yet another thing was that just as he was vicious and tyrannical, so were his begs, small and great, and his retainers and followers. The Ḥiṣārīs and in particular the followers of Khusrau Shāh

[1] *irildi*. The departure can hardly have been open because Aḥmad's begs favoured Maḥmūd; Malik-i-Muḥammad's party would be likely to slip away in small companies.

[2] This well-known Green, Grey or Blue palace or halting-place was within the citadel of Samarkand. *Cf.* f. 37. It served as a prison from which return was not expected.

[3] *Cf.* f. 27. He married a full-sister of Bāī-sunghar.

engaged themselves unceasingly with wine and fornication. Once one of them enticed and took away a certain man's wife.
Fol. 24. When her husband went to Khusrau Shāh and asked for justice, he received for answer: "She has been with you for several years; let her be a few days with him." Another thing was that the young sons of the townsmen and shopkeepers, nay! even of Turks and soldiers could not go out from their houses from fear of being taken for catamites. The Samarakandīs, having passed 20 or 25 years under Sl. Aḥmad Mīrzā in ease and tranquillity, most matters carried through lawfully and with justice by his Highness the Khwāja, were wounded and troubled in heart and soul, by this oppression and this vice. Low and high, the poor, the destitute, all opened the mouth to curse, all lifted the hand for redress.

> "Beware the steaming up of inward wounds,
> For an inward wound at the last makes head;
> Avoid while thou canst, distress to one heart,
> For a single sigh will convulse a world."[1]

By reason of his infamous violence and vice Sl. Maḥmud Mīrzā did not rule in Samarkand more than five or six months.

[1] *Gulistān* Part I. Story 27. For "steaming up," *see* Tennyson's Lotus-eaters Choric song, canto 8 (H.B.).

900 AH.—OCT. 2ND. 1494 TO SEP. 21ST. 1495 AD.[1]

THIS year Sl. Maḥmūd Mīrzā sent an envoy, named 'Abdu'l-qadūs Beg,[2] to bring me a gift from the wedding he had made with splendid festivity for his eldest son, Mas'ūd Mīrzā with (Ṣāliḥa-sulṭān), the Fair Begīm, the second daughter of his elder brother, Sl. Aḥmad Mīrzā. They had sent gold and silver almonds and pistachios.

There must have been relationship between this envoy and Ḥasan-i-yaq'ūb, and on its account he will have been the man sent to make Ḥasan-i-yaq'ūb, by fair promises, look towards Sl. Maḥmūd Mīrzā. Ḥasan-i-yaq'ūb returned him a smooth answer, made indeed as though won over to his side, and gave him leave to go. Five or six months later, his manners changed entirely; he began to behave ill to those about me and to others, and he carried matters so far that he would have dismissed me in order to put Jahāngīr Mīrzā in my place. Moreover his conversation with the whole body of begs and soldiers was not what should be; every-one came to know what was in his mind. Khwāja-i-Qāẓī and (Sayyid) Qāsim *Qūchīn* and 'Alī-dost Ṭaghāī met other well-wishers of mine in the presence of my grandmother, Āīsān-daulat Begīm and decided to give quietus to Ḥasan-i-yaq'ūb's disloyalty by his deposition.

Few amongst women will have been my grandmother's equals for judgment and counsel; she was very wise and far-sighted and most affairs of mine were carried through under her advice. She and my mother were (living) in the Gate-house of the outer fort;[3] Ḥasan-i-yaq'ūb was in the citadel.

[1] Elph. MS. f. 16*b*; First W.-i-B. I.O. 215 f. 19; Second W.-i-B. I.O. 217 f. 15*b*; Memoirs p. 27.

[2] He was a *Dūghlāt*, uncle by marriage of Ḥaidar Mīrzā and now holding Khost for Maḥmūd. *See* T.R. s.n. for his claim on Āīsān-daulat's gratitude.

[3] *tāsh qūrghān dā chiqār dā.* Here (as *e.g.* f. 110*b* l. 9) the Second W.-i-B. translates *tāsh* as though it meant *stone* instead of outer. *Cf.* f. 47 for an

When I went to the citadel, in pursuance of our decision, he had ridden out, presumably for hawking, and as soon as he had
Fol. 25. our news, went off from where he was towards Samarkand. The begs and others in sympathy with him,[1] were arrested; one was Muḥammad Bāqir Beg; Sl. Maḥmud *Dūldāī*, Sl. Muḥammad *Dūldāī's* father, was another; there were several more; to some leave was given to go for Samarkand. The Andijān Government and control of my Gate were settled on (Sayyid) Qāsim *Qūchīn*.

A few days after Ḥasan-i-yaq'ūb reached Kand-i-badām on the Samarkand road, he went to near the Khūqān sub-division (*aūrchīn*) with ill-intent on Akhsī. Hearing of it, we sent several begs and braves to oppose him; they, as they went, detached a scouting party ahead; he, hearing this, moved against the detachment, surrounded it in its night-quarters[2] and poured flights of arrows (*shība*) in on it. In the darkness of the night an arrow (*aūq*), shot by one of his own men, hit him just (*aūq*) in the vent (*qāchār*) and before he could take vent (*qāchār*),[3] he became the captive of his own act.

> "If you have done ill, keep not an easy mind,
> For retribution is Nature's law."[4]

This year I began to abstain from all doubtful food, my obedience extended even to the knife, the spoon and the table-cloth;[5] also the after-midnight Prayer (*taḥajjud*) was
Fol. 25*b*. less neglected.

---

adjectival use of *tāsh*, stone, with the preposition (*tāsh*) *din*. The places contrasted here are the citadel (*ark*) and the walled-town (*qūrghān*). The *chīqār* (exit) is the fortified Gate-house of the mud circumvallation. *Cf.* f. 46 for another example of *chīqār*.

[1] Elph. Ḥai. Kehr's MSS., *āning bīla bār kishi bār beglārnī tūtūrūldī*. This idiom recurs on f. 76*b* l. 8. A palimpsest entry in the Elph. MS. produces the statement that when Ḥasan fled, his begs returned to Andijān.

[2] Ḥai. MS. *awī mūnkūzī*, underlined by *sāgh-i-gāū*, cows' thatched house. [*T. mūnkūz*, lit. horn, means also cattle.] Elph. MS., *awī mūnkūsh*, underlined by *dar jā'ī khwāb alfakhta*, sleeping place. [T. *mūnkūsh*, retired.]

[3] The first *qāchār* of this pun has been explained as *gurez-gāh*, *sharm-gāh*, hinder parts, *fuite* and *vertèbre inférieur*. The Ḥ.S. (ii, 273 l. 3 fr. ft.) says the wound was in a vital (*maqattal*) part.

[4] From Niẓāmī's *Khusrau u Shirīn*, Lahore lith. ed. p. 137 l. 8. It is quoted also in the A.N. Bib. Ind. ed. ii, 207 (H.B. ii, 321). (H.B.).

[5] *See* Hughes *Dictionary of Islām s.nn.* Eating and Food.

(a. Death of Sl. Maḥmūd Mīrzā.)

In the month of the latter Rabī' (January 1495 AD.), Sl. Maḥmūd Mīrzā was confronted by violent illness and in six days, passed from the world. He was 43 (lunar) years old.

b. His birth and lineage.

He was born in 857 AH. (1453 AD.), was Sl. Abū-sa'īd Mīrzā's third son and the full-brother of Sl. Aḥmad Mīrzā.[1]

c. His appearance and characteristics.

He was a short, stout, sparse-bearded and somewhat ill-shaped person. His manners and his qualities were good, his rules and methods of business excellent; he was well-versed in accounts, not a *dinār* or a *dirhām*[2] of revenue was spent without his knowledge. The pay of his servants was never disallowed. His assemblies, his gifts, his open table, were all good. Everything of his was orderly and well-arranged;[3] no soldier or peasant could deviate in the slightest from any plan of his. Formerly he must have been hard set (*qātīrār*) on hawking but latterly he very frequently hunted driven game.[4] He carried violence and vice to frantic excess, was a constant wine-bibber and kept many catamites. If anywhere in his territory, there was a handsome boy, he used, by whatever means, to have him brought for a catamite; of his begs' sons and of his sons' begs' sons he made catamites; and laid command for this service on Fol. 26. his very foster brothers and on their own brothers. So common in his day was that vile practice, that no person was without his catamite; to keep one was thought a merit, not to keep one, a defect. Through his infamous violence and vice, his sons died in the day of their strength (*tamām juwān*).

[1] *Cf.* f. 6*b* and note. If 'Umar Shaikh were Maḥmūd's full-brother, his name might well appear here.

[2] *i.e.* "Not a farthing, not a half-penny."

[3] Here the Mems. enters a statement, not found in the Turkī text, that Maḥmūd's dress was elegant and fashionable.

[4] *n:h:l:m.* My husband has cleared up a mistake (Mems. p. 28 and *Mém.* i, 54) of supposing this to be the name of an animal. It is explained in the A.N. (i, 255. H.B. i, 496) as a Badakhshī equivalent of *tasqāwal*; *tasqāwal* var. *tāshqāwal*, is explained by the *Farhang-i-azfarī*, a Turkī-Persian Dict. seen in the Mullā Fīroz Library of Bombay, to mean *rāh band kunanda*, the stopping of the road. *Cf.* J.R.A.S. 1900 p. 137.

He had a taste for poetry and put a *dīwān*[1] together but his verse is flat and insipid,—not to compose is better than to compose verse such as his. He was not firm in the Faith and held his Highness Khwāja 'Ubaidu'l-lāh (*Aḥrārī*) in slight esteem. He had no heart (*yūruk*) and was somewhat scant in modesty,—several of his impudent buffoons used to do their filthy and abominable acts in his full Court, in all men's sight. He spoke badly, there was no understanding him at first.

d. His battles.

He fought two battles, both with Sl. Ḥusain Mīrzā (*Bāī-qarā*). The first was in Astarābād; here he was defeated. The second was at Chīkman (Sarāī),[2] near Andikhūd; here also he was defeated. He went twice to Kāfiristān, on the
Fol. 26*b*. south of Badakhshān, and made Holy War; for this reason they wrote him Sl. Maḥmūd *Ghāzī* in the headings of his public papers.

e. His countries.

Sl. Abū-sa'īd Mīrzā gave him Astarābād.[3] After the 'Irāq disaster (*i.e.*, his father's death,) he went into Khurāsān. At that time, Qambar-'alī Beg, the governor of Ḥiṣār, by Sl. Abū-sa'īd Mīrzā's orders, had mobilized the Hindūstān[4] army and was following him into 'Irāq; he joined Sl. Maḥmūd Mīrzā in Khurāsān but the Khurāsānīs, hearing of Sl. Ḥusain Mīrzā's approach, rose suddenly and drove them out of the country. On this Sl. Maḥmūd Mīrzā went to his elder brother, Sl. Aḥmad Mīrzā in Samarkand. A few months later Sayyid Badr and Khusrau Shāh and some braves under Aḥmad

[1] *i.e.* "a collection of poems in the alphabetical order of the various end rhymes." (Steingass.)

[2] At this battle Daulat-shāh was present. *Cf.* Browne's D.S. for Astarābād p. 523 and for Andikhūd p. 532. For this and all other references to D.S. and H.S. I am indebted to my husband.

[3] The following dates will help out Bābur's brief narrative. Maḥmūd *æt.* 7, was given Astarābād in 864 AH. (1459-60 AD.); it was lost to Ḥusain at Jauz-wilāyat and Maḥmūd went into Khurāsān in 865 AH.; he was restored by his father in 866 AH.; on his father's death (873 AH.-1469 AD.) he fled to Harāt, thence to Samarkand and from there was taken to Ḥiṣār *æt.* 16. *Cf.* D'Herbélot *s.n.* Abū-sa'ad; H.S. i, 209; Browne's D.S. p. 522.

[4] Presumably the "Hindūstān the Less" of Clavijo (Markham p. 3 and p. 113), approx. Qambar—'alī's districts. Clavijo includes Tirmiẕ under the name.

Mushtāq[1] took him and fled to Qambar-'alī in Ḥiṣār. From that time forth, Sl. Maḥmūd Mīrzā possessed the countries lying south of Quhqa (Quhlugha) and the Kohtin Range as far as the Hindū-kush Mountains, such as Tīrmīẓ, Chaghāniān, Ḥiṣār, Khutlān, Qūndūz and Badakhshān. He also held Sl. Aḥmad Mīrzā's lands, after his brother's death.

f. His children.

He had five sons and eleven daughters.

Sl. Mas'ūd Mīrzā was his eldest son; his mother was Khān-zāda Begīm, a daughter of the Great Mīr of Tīrmīẓ. Bāī-sunghar Mīrzā was another; his mother was Pasha (or Pāshā) Begīm. Sl. 'Alī Mīrzā was another; his mother was an Aūzbeg, a concubine called Zuhra Begī Āghā. Sl. Ḥusain Mīrzā was another; his mother was Khān-zāda Begīm, a grand-daughter of the Great Mīr of Tīrmīẓ; he went to God's mercy in his father's life-time, at the age of 13. Sl. Wais Mīrzā (Mīrzā Khān) was another; his mother, Sulṭān-nigār Khānīm was a daughter of Yūnas Khān and was a younger (half-) sister of my mother. The affairs of these four Mīrzās will be written of in this history under the years of their occurrence. Fol. 27.

Of Sl. Maḥmūd Mīrzā's daughters, three were by the same mother as Bāī-sunghar Mīrzā. One of these, Bāī-sunghar Mīrzā's senior, Sl. Maḥmūd Mīrzā made to go out to Malik-i-muḥammad Mīrzā, the son of his paternal uncle, Minūchihr Mīrzā.[2]

* * * * * *

Five other daughters were by Khān-zāda Begīm, the grand-daughter of the Great Mīr of Tīrmīẓ. The oldest of these,

[1] Perhaps a Ṣufī term,—longing for the absent friend. For particulars about this man *see* Ḥ.S. ii, 235 and Browne's D.S. p. 533.

[2] Here in the Ḥai. MS. is one of several blank spaces, waiting for information presumably not known to Bābur when writing. The space will have been in the archetype of the Ḥai. MS. and it makes for the opinion that the Ḥai. MS. is a direct copy of Bābur's own. This space is not left in the Elph. MS. but that MS. is known from its scribe's note (f. 198) down to f. 198 (Ḥai. MS. f. 243*b*) to have been copied from "other writings" and only subsequent to its f. 198 from Bābur's own. *Cf.* JRAS 1906 p. 88 and 1907 p. 143.

(Khān-zāda Begīm)[1] was given, after her father's death, to Abā-
Fol. 27b. bikr (*Dūghlāt*) *Kāshgharī*. The second was Bega Begīm. When Sl. Ḥusain Mīrzā besieged Ḥiṣār (901 AH.), he took her for Ḥaidar Mīrzā, his son by Pāyanda Begīm, Sl. Abū-sa'īd Mīrzā's daughter, and having done so, rose from before the place.[2] The third daughter was Āq (Fair) Begīm; the fourth[3]—,was betrothed to Jahāngīr Mīrzā (*aet.* 5, *circa* 895 AH.) at the time his father, 'Umar Shaikh Mīrzā sent him to help Sl. Maḥmūd Mīrzā with the Andijān army, against Sl. Ḥusain Mīrzā, then attacking Qūndūz.[4] In 910 AH. (1504 AD.) when Bāqī *Chaghānīānī*[5] waited on me on the bank of the Amū (Oxus), these (last-named two) Begīms were with their mothers in Tīrmīẕ and joined me then with Bāqī's family. When we reached Kahmard, Jahāngīr Mīrzā took ——— Begīm; one little daughter was born; she now[6] is in the Badakhshān country with her grandmother. The fifth daughter was *Zainab-sulṭān* Begīm; under my mother's insistance, I took her at the time of the capture of Kābul (910 AH.–Oct. 1504 AD.). She did not become very congenial; two or three years later, she left the world, through small-pox. Another daughter was Makhdūm-sulṭān Begīm, Sl. 'Alī Mīrzā's full-sister; she is now in the Badakhshān country. Two others of his daughters, Rajab-sulṭān and Muḥibb-sulṭān, were by mistresses (*ghūnchachī*).

g. His ladies (*khwātīnlār*) *and concubines* (*sarārī*).

His chief wife, Khān-zāda Begīm, was a daughter of the
Fol. 28. Great Mīr of Tīrmīẕ; he had great affection for her and must have mourned her bitterly; she was the mother of Sl. Mas'ūd Mīrzā. Later on, he took her brother's daughter, also called Khān-zāda Begīm, a grand-daughter of the Great Mīr of Tīrmīẕ.

[1] The T.R. (p. 330) supplies this name.

[2] *Cf.* f. 35*b*. This was a betrothal only, the marriage being made in 903 AH. *Cf.* H.S. ii, 260 and Gul-badan's H.N. f. 24*b*.

[3] Kehr's MS. supplies Aī (Moon) as her name but it has no authority. The Elph. MS. has what may be *lā nām*, no name, on its margin and over *tūrūtūnchī* (4th.) its usual sign of what is problematical.

[4] *See* H.S. ii, 250. Here Pīr-i-Muḥammad *Ailchī-būghā* was drowned. *Cf.* f. 29.

[5] Chaghānīān is marked in Erskine's (Mems.) map as somewhere about the head of (Fr. map 1904) the Ilyak Water, a tributary of the Kāfir-nighān.

[6] *i.e.* when Bābur was writing in Hindūstān.

She became the mother of five of his daughters and one of his sons. Pasha (or Pāshā) Begīm was another wife, a daughter of 'Alī-shukr Beg, a Turkmān Beg of the Black Sheep Bahārlū Aīmāq.[1] She had been the wife of Jahān-shāh (*Barānī*) of the Black Sheep Turkmāns. After Aūzūn (Long) Ḥasan Beg of the White Sheep had taken Āẕar-bāījān and 'Irāq from the sons of this Jahān-shāh Mīrzā (872 AH.-1467 AD.), 'Alī-shukr Beg's sons went with four or five thousand heads-of-houses of the Black Sheep Turkmāns to serve Sl. Abū-sa'īd Mīrzā and after the Mīrzā's defeat (873 AH. by Aūzūn Ḥasan), came down to these countries and took service with Sl. Maḥmūd Mīrzā. This happened after Sl. Maḥmūd Mīrzā came to Ḥiṣār from Samarkand, and then it was he took Pasha Begīm. She became the mother of one of his sons and three of his daughters. Sulṭān-nigār Khānīm was another of his ladies; her descent has been mentioned already in the account of the (Chaghatāī) Khāns. Fol. 28*b*.

He had many concubines and mistresses. His most honoured concubine (*mu'atabar ghūma*) was Zuhra Begī Āghā; she was taken in his father's life-time and became the mother of one son and one daughter. He had many mistresses and, as has been said, two of his daughters were by two of them.

h. His amirs.

Khusrau Shāh was of the Turkistānī Qīpchāqs. He had been in the intimate service of the Tarkhān begs, indeed had been a catamite. Later on he became a retainer of Mazīd Beg (Tarkhān) *Arghūn* who favoured him in all things. He was favoured by Sl. Maḥmūd Mīrzā on account of services done by him when, after the 'Irāq disaster, he joined the Mīrzā on his way to Khurāsān. He waxed very great in his latter days; his retainers, under Sl. Maḥmūd Mīrzā, were a clear five or six thousand. Not only Badakhshān but the whole country from the Amū to the Hindū-kush Mountains depended on him and he devoured its whole revenue (*darobast yīr īdī*). His open table was good, so too his open hand; though he was a rough getter,[2]

[1] For his family *see* f. 55*b* note to Yār-'alī *Balāl*.

[2] *bā wujūd turklūk muhkam paidā kunanda īdī.*

what he got, he spent liberally. He waxed exceeding great after Sl. Maḥmūd Mīrzā's death, in whose sons' time his retainers approached 20,000. Although he prayed and abstained from forbidden aliments, yet was he black-souled and vicious,
Fol. 29. dunder-headed and senseless, disloyal and a traitor to his salt. For the sake of this fleeting, five-days world,[1] he blinded one of his benefactor's sons and murdered another. A sinner before God, reprobate to His creatures, he has earned curse and execration till the very verge of Resurrection. For this world's sake he did his evil deeds and yet, with lands so broad and with such hosts of armed retainers, he had not pluck to stand up to a hen. An account of him will come into this history.

Pīr-i-muḥammad *Aīlchī-būghā*[2] *Qūchīn* was another. In Hazāraspī's fight[3] he got in on challenge with his fists in Sl. Abū-sa'īd Mīrzā's presence at the Gate of Balkh. He was a brave man, continuously serving the Mīrzā (Maḥmūd) and guiding him by his counsel. Out of rivalry to Khusrau Shāh, he made a night-attack when the Mīrzā was besieging Qūndūz, on Sl. Ḥusain Mīrzā, with few men, without arming[4] and without plan; he could do nothing; what was there he could do against such and so large a force? He was pursued, threw himself into the river and was drowned.

Ayūb (*Begchīk Mughūl*)[5] was another. He had served in Sl. Abū-sa'īd Mīrzā's Khurāsān Cadet Corps, a brave man, Bāīsunghar Mīrzā's guardian. He was choice in dress and food;

[1] Roebuck's *Oriental Proverbs* (p. 232) explains the *five* of this phrase where *seven* might be expected, by saying that of this Seven days' world (qy. days of Creation) one is for birth, another for death, and that thus five only are left for man's brief life.

[2] The cognomen *Aīlchī-būghā*, taken with the bearer's recorded strength of fist, may mean Strong man of Aīlchī (the capital of Khutan). One of Tīmūr's commanders bore the name. *Cf.* f. 21*b* for *būghū* as *athlete*.

[3] Hazāraspī seems to be Mīr Pīr Darwesh Hazāraspī. With his brother, Mīr 'Alī, he had charge of Balkh. *See Rauzatu'ṣ-ṣafā* B.M. Add. 23506, f. 242*b*; Browne's D.S. p. 432. It may be right to understand a hand-to-hand fight between Hazāraspī and Aīlchī-būghā. The affair was in 857 AH. (1453 AD.).

[4] *yārāq sīz*, perhaps trusting to fisticuffs, perhaps without mail. Bābur's summary has confused the facts. Muḥ. Aīlchī-būghā was sent by Sl. Maḥmūd Mīrzā from Ḥiṣār with 1,000 men and did not issue out of Qūndūz. (Ḥ.S. ii, 251.) His death occurred not before 895 AH.

[5] *See* T.R. *s.nn.* Mīr Ayūb and Ayūb.

a jester and talkative, nicknamed Impudence, perhaps because the Mīrzā called him so. Fol. 29*b*.

Walī was another, the younger, full-brother of Khusrau Shāh. He kept his retainers well. He it was brought about the blinding of Sl. Mas'ūd Mīrzā and the murder of Bāī-sunghar Mīrzā. He had an ill-word for every-one and was an evil-tongued, foul-mouthed, self-pleasing and dull-witted mannikin. He approved of no-one but himself. When I went from the Qūndūz country to near Dūshī (910 AH.-1503 AD.), separated Khusrau Shāh from his following and dismissed him, this person (*i.e.*, Walī) had come to Andar-āb and Sīr-āb, also in fear of the Aūzbegs. The Aīmāqs of those parts beat and robbed him[1] then, having let me know, came on to Kābul. Walī went to Shaibānī Khān who had his head struck off in the town of Samarkand.

Shaikh 'Abdu'l-lāh *Barlās*[2] was another; he had to wife one of the daughters of Shāh Sulṭān Muḥammad (*Badakhshī*) *i.e.*, the maternal aunt of Abā-bikr Mīrzā (*Mīrān-shāhī*) and of Sl. Maḥmūd Khān. He wore his tunic narrow and *pur shaqq*[3]; he was a kindly well-bred man.

Maḥmūd *Barlās* of the Barlāses of Nūndāk (Badakhshān) was another. He had been a beg also of Sl. Abū-sa'īd Mīrzā and had surrendered Karmān to him when the Mīrzā took the 'Irāq countries. When Abā-bikr Mīrzā (*Mīrān-shāhī*) came Fol. 30. against Ḥiṣār with Mazīd Beg Tarkhān and the Black Sheep Turkmāns, and Sl. Maḥmūd Mīrzā went off to his elder brother, Sl. Aḥmad Mīrzā in Samarkand, Maḥmūd *Barlās* did not surrender Ḥiṣār but held out manfully.[4] He was a poet and put a *dīwān* together.

(i. Historical narrative resumed).

When Sl. Maḥmūd Mīrzā died, Khusrau Shāh kept the event concealed and laid a long hand on the treasure. But

[1] This passage is made more clear by f. 120*b* and f. 125*b*.

[2] He is mentioned in 'Alī-sher *Nawā'ī's Majālis-i-nafā'is*; *see* B.M. Add. 7875, f. 278 and Rieu's Turkish Catalogue.

[3] ? full of splits or full handsome.

[4] This may have occurred after Abū-sa'īd Mīrzā's death whose son Abā-bikr was. *Cf.* f. 28. If so, over-brevity has obscured the statement.

how could such news be hidden? It spread through the town at once. That was a festive day for the Samarkand families; soldier and peasant, they uprose in tumult against Khusrau Shāh. Aḥmad Ḥājī Beg and the Tarkhānī begs put the rising down and turned Khusrau Shāh out of the town with an escort for Ḥiṣār.

As Sl. Maḥmūd Mīrzā himself after giving Ḥiṣār to Sl. Mas'ūd Mīrzā and Bukhārā to Bāī-sunghar Mīrzā, had dismissed both to their governments, neither was present when he died. The Ḥiṣār and Samarkand begs, after turning Khusrau Shāh out, agreed to send for Bāī-sunghar Mīrzā from Bukhārā, brought him to Samarkand and seated him on the throne. When he thus became supreme (*pādshāh*), he was 18 (lunar) years old.

At this crisis, Sl. Maḥmūd Khān (*Chaghatāī*), acting on the
Fol. 30*b*. word of Junaid *Barlās* and of some of the notables of Samarkand, led his army out to near Kān-bāī with desire to take that town. Bāī-sunghar Mīrzā, on his side, marched out in force. They fought near Kān-bāī. Ḥaidar *Kūkūldāsh*, the main pillar of the Mughūl army, led the Mughūl van. He and all his men dismounted and were pouring in flights of arrows (*shība*) when a large body of the mailed braves of Ḥiṣār and Samarkand made an impetuous charge and straightway laid them under their horses' feet. Their leader taken, the Mughūl army was put to rout without more fighting. Masses (*qālīn*) of Mughūls were wiped out; so many were beheaded in Bāī-sunghar Mīrzā's presence that his tent was three times shifted because of the number of the dead.

At this same crisis, Ibrāhīm *Sārū* entered the fort of Asfara, there read Bāī-sunghar Mīrzā's name in the *Khuṭba* and took up a position of hostility to me.

(*Author's note.*) Ibrāhīm *Sārū* is of the Minglīgh people;[1] he had served my father in various ways from his childhood but later on had been dismissed for some fault.

Fol. 31. The army rode out to crush this rebellion in the month of Sha'bān (May) and by the end of it, had dismounted round

[1] *minglīgh aildīn dūr*, perhaps of those whose hereditary Command was a Thousand, the head of a Ming (Pers. Hazāra), *i.e.* of the tenth of a *tūmān*.

Asfara. Our braves in the wantonness of enterprise, on the very day of arrival, took the new wall[1] that was in building outside the fort. That day Sayyid Qāsim, Lord of my Gate, outstripped the rest and got in with his sword; Sl. Aḥmad *Tambal* and Muḥammad-dost Ṭaghāī got theirs in also but Sayyid Qāsim won the Champion's Portion. He took it in Shāhrukhiya when I went to see my mother's brother, Sl. Maḥmūd Khān.

(*Author's note.*) The Championship Portion[2] is an ancient usage of the Mughūl horde. Whoever outdistanced his tribe and got in with his own sword, took the portion at every feast and entertainment.

My guardian, Khudāī-bīrdī Beg died in that first day's fighting, struck by a cross-bow arrow. As the assault was made without armour, several bare braves (*yikīt yīlāng*)[3] perished and many were wounded. One of Ibrāhīm *Sārū's* cross-bowmen was an excellent shot; his equal had never been seen; he it was hit most of those wounded. When Asfara had been taken, he entered my service.

As the siege drew on, orders were given to construct head-strikes[4] in two or three places, to run mines and to make every effort to prepare appliances for taking the fort. The siege lasted 40 days; at last Ibrāhīm *Sārū* had no resource but, through the mediation of Khwāja Moulānā-i-qāẓī, to elect to serve me. In the month of Shawwāl (June 1495 AD.) he came out, with his sword and quiver hanging from his neck, waited on me and surrendered the fort. Fol. 31*b*.

Khujand for a considerable time had been dependent on 'Umar Shaikh Mīrzā's Court (*dīwān*) but of late had looked towards Sl. Aḥmad Mīrzā on account of the disturbance in the Farghāna government during the interregnum.[5] As the

[1] *qūrghān-ning tāshidā yāngī tām qūpārīb sālā dūr.* I understand, that what was taken was a new circumvallation in whole or in part. Such double walls are on record. *Cf.* Appendix A.

[2] *bahādurlūq aūlūsh*, an actual portion of food.

[3] *i.e.* either unmailed or actually naked.

[4] The old English noun *strike* expresses the purpose of the *sar-kob*. It is "an instrument for scraping off what rises above the top" (Webster, whose example is grain in a measure). The *sar-kob* is an erection of earth or wood, as high as the attacked walls, and it enabled besiegers to strike off heads appearing above the ramparts.

[5] *i.e.* the dislocation due to 'Umar Shaikh's death.

opportunity offered, a move against it also was now made. Mīr Mughūl's father, 'Abdu'l-wahhāb *Shaghāwal*[1] was in it; he surrendered without making any difficulty at once on our arrival.

Just then Sl. Maḥmūd Khān was in Shāhrukhiya. It has been said already that when Sl. Aḥmad Mīrzā came into Andijān (899 AH.), he also came and that he laid siege to Akhsī. It occurred to me that if since I was so close, I went and waited on him, he being, as it were, my father and my elder brother, and if bye-gone resentments were laid aside, it would be good hearing and seeing for far and near. So said, I went.

I waited on The Khān in the garden Ḥaidar *Kūkūldāsh* had made outside Shāhrukhiya. He was seated in a large four-
Fol. 32. doored tent set up in the middle of it. Having entered the tent, I knelt three times,[2] he for his part, rising to do me honour. We looked one another in the eyes;[3] and he returned to his seat. After I had kneeled, he called me to his side and shewed me much affection and friendliness. Two or three days later, I set off for Akhsī and Andijān by the Kīndīrlīk Pass.[4] At Akhsī I made the circuit of my Father's

[1] *Cf.* f. 13. The H.S. (ii, 274) places his son, Mīr Mughūl, in charge, but otherwise agrees with the B.N.

[2] *Cf.* Clavijo, Markham p. 132. Sir Charles Grandison bent the knee on occasions but illustrated MSS. *e.g.* the B.M. *Tawārīkh-i-guzida Naṣrat-nāma* show that Bābur would kneel down on both knees. *Cf.* f. 123*b* for the fatigue of the genuflection.

[3] I have translated *kūrūshūb* thus because it appears to me that here and in other places, stress is laid by Bābur upon the mutual gaze as an episode of a ceremonious interview. The verb *kūrūshmak* is often rendered by the Persian translators as *daryāftan* and by the L. and E. Memoirs as *to embrace.* I have not found in the B.N. warrant for translating it as *to embrace; qūchūshmāq* is Bābur's word for this (f. 103). *Daryāftan*, taken as to grasp or see with the mind, to understand, well expresses mutual gaze and its sequel of mutual understanding. Sometimes of course, *kūrūsh*, the interview does not imply *kūrūsh*, the silent looking in the eyes with mutual understanding; it simply means *se voyer e.g.* f. 17. The point is thus dwelt upon because the frequent mention of an embrace gives a different impression of manners from that made by " interview " or words expressing mutual gaze.

[4] *dābān*. This word Réclus (vi, 171) quoting from Fedschenko, explains as a difficult rocky defile; *art*, again, as a dangerous gap at a high elevation; *bel*, as an easy low pass; and *kūtal*, as a broad opening between low hills. The explanation of *kūtal* does not hold good for Bābur's application of the word (f. 81*b*) to the Sara-tāq.

tomb. I left at the hour of the Friday Prayer (*i.e.*, about mid-day) and reached Andijān, by the Band-i-sālār Road between the Evening and Bedtime Prayers. This road *i.e.* the Band-i-sālār, people call a nine *yīghāch* road.[1]

One of the tribes of the wilds of Andijān is the Jīgrāk[2] a numerous people of five or six thousand households, dwelling in the mountains between Kāshghar and Farghāna. They have many horses and sheep and also numbers of yāks (*qūtās*), these hill-people keeping yāks instead of common cattle. As their mountains are border-fastnesses, they have a fashion of not paying tribute. An army was now sent against them under (Sayyid) Qāsim Beg in order that out of the tribute taken from them something might reach the soldiers. He took about 20,000 of their sheep and between 1000 and 1500 of their horses and shared all out to the men.

After its return from the Jīgrāk, the army set out for Aūrā-tīpā. Fol. 34. Formerly this was held by 'Umar Shaikh Mīrzā but it had gone out of hand in the year of his death and Sl. 'Alī Mīrzā was now in it on behalf of his elder brother, Bāi-sunghar Mīrzā. When Sl. 'Alī Mīrzā heard of our coming, he went off himself to the Macha hill-country, leaving his guardian, Shaikh Ẕū'n-nūn *Arghūn* behind. From half-way between Khujand and Aūrā-tīpā, Khalīfa[3] was sent as envoy to Shaikh Ẕū'n-nūn but that senseless mannikin, instead of giving him a plain answer, laid hands on him and ordered him to death. For Khalīfa to die cannot have been the Divine will; he escaped and came to me two or three days later, stripped bare and having suffered a hundred *tūmāns* (1,000,000) of hardships and fatigues. We went almost to Aūrā-tīpā but as, winter being near, people had carried away their corn and forage, after a few days we turned back for Andijān. After our retirement, The Khān's men moved on the place when the Aūrā-tīpā

[1] *Cf.* f. 4*b* and note. From Bābur's special mention of it, it would seem not to be the usual road.

[2] The spelling of this name is uncertain. Variants are many. Concerning the tribe *see* T.R. p. 165 n.

[3] Niẓāmu'd-dīn 'Alī *Barlās* : *see* Gul-badan's H.N. *s.n.* He served Bābur till the latter's death.

person[1] unable to make a stand, surrendered and came out. The Khān then gave it to Muḥammad Ḥusain *Kūrkān Dūghlāt* and in his hands it remained till 908 AH. (1503).[2]

[1] *i.e.* Ẕū'n-nūn or perhaps the garrison.
[2] *i.e.* down to Shaibānī's destruction of Chaghatāī rule in Tāshkīnt in 1503 AD.

901 AH.—SEP. 21st. 1495 to SEP. 9th. 1496 AD.[1]

(a. Sulṭān Ḥusain Mīrzā's campaign against Khusrau Shāh).

In the winter of this year, Sl. Ḥusain Mīrzā led his army out of Khurāsān against Ḥiṣār and went to opposite Tīrmīẕ. Sl. Mas'ūd Mīrzā, for his part, brought an army (from Ḥiṣār) and sat down over against him in Tīrmīẕ. Khusrau Shāh strengthened himself in Qūndūz and to help Sl. Mas'ūd Mīrzā sent his younger brother, Walī. They (*i.e.*, the opposed forces) spent most of that winter on the river's banks, no crossing being effected. Sl. Ḥusain Mīrzā was a shrewd and experienced commander; he marched up the river,[2] his face set for Qūndūz and by this having put Sl. Mas'ūd Mīrzā off his guard, sent 'Abdu'l-laṭīf *Bakhshī* (pay-master) with 5 or 600 serviceable men, down the river to the Kilīf ferry. These crossed and had entrenched themselves on the other bank before Sl. Mas'ūd Mīrzā had heard of their movement. When he did hear of it, whether because of pressure put upon him by Bāqī *Chaghāniānī* to spite (his half-brother) Walī, or whether from his own want of heart, he did not march against those who had crossed but disregarding Walī's urgency, at once broke up his camp and turned for Ḥiṣār.[3]

Sl. Ḥusain Mīrzā crossed the river and then sent, (1) against Khusrau Shāh, Badī'u'z-zamān Mīrzā and Ibrāhīm Ḥusain Mīrzā with Muḥammad Walī Beg and Ẕū'n-nūn *Arghūn*, and Fol. 33*b*.

[1] Elph. MS. f. 23; W.-i-B. I.O. 215 f. 26 and 217 f. 21; Mems. p. 35.
Bābur's own affairs form a small part of this year's record; the rest is drawn from the Ḥ.S. which in its turn, uses Bābur's f. 34 and f. 37*b*. Each author words the shared material in his own style; one adding magniloquence, the other retracting to plain statement, indeed summarizing at times to obscurity. Each passes his own judgment on events, *e.g.* here Khwānd-amīr's is more favourable to Ḥusain Bāī-qarā's conduct of the Ḥiṣār campaign than Bābur's. *Cf.* Ḥ.S. ii, 256-60 and 274.

[2] This feint would take him from the Oxus.

[3] Tīrmīẕ to Ḥiṣār, 96m. (Réclus vi, 255).

(2) against Khutlān, Muẓaffar Ḥusain Mīrzā with Muḥammad *Barandūq Barlās*. He himself moved for Ḥiṣār.

When those in Ḥiṣār heard of his approach, they took their precautions; Sl. Mas'ūd Mīrzā did not judge it well to stay in the fort but went off up the Kām Rūd valley[1] and by way of Sara-tāq to his younger brother, Bāī-sunghar Mīrzā in Samarkand. Walī, for his part drew off to (his own district) Khutlān. Bāqī *Chaghāniānī*, Maḥmūd *Barlās* and Qūch Beg's father, Sl. Aḥmad strengthened the fort of Ḥiṣār. Ḥamza Sl. and Mahdī Sl. (*Aūzbeg*) who some years earlier had left Shaibānī Khān for (the late) Sl. Maḥmūd Mīrzā's service, now, in this dispersion, drew off with all their Aūzbegs, for Qarā-tīgīn. With them went Muḥammad *Dūghlāt*[2] and Sl. Ḥusain *Dūghlāt* and all the Mughūls located in the Ḥiṣār country.

Upon this Sl. Ḥusain Mīrzā sent Abū'l-muḥsin Mīrzā after Sl. Mas'ūd Mīrzā up the Kām Rūd valley. They were not strong enough for such work when they reached the defile.[3] There Mīrzā Beg *Fīringī-bāz*[4] got in his sword. In pursuit of Ḥamza Sl. into Qarā-tīgīn, Sl. Ḥusain Mīrzā sent Ibrāhīm Tarkhān and Yaq'ūb-i-ayūb. They overtook the sulṭāns and

Fol. 33. fought. The Mīrzā's detachment was defeated; most of his begs were unhorsed but all were allowed to go free.

(*b. Bābur's reception of the Aūzbeg sulṭāns.*)

As a result of this exodus, Ḥamza Sl. with his son, Mamāq Sl., and Mahdī Sl. and Muḥammad *Dūghlāt*, later known as *Ḥiṣārī* and his brother, Sl. Ḥusain *Dūghlāt* with the Aūzbegs dependent on the sulṭāns and the Mughūls who had been located in Ḥiṣār as (the late) Sl. Maḥmūd Mīrzā's retainers, came, after letting me know (their intention), and waited upon me in Ramẓān (May-June) at Andijān. According to the

[1] Ḥ.S. Wazr-āb valley. The usual route is up the Kām Rūd and over the Mūra pass to Sara-tāq. *Cf.* f. 81*b*.

[2] *i.e.* the Ḥiṣārī mentioned a few lines lower and on f. 99*b*. Nothing on f. 99*b* explains his cognomen.

[3] The road is difficult. *Cf.* f. 81*b*.

[4] Khwānd-amīr also singles out one man for praise, Sl. Maḥmūd *Mīr-i-ākhwur*; the two names probably represent one person. The sobriquet may refer to skill with a matchlock, to top-spinning (*firnagī-bāz*) or to some lost joke. (Ḥ.S. ii, 257.)

custom of Tīmūriya sulṭāns on such occasions, I had seated myself on a raised seat (*tūshāk*); when Ḥamza SL. and Mamāq Sl. and Mahdī Sl. entered, I rose and went down to do them honour; we looked one another in the eyes and I placed them on my right, *bāghīsh dā*.[1] A number of Mughūls also came, under Muḥammad *Ḥiṣārī*; all elected for my service.

(*c. Sl. Ḥusain Mīrzā's affairs resumed*).

Sl. Ḥusain Mīrzā, on reaching Ḥiṣār, settled down at once to besiege it. There was no rest, day nor night, from the labours of mining and attack, of working catapults and mortars. Mines were run in four or five places. When one had gone well forward towards the Gate, the townsmen, countermining, struck it and forced smoke down on the Mīrzā's men; they, in turn, closed the hole, thus sent the smoke straight back and made the townsmen flee as from the very maw of death. In the end, the townsmen drove the besiegers out by pouring jar after jar of water in on them. Another day, a party dashed out from the town and drove off the Mīrzā's men from their own mine's mouth. Once the discharges from catapults and mortars in the Mīrzā's quarters on the north cracked a tower of the fort; it fell at the Bed-time Prayer; some of the Mīrzā's braves begged to assault at once but he refused, saying, "It is night." Before the shoot of the next day's dawn, the besieged had rebuilt the whole tower. That day too there was no assault; in fact, for the two to two and a half months of the siege, no attack was made except by keeping up the blockade,[2] by mining, rearing head-strikes,[3] and discharging stones. Fol. 34b.

[1] This pregnant phrase has been found difficult. It may express that Bābur assigned the sulṭāns places in their due precedence; that he seated them in a row; and that they sat cross-legged, as men of rank, and were not made, as inferiors, to kneel and sit back on their heels. Out of this last meaning, I infer comes the one given by dictionaries, "to sit at ease," since the cross-legged posture is less irksome than the genuflection, not to speak of the ease of mind produced by honour received. *Cf.* f. 18*b* and note on Aḥmad's posture; Redhouse *s.nn. bāghīsh* and *bāghdāsh*; and B.M. Tawārīkh-i-guzīda naṣrat-nāma, in the illustrations of which the chief personage, only, sits cross-legged.

[2] *siyāsat*. My translation is conjectural only.

[3] *sar-kob*. The old English noun *strike*, "an instrument for scraping off what appears above the top," expresses the purpose of the wall-high erections of wood or earth (*L. agger*) raised to reach what shewed above ramparts. *Cf.* Webster.

When Badī'u'z-zamān Mīrzā and whatever (*nī kīm*) troops had been sent with him against Khusrau Shāh, dismounted some 16 m. (3 to 4 *yīghāch*) below Qūndūz,[1] Khusrau Shāh arrayed whatever men (*nī kīm*) he had, marched out, halted one night on the way, formed up to fight and came down upon the Mīrzā and his men. The Khurāsānīs may not have been twice as many as his men but what question is there they were half
Fol. 35. as many more? None the less did such Mīrzās and such Commander-begs elect for prudence and remain in their entrenchments! Good and bad, small and great, Khusrau Shāh's force may have been of 4 or 5,000 men!

This was the one exploit of his life,—of this man who for the sake of this fleeting and unstable world and for the sake of shifting and faithless followers, chose such evil and such ill-repute, practised such tyranny and injustice, seized such wide lands, kept such hosts of retainers and followers,—latterly he led out between 20 and 30,000 and his countries and his districts (*parganāt*) exceeded those of his own ruler and that ruler's sons,[2] —for an exploit such as this his name and the names of his adherents were noised abroad for generalship and for this they were counted brave, while those timorous laggards, in the trenches, won the resounding fame of cowards.

Badī'u'z-zamān Mīrzā marched out from that camp and after a few stages reached the Alghū Mountain of Tāliqān[3] and there made halt. Khusrau Shāh, in Qūndūz, sent his brother, Walī, with serviceable men, to Ishkīmīsh, Fulūl and the hill-skirts thereabouts to annoy and harass the Mīrzā from outside also. Muḥibb-'alī, the armourer, (*qūrchī*) for his part, came down
Fol. 35*b*. (from Walī's Khutlān) to the bank of the Khutlān Water, met in with some of the Mīrzā's men there, unhorsed some, cut off a few heads and got away. In emulation of this, Sayyidīm 'Alī[4] the door-keeper, and his younger brother, Qulī Beg and

[1] Presumably lower down the Qūndūz Water.

[2] *aūz pādshāhī u mīrzālārīdīn artīb.*

[3] *sic.* Ḥai. MS.; Elph. MS. "near Tāliqān; some W.-i-B. MSS. "Great Garden." Gul-badan mentions a Tāliqān Garden. Perhaps the Mīrzā went so far east because, Ẕū'n-nūn being with him, he had Qandahār in mind. *Cf.* f. 42*b*.

[4] *i.e.* Sayyid Muḥammad 'Alī. *See* f. 15 n. to Sherīm. Khwāja Changāl lies 14 m. below Tāliqān on the Tāliqān Water. (Erskine.)

Bihlūl-i-ayūb and a body of their men got to grips with the Khurāsānīs on the skirt of 'Ambar Koh, near Khwāja Changāl but, many Khurāsānīs coming up, Sayyidīm 'Alī and Bābā Beg's (son) Qulī Beg and others were unhorsed.

At the time these various news reached Sl. Ḥusain Mīrzā, his army was not without distress through the spring rains of Ḥiṣār; he therefore brought about a peace; Maḥmūd *Barlās* came out from those in the fort; Ḥājī Pīr the Taster went from those outside; the great commanders and what there was (*nī kīm*) of musicians and singers assembled and the Mīrzā took (Bega Begīm), the eldest[1] daughter of Sl. Maḥmūd Mīrzā by Khān-*zāda* Begīm, for Ḥaidar Mīrzā, his son by Pāyanda Begīm and through her the grandson of Sl. Abū-sa'īd Mīrzā. This done, he rose from before Ḥiṣār and set his face for Qūndūz.

At Qūndūz also Sl. Ḥusain Mīrzā made a few trenches and took up the besieger's position but by Badī'u'z-zamān Mīrzā's intervention peace at length was made, prisoners were exchanged and the Khurāsānīs retired. The twice-repeated[2] attacks made by Sl. Ḥusain Mīrzā on Khusrau Shāh and his unsuccessful retirements were the cause of Khusrau Shāh's great rise and of action of his so much beyond his province. Fol. 36.

When the Mīrzā reached Balkh, he, in the interests of Mā warā'u'n-nahr gave it to Badī'u'z-zamān Mīrzā, gave Badī'u'z-zamān Mīrzā's district of Astarābād to (a younger son), Muẓaffar Ḥusain Mīrzā and made both kneel at the same assembly, one for Balkh, the other for Astarābād. This offended Badī'u'z-zamān Mīrzā and led to years of rebellion and disturbance.[3]

(*d. Revolt of the Tarkhānīs in Samarkand*).

In Ramẓān of this same year, the Tarkhānīs revolted in Samarkand. Here is the story:—Bāī-sunghar Mīrzā was not so friendly and familiar with the begs and soldiers of Samarkand as he was with those of Ḥiṣār.[4] His favourite beg was Shaikh

[1] f. 27*b*, second.
[2] The first was *circa* 895 AH.-1490 AD. *Cf.* f. 27*b*.
[3] Bābur's wording suggests that their common homage was the cause of Badī'u'z-zamān's displeasure but *see* f. 41.
[4] The Mīrzā had grown up with Ḥiṣārīs. *Cf.* H.S. ii, 270.

'Abdu'l-lāh *Barlās*[1] whose sons were so intimate with the Mīrzā that it made a relation as of Lover and Beloved. These things displeased the Tarkhāns and the Samarkandī begs; Darwesh Muḥammad Tarkhān went from Bukhārā to Qarshī, brought Sl. 'Alī Mīrzā to Samarkand and raised him to be supreme. People then went to the New Garden where Bāī-
Fol. 36*b*. sunghar Mīrzā was, treated him like a prisoner, parted him from his following and took him to the citadel. There they seated both mīrzās in one place, thinking to send Bāī-sunghar Mīrzā to the Gūk Sarāī close to the Other Prayer. The Mīrzā, however, on plea of necessity, went into one of the palace-buildings on the east side of the Bū-stān Sarāī. Tarkhānīs stood outside the door and with him went in Muḥammad Qulī *Qūchīn* and Ḥasan, the sherbet-server. To be brief:—A gateway, leading out to the back, must have been bricked up for they broke down the obstacle at once. The Mīrzā got out of the citadel on the Kafshīr side, through the water-conduit (*āb-mūrī*), dropped himself from the rampart of the water-way (*dū-tahī*), and went to Khwājakī Khwāja's[2] house in Khwāja Kafshīr. When the Tarkhānīs, in waiting at the door, took the precaution of looking in, they found him gone. Next day the Tarkhānīs went in a large body to Khwājakī Khwāja's gate but the Khwāja said, "No!"[3] and did not give him up. Even they could not take him by force, the Khwāja's dignity was too great for them to be able to use force. A few days later, Khwāja Abu'l-makāram[4] and Aḥmad Ḥājī Beg and other begs, great and
Fol. 37. small, and soldiers and townsmen rose in a mass, fetched the Mīrzā away from the Khwāja's house and besieged Sl. 'Ali Mīrzā and the Tarkhāns in the citadel. They could not hold out for even a day; Muḥ. Mazīd Tarkhān went off through the Gate of the Four Roads for Bukhārā;

[1] As the husband of one of the six Badakhshī Begīms, he was closely connected with local ruling houses. *See* T.R. p. 107.

[2] *i.e.* Muḥammad 'Ubaidu'l-lāh the elder of *Aḥrārī's* two sons. d. 911 AH. *See Rashaḥāt-i-'ain-alḥayāt* (I.O. 633) f. 269-75; and *Khizīnatu'l-aṣfiya* lith. ed. i, 597.

[3] *Bū yūq tūr*, *i.e.* This is not to be.

[4] d. 908 AH. He was not, it would seem, of the *Aḥrārī* family. His own had provided Pontiffs (*Shaikhu'l-islām*) for Samarkand through 400 years. *Cf. Shaibānī-nāma*, Vambéry, p. 106; also, for his character, p. 96.

Sl. 'Alī Mīrzā and Darwesh Muḥ. Tarkhān were made prisoner.

Bāī-sunghar Mīrzā was in Aḥmad Ḥājī Beg's house when people brought Darwesh Muḥammad Tarkhān in. He put him a few questions but got no good answer. In truth Darwesh Muḥammad's was a deed for which good answer could not be made. He was ordered to death. In his helplessness he clung to a pillar[1] of the house; would they let him go because he clung to a pillar? They made him reach his doom (*siyāsat*) and ordered Sl. 'Alī Mīrzā to the Gūk Sarāī there to have the fire-pencil drawn across his eyes.

(*Author's note.*) The Gūk Sarāī is one of Tīmūr Beg's great buildings in the citadel of Samarkand. It has this singular and special characterstic, if a Tīmūrid is to be seated on the throne, here he takes his seat; if one lose his head, coveting the throne, here he loses it; therefore the name Gūk Sarāī has a metaphorical sense (*kināyat*) and to say of any ruler's son, "They have taken him to the Gūk Sarāī," means, to death.[2]

To the Gūk Sarāī accordingly Sl. 'Alī Mīrzā was taken but when the fire-pencil was drawn across his eyes, whether by the surgeon's choice or by his inadvertence, no harm was done. Fol. 37*b*. This the Mīrzā did not reveal at once but went to Khwāja Yahya's house and a few days later, to the Tarkhāns in Bukhārā.

Through these occurrences, the sons of his Highness Khwāja 'Ubaidu'l-lāh became settled partisans, the elder (Muḥammad 'Ubaidu'l-lāh, Khwājakī Khwāja) becoming the spiritual guide of the elder prince, the younger (Yahya) of the younger. In a few days, Khwāja Yahya followed Sl. 'Alī Mīrzā to Bukhārā.

Bāī-sunghar Mīrzā led out his army against Bukhārā. On his approach, Sl. 'Alī Mīrzā came out of the town, arrayed for battle. There was little fighting; Victory being on the side of Sl. 'Alī Mīrzā, Bāī-sunghar Mīrzā sustained defeat. Aḥmad Ḥājī Beg and a number of good soldiers were taken; most of the men were put to death. Aḥmad Ḥājī Beg himself the slaves and slave-women of Darwesh Muḥammad Tarkhān, issuing out

[1] *i.e.* he claimed sanctuary.

[2] *Cf.* f. 45*b* and Pétis de la Croix's *Histoire de Chīngīz Khān* pp. 171 and 227. What Tīmūr's work on the Gūk Sarāī was is a question for archæologists.

of Bukhārā, put to a dishonourable death on the charge of their master's blood.

(*e. Bābur moves against Samarkand*).

These news reached us in Andijān in the month of Shawwāl (mid-June to mid-July) and as we (*act.* 14) coveted Samarkand, we got our men to horse. Moved by a like desire, Sl. Mas'ūd Mīrzā, his mind and Khusrau Shāh's mind set at ease by Sl.
Fol. 38. Ḥusain Mīrzā's retirement, came over by way of Shahr-i-sabz.[1] To reinforce him, Khusrau Shāh laid hands (*qāptī*) on his younger brother, Walī. We (three mīrzās) beleaguered the town from three sides during three or four months; then Khwāja Yahya came to me from Sl. 'Alī Mīrzā to mediate an agreement with a common aim. The matter was left at an interview arranged (*kūrūshmak*); I moved my force from Soghd to some 8m. below the town; Sl. 'Alī Mīrzā from his side, brought his own; from one bank, he, from the other, I crossed to the middle of[2] the Kohik water, each with four or five men; we just saw one another (*kūrūshūb*), asked each the other's welfare and went, he his way, I mine.

I there saw, in Khwāja Yahya's service, Mullā *Binā'ī* and Muḥammad Ṣāliḥ;[3] the latter I saw this once, the former was long in my service later on. After the interview (*kūrūshkān*) with Sl. 'Alī Mīrzā, as winter was near and as there was no great scarcity amongst the Samarkandīs, we retired, he to Bukhārā, I to Andijān.

Sl. Mas'ūd Mīrzā had a penchant for a daughter of Shaikh 'Abdu'l-lāh *Barlās*, she indeed was his object in coming to Samarkand. He took her, laid world-gripping ambition aside
Fol. 38*b*. and went back to Ḥiṣār.

When I was near Shīrāz and Kān-bāī, Mahdī Sl. deserted to Samarkand; Ḥamza Sl. went also from near *Zamīn* but with leave granted.

[1] *i.e.* over the Aītmak Pass. *Cf.* f. 49.

[2] Ilai. MS. *ārālighigha*. Elph. MS. *ārāl*, island.

[3] *See* f. 179*b* for *Binā'ī*. Muḥammad Ṣāliḥ Mīrzā *Khwārizmī* is the author of the *Shaibānī-nāma*.

902 AH.—SEP. 9TH. 1496 TO AUG. 30TH. 1497 AD.[1]

(*a. Bābur's second attempt on Samarkand.*)

This winter, Bāī-sunghar Mīrzā's affairs were altogether in a good way. When 'Abdu'l-karīm *Ushrit* came on Sl. 'Alī Mīrzā's part to near Kūfīn, Mahdī Sl. led out a body of Bāī-sunghar Mīrzā's troops against him. The two commanders meeting exactly face to face, Mahdī Sl. pricked 'Abdu'l-karīm's horse with his Chirkas[2] sword so that it fell, and as 'Abdu'l-karīm was getting to his feet, struck off his hand at the wrist. Having taken him, they gave his men a good beating.

These (Aūzbeg) sulṭāns, seeing the affairs of Samarkand and the Gates of the (Tīmūrid) Mīrzās tottering to their fall, went off in good time (*āīrtā*) into the open country (?)[3] for Shaibānī.

Pleased[4] with their small success (over 'Abdu'l-karīm), the Samarkandīs drew an army out against Sl. 'Alī Mīrzā; Bāī-sunghar Mīrzā went to Sar-i-pul (Bridge-head), Sl. 'Alī Mīrzā to Khwāja Kārzūn. Meantime, Khwāja Abū'l-makāram, at the instigation of Khwāja Munīr of Aūsh, rode light against Fol. 39.
Bukhārā with Wais *Lāgharī* and Muḥammad Bāqir of the Andijān begs, and Qāsim *Dūldāī* and some of the Mīrzā's household. As the Bukhāriots took precautions when the invaders got near the town, they could make no progress. They therefore retired.

[1] Elph. MS. f. 27; W.-i-B. I.O. 215 f. 30*b* and 217 f. 25; Mems. p. 42.

[2] *i.e.* Circassian. Muḥammad Ṣāliḥ (Sh.N. Vambéry p. 276 l. 58) speaks of other Aūzbegs using Chirkas swords.

[3] *aīrtā yāzīghā*. My translation is conjectural. *Aīrtā* implies *i.a.* foresight. *Yāzīghā* allows a pun at the expense of the sulṭāns; since it can be read both as *to the open country* and as *for their* (*next*, *aīrtā*) *misdeeds*. My impression is that they took the opportunity of being outside Samarkand with their men, to leave Bāī-sunghar and make for Shaibānī, then in Turkistān. Muḥammad Ṣāliḥ also marking the tottering Gate of Sl. 'Alī Mīrzā, left him now, also for Shaibānī. (Vambéry cap. xv.)

[4] *aūmāq*, to amuse a child in order to keep it from crying.

At the time when (last year) Sl. 'Alī Mīrzā and I had our interview, it had been settled[1] that this summer he should come from Bukhārā and I from Andijān to beleaguer Samarkand. To keep this tryst, I rode out in Ramẓān (May) from Andijān. Hearing when close to Yār Yīlāq, that the (two) Mīrzās were lying front to front, we sent Tūlūn Khwāja *Mūghūl*[2] ahead, with 2 or 300 scouting braves (*qāzāq yīkītlār*). Their approach giving Bāī-sunghar Mīrzā news of our advance, he at once broke up and retired in confusion. That same night our detachment overtook his rear, shot a mass (*qālīn*) of his men and brought in masses of spoil.

Two days later we reached Shīrāz. It belonged to Qāsim Beg *Dūldāī*; his *dārogha* (Sub-governor) could not hold it and surrendered.[3] It was given into Ibrāhīm *Sārū's* charge. After making there, next day, the Prayer of the Breaking of the Fast (*'Īdu'l-fiṭr*), we moved for Samarkand and dismounted in the reserve (*qūrūgh*) of Āb-i-yār (Water of Might). That day waited on me with 3 or 400 men, Qāsim *Dūldāī*,
Fol. 39*b*. Wais *Lāgharī*, Muḥammad Sīghal's grandson, Ḥasan,[4] and Sl. Muḥammad Wais. What they said was this: 'Bāī-sunghar Mīrzā came out and has gone back; we have left him therefore and are here for the *pādshāh's* service,' but it was known later that they must have left the Mīrzā at his request to defend Shīrāz, and that the Shīrāz affair having become what it was, they had nothing for it but to come to us.

When we dismounted at Qarā-būlāq, they brought in several Mughūls arrested because of senseless conduct to humble village elders coming in to us.[5] Qāsim Beg *Qūchīn* for discipline's

[1] *i.e.* with Khwāja Yahya presumably. *See* f. 38.

[2] This man is mentioned also in the *Tawārīkh-i-guzīda Naṣratnāma* B.M. Or. 3222 f. 124*b*.

[3] H.S., on the last day of Ramẓān (June 28th. 1497 AD.).

[4] Muḥammad *Sīghal* appears to have been a marked man. I quote from the T.G.N.N. (*see supra*), f. 123*b* foot, the information that he was the grandson of Ya'qūb Beg. Zenker explains *Sīghalī* as the name of a Chaghatāī family. An *Ayūb-i-Ya'qūb Begchīk Mughūl* may be an uncle. See f. 43 for another grandson.

[5] *baẓ'ī kīrkān-kīnt-kīsākkā bāsh-sīz-qīlghān Mughūllārnī tūtūb.* I take the word *kīsāk* in this highly idiomatic sentence to be a diminutive of *kīs*, old person, on the analogy of *mīr, mīrāk, mard, mardak*. [The H.S. uses *Kisāk* (ii, 261) as a proper noun.] The alliteration in *kāf* and the mighty adjective here are noticeable.

sake (*siyāsat*) had two or three of them cut to pieces. It was on this account he left me and went to Ḥiṣār four or five years later, in the guerilla times, (907 AH.) when I was going from the Macha country to The Khān.[1]

Marching from Qarā-būlāq, we crossed the river (*i.e.* the Zar-afshān) and dismounted near Yām.[2] On that same day, our men got to grips with Bāī-sunghar Mīrzā's at the head of the Avenue. Sl. Aḥmad *Taṃbal* was struck in the neck by a spear but not unhorsed. Khwājakī Mullā-i-ṣadr, Khwāja-i-kalān's eldest brother, was pierced in the nape of the neck[3] by an arrow and went straightway to God's mercy. An excellent soldier, my father before me had favoured him, making him Keeper of the Seal; he was a student of theology, had great Fol. 40. acquaintance with words and a good style; moreover he undertook hawking and rain-making with the jade-stone.

While we were at Yām, people, dealers and other, came out in crowds so that the camp became a bazar for buying and selling. One day, at the Other Prayer, suddenly, a general hubbub arose and all those Musalmān (traders) were plundered. Such however was the discipline of our army that an order to restore everything having been given, the first watch (*pahār*) of the next day had not passed before nothing, not a tag of cotton, not a broken needle's point, remained in the possession of any man of the force, all was back with its owners.

Marching from Yām, it was dismounted in Khān Yūrtī (The Khān's Camping Ground),[4] some 6 m. (3 *kuroh*) east of Samarkand. We lay there for 40 or 50 days. During the time, men from their side and from ours chopped at one another (*chāpqūlāshtīlār*) several times in the Avenue. One day when Ibrāhīm *Begchīk* was chopping away there, he was cut on the face;

[1] Qāsim feared to go amongst the Mughūls lest he should meet retaliatory death. *Cf.* f. 99*b*.

[2] This appears from the context to be Yām (Jām) -bāī and not the Djouma (Jām) of the Fr. map of 1904, lying farther south. The Avenue named seems likely to be Tīmūr's of f. 45*b* and to be on the direct road for Khujand. *See* Schuyler i, 232.

[3] *būghān buyinī.* W.-i-B. 215, *yān*, thigh, and 217 *gardan*, throat. I am in doubt as to the meaning of *būghān*; perhaps the two words stand for joint at the nape of the neck. Khwāja-i-kalān was one of seven brothers, six died in Bābur's service, he himself served till Bābur's death.

[4] *Cf.* f. 48.

thereafter people called him *Chāpūk* (*Balafré*). Another time, this also in the Avenue, at the Maghāk (Fosse) Bridge[1] Abū'l-qāsim (*Kohbur Chaghatāī*) got in with his mace. Once, again
Fol. 40*b*. in the Avenue, near the Mill-sluice, when Mīr Shāh *Qūchīn* also got in with his mace, they cut his neck almost half-through; most fortunately the great artery was not severed.

While we were in Khān Yūrtī, some in the fort sent the deceiving message,[2] 'Come you to-night to the Lovers' Cave side and we will give you the fort.' Under this idea, we went that night to the Maghāk Bridge and from there sent a party of good horse and foot to the rendezvous. Four or five of the household foot-soldiers had gone forward when the matter got wind. They were very active men; one, known as Ḥājī, had served me from my childhood; another people called Maḥmūd *Kūndūr-sangak*.[3] They were all killed.

While we lay in Khān Yūrtī, so many Samarkandīs came out that the camp became a town where everything looked for in a town was to be had. Meantime all the forts, Samarkand excepted, and the Highlands and the Lowlands were coming in to us. As in Aūrgūt, however, a fort on the skirt of the Shavdār (var. Shādwār) range, a party of men held fast[4], of necessity we moved out from Khān Yūrtī against them. They could not maintain themselves, and surrendered, making
Fol. 41. Khwāja-i-qāẓī their mediator. Having pardoned their offences against ourselves, we went back to beleaguer Samarkand.

(*b. Affairs of Sl. Ḥusain Mīrzā and his son, Badī'u'z-zamān Mīrzā.*)[5]

This year the mutual recriminations of Sl. Ḥusain Mīrzā and Badī'u'z-zamān Mīrzā led on to fighting; here are the par-

[1] Khorochkine (Radlov's *Réceuil d'Itinéraires* p. 241) mentions Pul-i-mougak, a great stone bridge thrown across a deep ravine, east of Samarkand. *For* Kūl-i-maghāk, deep pool, or pool of the fosse, *see* f. 48*b*.

[2] From Khwānd-amīr's differing account of this affair, it may be surmised that those sending the message were not treacherous; but the message itself was deceiving inasmuch as it did not lead Bābur to expect opposition. *Cf.* f. 43 and note.

[3] Of this nick-name several interpretations are allowed by the dictionaries.

[4] *See* Schuyler i, 268 for an account of this beautiful Highland village.

[5] Here Bābur takes up the thread, dropped on f. 36, of the affairs of the Khurāsānī mīrzās. He draws on other sources than the Ḥ.S.; perhaps on

ticulars:—Last year, as has been mentioned, Badī'u'z-zamān Mīrzā and Muẓaffar Ḥusain Mīrzā had been made to kneel for Balkh and Astarābād. From that time till this, many envoys had come and gone, at last even 'Alī-sher Beg had gone but urge it as all did, Badī'u'z-zamān Mīrzā would not consent to give up Astarābād. 'The Mīrzā,' he said, 'assigned[1] it to my son, Muḥammad Mū'min Mīrzā at the time of his circumcision.' A conversation had one day between him and 'Alī-sher Beg testifies to his acuteness and to the sensibility of 'Alī-sher Beg's feelings. After saying many things of a private nature in the Mīrzā's ear, 'Alī-sher Beg added, 'Forget these matters.'[2] 'What matters?' rejoined the Mīrzā instantly. 'Alī-sher Beg was much affected and cried a good deal.

At length the jarring words of this fatherly and filial discussion went so far that *his* father against his father, and *his* son against his son drew armies out for Balkh and Astarābād.[3]

Up (from Harāt) to the Pul-i-chirāgh meadow, below Garzawān,[4] went Sl. Ḥusain Mīrzā; down (from Balkh) came Fol. 41*b*.
Badī'u'z-zamān Mīrzā. On the first day of Ramẓān (May 2nd.) Abū'l-muḥsin Mīrzā advanced, leading some of his father's light troops. There was nothing to call a battle; Badī'u'z-zamān Mīrzā was routed and of his braves masses were made prisoner. Sl. Ḥusain Mīrzā ordered that all prisoners should

---

his own memory, perhaps on information given by Khurāsānīs with him in Hindūstān *e.g.* Ḥusain's grandson. *See* f. 167*b*. *Cf.* Ḥ.S. ii, 261.

[1] *bāghishlāb tūr*. *Cf.* f. 34 note to *bāghish dā*.

[2] *Bū sozlār aūnūlūng*. Some W.-i-B. MSS., *Farāmosh bakunīd* for *nakunīd*, thus making the Mīrzā not acute but rude, and destroying the point of the story *i.e.* that the Mīrzā pretended so to have forgotten as to have an empty mind. Khwānd-amīr states that 'Alī-sher prevailed at first; his tears therefore may have been of joy at the success of his pacifying mission.

[3] *i.e.* B.Z.'s father, Ḥusain, against Mū'min's father, B.Z. and Ḥusain's son, Muẓaffar Ḥusain against B. Z.'s son Mū'min;—a veritable conundrum.

[4] Garzawān lies west of Balkh. Concerning Pul-i-chirāgh Col. Grodekoff's *Ride to Harāt* (Marvin p. 103 ff.) gives pertinent information. It has also a map showing the Pul-i-chirāgh meadow. The place stands at the mouth of a triply-bridged defile, but the name appears to mean Gate of the Lamp (*cf.* Gate of Tīmūr), and not Bridge of the Lamp, because the Ḥ.S. and also modern maps write *bīl* (*bel*), pass, where the Turkī text writes *pul*, bridge, narrows, pass.

The lamp of the name is one at the shrine of a saint, just at the mouth of the defile. It was alight when Col. Grodekoff passed in 1879 and to it, he says, the name is due now—as it presumably was 400 years ago and earlier.

be beheaded; this not here only but wherever he defeated a rebel son, he ordered the heads of all prisoners to be struck off. And why not? Right was with him. The (rebel) Mīrzās were so given over to vice and social pleasure that even when a general so skilful and experienced as their father was within half-a-day's journey of them, and when before the blessed month of Ramẓān, one night only remained, they busied themselves with wine and pleasure, without fear of their father, without dread of God. Certain it is that those so lost (*yūtkān*) will perish and that any hand can deal a blow at those thus going to perdition (*aūtkān*). During the several years of Badī'u'z-zamān Mīrzā's rule in Astarābād, his coterie and his following, his bare (*yālāng*) braves even, were in full splendour[4] and adornment. He had many gold and silver drinking cups
Fol. 42. and utensils, much silken plenishing and countless tīpūchāq horses. He now lost everything. He hurled himself in his flight down a mountain track, leading to a precipitous fall. He himself got down the fall, with great difficulty, but many of his men perished there.[1]

After defeating Badī'u'z-zamān Mīrzā, Sl. Ḥusain Mīrzā moved on to Balkh. It was in charge of Shaikh 'Alī Ṭaghāī; he, not able to defend it, surrendered and made his submission. The Mīrzā gave Balkh to Ibrāhīm Ḥusain Mīrzā, left Muḥammad Walī Beg and Shāh Ḥusain, the page, with him and went back to Khurāsān.

Defeated and destitute, with his braves bare and his bare foot-soldiers[2], Badī'u'z-zamān Mīrzā drew off to Khusrau Shāh in Qūndūz. Khusrau Shāh, for his part, did him good service, such service indeed, such kindness with horses and camels, tents and pavilions and warlike equipment of all sorts, both for himself and those with him, that eye-witnesses said between this and his former equipment the only difference might be in the gold and silver vessels.

[1] Khwānd-amīr heard from the Mīrzā on the spot, when later in his service, that he was let down the precipice by help of turban-sashes tied together.

[2] *yikit yīlāng u yāyāq yāling*; a jingle made by due phonetic change of vowels; a play too on *yālāng*, which first means stripped *i.e.* robbed and next unmailed, perhaps sometimes bare-bodied in fight.

(*c. Dissension between Sl. Mas'ūd Mīrzā and Khusrau Shāh.*)

Ill-feeling and squabbles had arisen between Sl. Mas'ūd Mīrzā and Khusrau Shāh because of the injustices of the one and the self-magnifyings of the other. Now therefore Khusrau Shāh joined his brothers, Walī and Bāqī to Badī'u'z-zamān Mīrzā and sent the three against Ḥiṣār. They could not even Fol. 42*b*.
get near the fort, in the outskirts swords were crossed once or twice; one day at the Bird-house[1] on the north of Ḥiṣār, Muḥibb-'alī, the armourer (*qūrchī*), outstripped his people and struck in well; he fell from his horse but at the moment of his capture, his men attacked and freed him. A few days later a somewhat compulsory peace was made and Khusrau Shāh's army retired.

Shortly after this, Badī'u'z-zamān Mīrzā drew off by the mountain-road to Ẕū'n-nūn *Arghūn* and his son, Shujā' *Arghūn* in Qandahār and Zamīn-dāwar. Stingy and miserly as Ẕū'n-nūn was, he served the Mīrzā well, in one single present offering 40,000 sheep.

Amongst curious happenings of the time one was this: Wednesday was the day Sl. Ḥusain Mīrzā beat Badī'u'z-zamān Mīrzā; Wednesday was the day Muẓaffar Ḥusain Mīrzā beat Muḥammad Mū'min Mīrzā; Wednesday, more curious still, was the name of the man who unhorsed and took prisoner, Muḥammad Mū'min Mīrzā.[2]

[1] *qūsh-khāna*. As the place was outside the walls, it may be a good hawking ground and not a falconry.

[2] The Ḥ.S., mentions (ii, 222) a Sl. Aḥmad of Chār-shamba, a town mentioned *e.g.* by Grodekoff p. 123. It also spoils Bābur's coincidence by fixing Tuesday, Shab'ān 29th. for the battle. Perhaps the commencement of the Muḥammadan day at sunset, allows of both statements.

903 AH.—AUG. 30TH. 1497 TO AUG. 19TH. 1498 AD.[1]

(*a. Resumed account of Bābur's second attempt on Samarkand.*)

When we had dismounted in the Qulba (Plough) meadow,[2] behind the Bāgh-i-maidān (Garden of the plain), the Samarkandīs came out in great numbers to near Muḥammad Chap's
Fol. 43. Bridge. Our men were unprepared; and before they were ready, Bābā 'Alī's (son) Bābā Qulī had been unhorsed and taken into the fort. A few days later we moved to the top of Qulba, at the back of Kohik.[3] That day Sayyid Yūsuf,[4] having been sent out of the town, came to our camp and did me obeisance.

The Samarkandīs, fancying that our move from the one ground to the other meant, 'He has given it up,' came out, soldiers and townsmen in alliance (through the Turquoise Gate), as far as the Mīrzā's Bridge and, through the Shaikh-zāda's Gate, as far as Muḥammad Chap's. We ordered our braves to arm and ride out; they were strongly attacked from both sides, from Muḥammad Chap's Bridge and from the Mīrzā's, but God brought it right! our foes were beaten. Begs of the best and the boldest of braves our men unhorsed and brought in. Amongst them Ḥāfiẓ *Dūldāī's* (son) Muḥammad *Mīskīn*[5] was taken, after his index-finger had been struck off; Muḥammad Qāsim *Nabīra* also was unhorsed and brought in by his own younger brother, Ḥasan *Nabīra*.[6] There were many other such soldiers and known men. Of the town-

[1] Elph. MS. f. 30*b*; W.-i-B. I.O. 215 f. 34 and 217 f. 26*b*; Mems. p. 46. The abruptness of this opening is due to the interposition of Sl. Ḥusain M.'s affairs between Bābur's statement on f. 41 that he returned from Aūrgūt and this first of 903 AH. that on return he encamped in Qulba.

[2] *See* f. 48*b*.

[3] *i.e.* Chūpān-ātā; *see* f. 45 and note.

[4] *Aūghlāqchī*, the Grey Wolfer of f. 22.

[5] A sobriquet, the *suppliant* or perhaps something having connection with musk. Ḥ.S. ii, 278, son of Ḥ.D.

[6] *i.e.* grandson (of Muḥammad Sīghal). *Cf.* f. 39.

rabble, were brought in Diwāna, the tunic-weaver and *Kāl-qāshūq*,[1] headlong leaders both, in brawl and tumult; they were ordered to death with torture in blood-retaliation for our foot-soldiers, killed at the Lovers' Cave.[2] This was a complete reverse for the Samarkandīs; they came out no more even when our men used to go to the very edge of the ditch and bring back their slaves and slave-women. Fol. 43*b*.

The Sun entered the Balance and cold descended on us.[3] I therefore summoned the begs admitted to counsel and it was decided, after discussion, that although the towns-people were so enfeebled that, by God's grace, we should take Samarkand, it might be to-day, it might be to-morrow, still, rather than suffer from cold in the open, we ought to rise from near it and go for winter-quarters into some fort, and that, even if we had to leave those quarters later on, this would be done without further trouble. As Khwāja Dīdār seemed a suitable fort, we marched there and having dismounted in the meadow lying before it, went in, fixed on sites for the winter-houses and covered shelters,[4] left overseers and inspectors of the work and returned to our camp in the meadow. There we lay during the few days before the winter-houses were finished.

Meantime Bāī-sunghar Mīrzā had sent again and again to ask help from Shaibānī Khān. On the morning of the very day on which, our quarters being ready, we had moved into Khwāja Dīdār, the Khān, having ridden light from Turkistān, Fol. 44. stood over against our camping-ground. Our men were not all at hand; some, for winter-quarters, had gone to Khwāja Rabāṭī, some to Kabud, some to Shīrāz. None-the-less, we formed up those there were and rode out. Shaibānī Khān made no stand but drew off towards Samarkand. He went right up to the fort but because the affair had not gone as

[1] This seeming sobriquet may show the man's trade. *Kāl* is a sort of biscuit; *qāshūq* may mean a spoon.

[2] The Ḥ.S. does not ascribe treachery to those inviting Bābur into Samarkand but attributes the murder of his men to others who fell on them when the plan of his admission became known. The choice here of "town-rabble" for retaliatory death supports the account of Ḥ.S. ii.

[3] "It was the end of September or beginning of October" (Erskine).

[4] *awī u kīpa yīwlār*. *Awī* is likely to represent *kibitkas*. For *kīpa yīr*, *see* Zenker p. 782.

Bāī-sunghar Mīrzā wished, did not get a good reception. He therefore turned back for Turkistān a few days later, in disappointment, with nothing done.

Bāī-sunghar Mīrzā had sustained a seven months' siege; his one hope had been in Shaibānī Khān; this he had lost and he now with 2 or 300 of his hungry suite, drew off from Samarkand, for Khusrau Shāh in Qūndūz.

When he was near Tīrmīẕ, at the Amū ferry, the Governor of Tīrmīẕ, Sayyid Ḥusain Akbar, kinsman and confidant both of Sl. Mas'ūd Mīrzā, heard of him and went out against him. The Mīrzā himself got across the river but Mīrīm Tarkhān was drowned and all the rest of his people were captured, together with his baggage and the camels loaded with his personal effects; even his page, Muḥammad Ṭāhir, falling into Sayyid Ḥusain Akbar's hands. Khusrau Shāh, for his part, looked kindly on the Mīrzā.

Fol. 44*b*. When the news of his departure reached us, we got to horse and started from Khwāja Dīdār for Samarkand. To give us honourable meeting on the road, were nobles and braves, one after another. It was on one of the last ten days of the first Rabī' (end of November 1497 AD.), that we entered the citadel and dismounted at the Bū-stān Sarāī. Thus, by God's favour, were the town and the country of Samarkand taken and occupied.

(*b. Description of Samarkand.*)[1]

Few towns in the whole habitable world are so pleasant as Samarkand. It is of the Fifth Climate and situated in lat. 40° 6′ and long. 99°.[2] The name of the town is Samarkand; its country people used to call Mā warā'u'n-nahr (Transoxania).

[1] Interesting reference may be made, amongst the many books on Samarkand, to Sharafu'd-dīn 'Alī *Yazdī's Ẓafar-nāma* Bib. Ind. ed. i, 300, 781, 799, 800 and ii, 6, 194, 596 etc.; to Ruy Gonzalves di Clavijo's *Embassy to Tīmūr* (Markham) cap. vi and vii; to Ujfalvy's *Turkistan* ii, 79 and Madame Ujfalvy's *De Paris à Samarcande* p. 161,—these two containing a plan of the town; to Schuyler's *Turkistan*; to Kostenko's *Turkistan Gazetteer* i, 345; to Réclus, vi, 270 and plan; and to a beautiful work of the St. Petersburg Archæological Society, *Les Mosquées de Samarcande*, of which the B.M. has a copy.

[2] This statement is confused in the Elp. and Ḥai. MSS. The second appears to give, by *abjad*, lat. 40′ 6″ and long. 99′. Mr. Erskine (p. 48) gives

They used to call it *Baldat-i-maḥfūẓa* because no foe laid hands on it with storm and sack.[1] It must have become [2] Musalmān in the time of the Commander of the Faithful, his Highness 'Usmān. Quṣam ibn 'Abbās, one of the Companions[3] must have gone there; his burial-place, known as the Tomb of Shāh-i-zinda (The Living Shāh, *i.e.*, Fāqīr) is outside the Iron Gate. Iskandar must have founded Samarkand. The Turk and Mughūl hordes call it Sīmīz-kīnt.[4] Tīmūr Beg made it his capital; no ruler so great will ever have made it a capital before (*qīlghān aīmās dūr*). I ordered people to pace round the ramparts of the walled-town; it came out at 10,000 steps.[5] Samarkandīs are all orthodox (*sunnī*), pure-in-the Faith, law-abiding and religious. The number of Leaders of Islām said to have arisen in Mā warā'u'n-nahr, since the days of his Highness the Prophet, are not known to have arisen in any other country.[6] From the Mātarīd suburb of Samarkand came Shaikh Abū'l-manṣūr, one of the Expositors of the Word.[7] Of the two sects of Expositors, the Mātarīdiyah Fol. 45.

---

lat. 39' 57" and long. 99' 16", noting that this is according to Ūlūgh Beg's Tables and that the long. is calculated from Ferro. The Ency. Br. of 1910-11 gives lat. 39' 39" and long. 66' 45".

1 The enigmatical cognomen, Protected Town, is of early date; it is used *i.a.* by Ibn Batūta in the 14th. century. Bābur's tense refers it to the past. The town had frequently changed hands in historic times before he wrote. The name may be due to immunity from damage to the buildings in the town. Even Chīngīz Khān's capture (1222 AD.) left the place well-preserved and its lands cultivated, but it inflicted great loss of men. *Cf.* Schuyler i, 236 and his authorities, especially Bretschneider.

2 Here is a good example of Bābur's caution in narrative. He does not affirm that Samarkand became Musalmān, or (*infra*) that Quṣam ibn 'Abbās went, or that Alexander founded but in each case uses the presumptive past tense, resp. *būlghān dūr, bārghān dūr, bīnā qīlghān dūr*, thus showing that he repeats what may be inferred or presumed and not what he himself asserts.

3 *i.e.* of Muḥammad. See Ẓ.N. ii, 193.

4 *i.e.* Fat Village. His text misleading him, Mr. Erskine makes here the useful irrelevant note that Persians and Arabs call the place Samar-qand and Turks, Samar-kand, the former using *qaf* (q), the latter *kaf* (k). Both the Elph. and the Ḥai. MSS. write Samarqand.

For use of the name Fat Village, *see* Clavijo (Markham p. 170), Simesquintc, and Bretschneider's *Mediæval Geography* pp. 61, 64, 66 and 163.

5 *qadam*. Kostenko (i, 344) gives 9 m. as the circumference of the old walls and 1⅞ m. as that of the citadel. *See* Mde. Ujfalvy p. 175 for a picture of the walls.

6 *Ma'lūm aīmās kīm müncha paidā būlmīsh būlghāī*; an idiomatic phrase.

7 d. 333 AH. (944 AD.). *See* D'Herbélot art. Mātridī p. 572.

and the Ash'ariyah,[1] the first is named from this Shaikh Abū'l-manṣūr. Of Mā warā'u'n-nahr also was Khwāja Ismā'īl *Khartank*, the author of the *Ṣāḥiḥ-i-bukhārī*.[2] From the Farghāna district, Marghīnān—Farghāna, though at the limit of settled habitation, is included in Mā warā'u'n-nahr,—came the author of the *Hidāyat*,[3] a book than which few on Jurisprudence are more honoured in the sect of Abū Ḥanīfa.

On the east of Samarkand are Farghāna and Kāshghar; on the west, Bukhārā and Khwārizm; on the north, Tāshkīnt and Shāhrukhiya,—in books written Shāsh and Banākat; and on the south, Balkh and Tīrmīẕ.

The Kohik Water flows along the north of Samarkand, at the distance of some 4 miles (2 *kuroh*); it is so-called because it comes out from under the upland of the Little Hill (*Kohik*)[4] lying between it and the town. The Dar-i-gham Water (canal) flows along the south, at the distance of some two miles (1 *sharī'*). This is a large and swift torrent,[5] indeed it is like a large river, cut off from the Kohik Water. All the gardens and suburbs and some of the *tūmāns* of Samarkand are cultivated by it. By the Kohik Water a stretch of from 30 to 40 *yīghāch*,[6] by road, is made habitable and cultivated, as far as Bukhārā

[1] *See* D'Herbélot art. Aschair p. 124.

[2] Abū 'Abdu'l-lāh bin Ismā'īlu'l-jausī b. 194 AH. d. 256 AH. (810-870 AD.). *See* D'Herbélot art. Bokhārī p. 191, art. Giorag p. 373, and art. Ṣāḥiḥu'l-bokhārī p. 722. He passed a short period, only, of his life in Khartank, a suburb of Samarkand.

[3] *Cf.* f. 3*b* and n. 1.

[4] This though 2475 ft. above the sea is only some 300 ft. above Samarkand. It is the Chūpān-ātā (Father of Shepherds) of maps and on it Tīmūr built a shrine to the local patron of shepherds. The Zar-afshān, or rather, its Qarā-sū arm, flows from the east of the Little Hill and turns round it to flow west. Bābur uses the name *Kohik Water* loosely; *e.g.* for the whole Zar-afshān when he speaks (*infra*) of cutting off the Dar-i-gham canal but for its southern arm only, the Qarā-sū in several places, and once, for the Dar-i-gham canal. *See* f. 49*b* and Kostenko i. 192.

[5] *rūd*. The Zar-afshān has a very rapid current. *See* Kostenko i, 196, and for the canal, i, 174. The name Dar-i-gham is used also for a musical note having charm to witch away grief; and also for a town noted for its wines.

[6] What this represents can only be guessed; perhaps 150 to 200 miles. Abū'l-fidā (Reinaud ii, 213) quotes Ibn Haukal as saying that from Bukhārā up to "Bottam" (this seems to be where the Zar-afshān emerges into the open land) is eight days' journey through an unbroken tangle of verdure and gardens.

and Qarā-kūl. Large as the river is, it is not too large for its dwellings and its culture; during three or four months of the year, indeed, its waters do not reach Bukhārā.[1] Grapes, melons, apples and pomegranates, all fruits indeed, are good in Samarkand; two are famous, its apple and its *ṣāḥibī* (grape).[2] Its winter is mightily cold; snow falls but not so much as in Kābul; in the heats its climate is good but not so good as Kābul's. Fol. 45*b*.

In the town and suburbs of Samarkand are many fine buildings and gardens of Tīmur Beg and Aūlūgh Beg Mīrzā.[3]

In the citadel,[4] Tīmūr Beg erected a very fine building, the great four-storeyed kiosque, known as the Gūk Sarāī.[5] In the walled-town, again, near the Iron Gate, he built a Friday Mosque[6] of stone (*sangīn*); on this worked many stone-cutters, brought from Hindūstān. Round its frontal arch is inscribed in letters large enough to be read two miles away, the Qu'rān verse, *Wa az yerfa' Ibrāhīm al Qawā'id alī akhara.*[7] This also is a very fine building. Again, he laid out two gardens, on the

[1] *See* Schuyler i, 286 on the apportionment of water to Samarkand and Bukhārā.

[2] It is still grown in the Samarkand region, and in Mr. Erskine's time a grape of the same name was cultivated in Aurangābād of the Deccan.

[3] *i.e. Shāhrukhī*, Tīmūr's grandson, through Shāhrukh. It may be noted here that Bābur never gives Tīmūr any other title than Beg and that he styles all Tīmūrids, Mīrzā (Mīr-born).

[4] Mr. Erskine here points out the contradiction between the statements (1) of Ibn Haukal, writing, in 367 AH. (977 AD.), of Samarkand as having a citadel (*ark*), an outer-fort (*qūrghān*) and Gates in both circumvallations; and (2) of Sharafu'd-dīn *Yazdī* (Z.N.) who mentions that when, in Tīmūr's day, the Getes besieged Samarkand, it had neither walls nor gates. *See* Ouseley's Ibn Haukal p. 253; Z.N. Bib. Ind. ed. i, 109 and Pétis de la Croix's Z.N. (*Histoire de Tīmūr Beg*) i, 91.

[5] Here still lies the Ascension Stone, the *Gūk-tāsh*, a block of greyish white marble. Concerning the date of the erection of the building and meaning of its name, *see e.g.* Pétis de la Croix's *Histoire de Chīngīz Khān* p. 171; Mems. p. 40 note; and Schuyler *s.n.*

[6] This seems to be the Bībī Khānīm Mosque. The author of *Les Mosquées de Samarcande* states that Tīmūr built Bībī Khānīm and the Gūr-i-amīr (Amīr's tomb); decorated Shāh-i-zinda and set up the Chūpān-ātā shrine. *Cf.* f 46 and note to Jahāngīr Mīrzā, as to the Gūr-i-amīr.

[7] Cap. II. Quoting from Sale's *Qur'ān* (i 24) the verse is, "And Ibrāhīm and Ismā'īl raised the foundations of the house, saying, 'Lord! accept it from us, for Thou art he who hearest and knowest; Lord! make us also resigned to Thee, and show us Thy holy ceremonies, and be turned to us, for Thou art easy to be reconciled, and merciful.'"

east of the town, one, the more distant, the Bāgh-i-bulandī,[1] the other and nearer, the Bāgh-i-dilkushā.[2] From Dilkushā to the Turquoise Gate, he planted an Avenue of White Poplar,[3] and in the garden itself erected a great kiosque, painted inside
Fol. 46. with pictures of his battles in Hindūstān. He made another garden, known as the Naqsh-i-jahān (World's Picture), on the skirt of Kohik, above the Qarā-sū or, as people also call it, the Āb-i-raḥmat (Water-of-mercy) of Kān-i-gil.[4] It had gone to ruin when I saw it, nothing remaining of it except its name. His also are the Bāgh-i-chanār,[5] near the walls and below the town on the south,[6] also the Bāgh-i-shamāl (North Garden) and the Bāgh-i-bihisht (Garden of Paradise). His own tomb and those of his descendants who have ruled in Samarkand, are in a College, built at the exit (*chāqār*) of the walled-town, by Muḥammad Sulṭān Mīrzā, the son of Tīmūr Beg's son, Jahāngīr Mīrzā.[7]

Amongst Aūlūgh Beg Mīrzā's buildings inside the town are a College and a monastery (*Khānqāh*). The dome of the monastery is very large, few so large are shown in the world. Near these two buildings, he constructed an excellent Hot Bath (*ḥammām*) known as the Mīrzā's Bath; he had the pavements in this made of all sorts of stone (? mosaic); such

[1] or, *buland*, Garden of the Height or High Garden. The Turkī texts have what can be read as *buldī* but the Ẓ.N. both when describing it (ii, 194) and elsewhere (*e.g.* ii, 596) writes *buland*. *Buldī* may be a clerical error for *bulandī*, the height, a name agreeing with the position of the garden.

[2] In the Heart-expanding Garden, the Spanish Ambassadors had their first interview with Tīmūr. *See* Clavijo (Markham p. 130). Also the Ẓ.N. ii, 6 for an account of its construction.

[3] Judging from the location of the gardens and of Bābur's camps, this appears to be the Avenue mentioned on f. 39*b* and f. 40.

[4] *See infra* f. 48 and note.

[5] The Plane-tree Garden. This seems to be Clavijo's *Bayginar*, laid out shortly before he saw it (Markham p. 136).

[6] The citadel of Samarkand stands high; from it the ground slopes west and south; on these sides therefore gardens outside the walls would lie markedly below the outer-fort (*tāsh-qūrghān*). Here as elsewhere the second W.-i-B. reads *stone* for *outer* (*Cf.* index *s.n. tāsh*). For the making of the North garden *see* Ẓ.N. i, 799.

[7] Tīmūr's eldest son, d. 805 AH. (1402 AD.), before his father, therefore. Bābur's wording suggests that in his day, the Gūr-i-amīr was known as the Madrāsa. *See* as to the buildings Ẓ.N. i, 713 and ii, 492, 595, 597, 705; Clavijo (Markham p. 164 and p. 166); and *Les Mosquées de Samarcande*.

another bath is not known in Khurāsān or in Samarkand.[1] Fol. 46b. Again;—to the south of the College is his mosque, known as the Masjid-i-maqaṭa' (Carved Mosque) because its ceiling and its walls are all covered with *islīmī*[2] and Chinese pictures formed of segments of wood.[3] There is great discrepancy between the *qibla* of this mosque and that of the College; that of the mosque seems to have been fixed by astronomical observation.

Another of Aūlūgh Beg Mīrzā's fine buildings is an observatory, that is, an instrument for writing Astronomical Tables.[4] This stands three storeys high, on the skirt of the Kohik upland. By its means the Mīrzā worked out the Kūrkānī Tables, now used all over the world. Less work is done with any others. Before these were made, people used the Aīl-khānī Tables, put together at Marāgha, by Khwāja Naṣīr *Tūsī*,[5] in the time of Hulākū Khān. Hulākū Khān it is, people call *Aīl-khānī*.[6]

(*Author's note.*) Not more than seven or eight observatories seem to have been constructed in the world. Māmūm Khalīfa[7] (Caliph) made one with which the *Mamūmī* Tables were written. Batalmūs (Ptolemy) constructed another. Another was made, in Hindūstān, in the time of Rājā Vikramāditya *Hindū*, in Ujjain and Dhar, that is, the Mālwa country, now known as Māndū. The Hindūs of Hindūstān use the Tables of this Observatory. They were put together 1,584 years ago.[8] Fol. 47. Compared with others, they are somewhat defective.

---

[1] Hindūstān would make a better climax here than Samarkand does.

[2] These appear to be pictures or ornamentations of carved wood. Redhouse describes *islīmī* as a special kind of ornamentation in curved lines, similar to Chinese methods.

[3] *i.e.* the Black Stone (*ka'ba*) at Makkah to which Musalmāns turn in prayer.

[4] As ancient observatories were themselves the instruments of astronomical observation, Bābur's wording is correct. Aūlūgh Beg's great quadrant was 180 ft. high; Abū-muḥammad *Khujandī's* sextant had a radius of 58 ft. Jā'ī Singh made similar great instruments in Jā'īpūr, Dihlī has others. *Cf.* Greaves Misc. Works i, 50; Mems. p. 51 note; *Āiyīn-i-akbarī* (Jarrett) ii, 5 and note; Murray's Hand-book to Bengal p. 331; Indian Gazetteer xiii, 400.

[5] b. 597 AH. d. 672 AH. (1201-1274 AD.). *See* D'Herbélot's art. Naṣīr-i-dīn p. 662; Abū'l-fidā (Reinaud, Introduction i, cxxxviii) and Beale's Biographical Dict. *s.n.*

[6] a grandson of Chīngīz Khān, d. 663 AH. (1265 AD.). The cognomen *Aīl-khānī* (*Īl-khānī*) may mean Khān of the Tribe.

[7] Harūnu'r-rashīd's second son; d. 218 AH. (833 AD.).

[8] Mr. Erskine notes that this remark would seem to fix the date at which Bābur wrote it as 934 AH. (1527 AD.), that being the 1584th. year of the era of Vikramāditya, and therefore at three years before Bābur's death. (The Vikramāditya era begun 57 BC.)

Aūlūgh Beg Mīrzā again, made the garden known as the Bāgh-i-maidān (Garden of the Plain), on the skirt of the Kohik upland. In the middle of it he erected a fine building they call Chihil Sitūn (Forty Pillars). On both storeys are pillars, all of stone (*tāshdīn*).[1] Four turrets, like minarets, stand on its four corner-towers, the way up into them being through the towers. Everywhere there are stone pillars, some fluted, some twisted, some many-sided. On the four sides of the upper storey are open galleries enclosing a four-doored hall (*chār-dara*); their pillars also are all of stone. The raised floor of the building is all paved with stone.

He made a smaller garden, out beyond Chihil Sitūn and towards Kohik, also having a building in it. In the open gallery of this building he placed a great stone throne, some 14 or 15 yards (*qārī*) long, some 8 yards wide and perhaps 1 yard high. They brought a stone so large by a very long road.[2] There is a crack in the middle of it which people say must have come after it was brought here. In the same
Fol. 47*b*. garden he also built a four-doored hall, know as the Chīnī-khāna (Porcelain House) because its *īzāra*[3] are all of porcelain; he sent to China for the porcelain used in it. Inside the walls again, is an old building of his, known as the Masjid-i-laqlaqa (Mosque of the Echo). If anyone stamps on the ground under the middle of the dome of this mosque, the sound echoes back from the whole dome; it is a curious matter of which none know the secret.

In the time also of Sl. Aḥmad Mīrzā the great and lesser begs laid out many gardens, large and small.[4] For beauty, and air, and view, few will have equalled Darwesh Muḥammad Tarkhān's Chār-bāgh (Four Gardens).[5] It lies overlooking the whole of Qulba Meadow, on the slope below the Bāgh-i-

[1] *Cf.* index *s.n. tāsh.*

[2] This remark may refer to the 34 miles between the town and the quarries of its building stone. *See* f. 49 and note to Aītmāk Pass.

[3] Steingass, any support for the back in sitting, a low wall in front of a house. *See* Vullers p. 148 and *Burhān-i-qāṭi'*; p. 119. Perhaps a *dado*.

[4] *beg u begāt, bāgh u bāghcha.*

[5] Four Gardens, a quadrilateral garden, laid out in four plots. The use of the name has now been extended for any well-arranged, large garden, especially one belonging to a ruler (Erskine).

maidān. Moreover it is arranged symmetrically, terrace above terrace, and is planted with beautiful *nārwān*[1] and cypresses and white poplar. A most agreeable sojourning place, its one defect is the want of a large stream.

Samarkand is a wonderfully beautified town. One of its specialities, perhaps found in few other places,[2] is that the different trades are not mixed up together in it but each has its own *bāzār*, a good sort of plan. Its bakers and its cooks are good. The best paper in the world is made there; the water for the paper-mortars[3] all comes from Kān-i-gil,[4] a meadow on the banks of the Qarā-sū (Blackwater) or Āb-i-raḥmat (Water Fol. 48. of Mercy). Another article of Samarkand trade, carried to all sides and quarters, is cramoisy velvet.

Excellent meadows lie round Samarkand. One is the famous Kān-i-gil, some 2 miles east and a little north of the town. The Qarā-sū or Āb-i-raḥmat flows through it, a stream (with driving power) for perhaps seven or eight mills. Some say the original name of the meadow must have been Kān-i-ābgīr (Mine of Quagmire) because the river is bordered by quagmire, but the histories all write Kān-i-gil (Mine of clay). It is an excellent meadow. The Samarkand sulṭans always made it their reserve,[5] going out to camp in it each year for a month or two.

1 As two of the trees mentioned here are large, it may be right to translate *nārwān*, not by pomegranate, but as the hard-wood elm, Madame Ujfalvy's '*karagatch*' (p. 168 and p. 222). The name *qarā-yighāch* (*karagatch*), dark tree, is given to trees other than this elm on account of their deep shadow.

2 Now a common plan indeed! *See* Schuyler i, 173.

3 *juwāz-i-kaghazlār (ning) sū'ī*, *i.e.* the water of the paper-(pulping)-mortars. Owing to the omission from some MSS. of the word *sū*, water, *juwāz* has been mistaken for a kind of paper. *See* Mems. p. 52 and *Mems.* i, 102; A.Q.R. July 1910, p. 2, art. Paper-mills of Samarkand (H.B.); and Madame Ujfalvy p. 188. Kostenko, it is to be noted, does not include paper in his list (i, 346) of modern manufactures of Samarkand.

4 Mine of mud or clay. My husband has given me support for reading *gil*, and not *gul*, rose;—(1) In two good MSS. of the W.-i-B. the word is pointed with *kasra*, *i.e.* as for *gil*, clay; and (2) when describing a feast held in the garden by Tīmūr, the Ẓ.N. says the mud-mine became a rose-mine, *shuda Kān-i-gil Kān-i-gul*. [Mr. Erskine refers here to Pétis de la Croix's *Histoire de Timūr Beg* (*i.e.* Ẓ.N.) i, 96 and ii, 133 and 421.]

5 *qūrūgh*. Vullers, classing the word as Arabic, Zenker, classing it as Eastern Turkī, and Erskine (p. 42 n.) explain this as land reserved for the

6

Higher up (on the river) than Kān-i-gil and to the s.e. of it is a meadow some 4 miles east of the town, known as Khān Yūrtī (Khān's Camping-ground). The Qarā-sū flows through this meadow before entering Kān-i-gil. When it comes to Khān Yūrtī it curves back so far that it encloses, with a very narrow outlet, enough ground for a camp. Having noticed these advantages, we camped there for a time during
Fol. 48b. the siege of Samarkand.[1]

Another meadow is the Būdana Qūrūgh (Quail Reserve), lying between Dil-kushā and the town. Another is the Kūl-i-maghāk (Meadow of the deep pool) at some 4 miles from the town. This also is a round[2] meadow. People call it Kul-i-maghāk meadow because there is a large pool on one side of it. Sl. 'Alī Mīrzā lay here during the siege, when I was in Khān Yūrtī. Another and smaller meadow is Qulba (Plough); it has Qulba Village and the Kohik Water on the north, the Bāgh-i-maidān and Darwesh Muḥammad Tarkhān's Chār-bāgh on the south, and the Kohik upland on the west.

Samarkand has good districts and *tūmāns*. Its largest district, and one that is its equal, is Bukhārā, 25 *yīghāch*[3] to the west. Bukhārā in its turn, has several *tūmāns;* it is a fine town; its fruits are many and good, its melons excellent; none in Mā warā'u'n-nahr matching them for quality and quantity. Although the Mīr Tīmūrī melon of Akhsī[4] is sweeter and more delicate than any Bukhārā melon, still in Bukhārā many kinds of melon are good and plentiful. The Bukhārā plum is famous; no other equals it. They skin it,[5] dry it and
Fol. 49. carry it from land to land with rarities (*tabarrūklār bīla*); it is an excellent laxative medicine. Fowls and geese are much

---

summer encampment of princes. Shaw (Voc. p. 155), deriving it from *qūrūmāq*, to frighten, explains it as a fenced field of growing grain.

[1] *Cf.* f. 40. There it is located at one *yīghāch* and here at 3 *kurohs* from the town.

[2] *taur*. *Cf.* Zenker *s.n.* I understand it to lie, as Khān Yūrtī did, in a curve of the river.

[3] 162 m. by rail.

[4] *Cf.* f. 3.

[5] *tirisini sūiūb*. The verb *sūimāk*, to despoil, seems to exclude the common plan of stoning the fruit. *Cf.* f. 3*b*, *dānasini alip*, taking out the stones.

looked after (*parwārī*) in Bukhārā. Bukhārā wine is the strongest made in Mā warā'u'n-nahr; it was what I drank when drinking in those countries at Samarkand.[1]

Kesh is another district of Samarkand, 9 *yīghāch*[2] by road to the south of the town. A range called the Aītmāk Pass (*Dābān*)[3] lies between Samarkand and Kesh; from this are taken all the stones for building. Kesh is called also Shahr-i-sabz (Green-town) because its barren waste (*ṣahr*) and roofs and walls become beautifully green in spring. As it was Tīmūr Beg's birth-place, he tried hard to make it his capital. He erected noble buildings in it. To seat his own Court, he built a great arched hall and in this seated his Commander-begs and his Dīwān-begs, on his right and on his left. For those attending the Court, he built two smaller halls, and to seat petitioners to his Court, built quite small recesses on the four sides of the Court-house.[4] Few arches so fine can be shown in the world. It is said to be higher than the Kisrī Arch.[5] Tīmūr Beg also built in Kesh a college and a mausoleum, in which are the tombs of Jahāngīr Mīrzā and others of his descendants.[6] As Kesh did not offer the same facilities as Fol. 49b

[1] *Mīn Samarkandīā aūl* (*or auwal*) *aīchkāndā Bukhārā chāghīrlār nī aīchār aīdīm.* These words have been understood to refer to Bābur's initial drinking of wine but this reading is negatived by his statement (f. 189) that he first drank wine in Harāt in 912 AH. I understand his meaning to be that the wine he drank in Samarkand was Bukhārā wine. The time cannot have been earlier than 917 AH. The two words *aūl aīchkāndā*, I read as parallel to *aūl* (*bāghrī qarā*) (f. 280) 'that drinking,' 'that bird,' *i.e.* of those other countries, not of Hindūstān where he wrote.

It may be noted that Bābur's word for wine, *chāghīr*, may not always represent wine of the grape but may include wine of the apple and pear (cider and perry), and other fruits. Cider, its name seeming to be a descendant of *chāghīr*, was introduced into England by Crusaders, its manufacture having been learned from Turks in Palestine.

[2] 48 m. 3 fur. by way of the Aītmāk Pass (mod. Takhta Qarachi), and, Réclus (vi, 256) Buz-gala-khāna, Goat-house.

[3] The name Aītmāk, to build, appears to be due to the stone quarries on the range. The pass-head is 34 m. from Samarkand and 3000 ft. above it. *See* Kostenko ii, 115 and Schuyler ii, 61 for details of the route.

[4] The description of this hall is difficult to translate. Clavijo (Markham 124) throws light on the small recesses. *Cf.* Z.N. i, 781 and 300 and Schuyler ii, 68.

[5] The Ṭāq-i-kisrī, below Bāghdād, is 105 ft. high, 84 ft. span and 150 ft. in depth (Erskine).

[6] *Cf.* f. 46. Bābur does not mention that Tīmūr's father was buried at Kesh. Clavijo (Markham p. 123) says it was Tīmūr's first intention to be buried near his father, in Kesh.

Samarkand for becoming a town and a capital, he at last made clear choice of Samarkand.

Another district is Qarshī, known also as Nashaf and Nakhshab.[1] Qarshī is a Mughūl name. In the Mughūl tongue they call a *kūr-khāna* Qarshī.[2] The name must have come in after the rule of Chīngīz Khān. Qarshī is somewhat scantily supplied with water; in spring it is very beautiful and its grain and melons are good. It lies 18 *yīghāch*[3] by road south and a little inclined to west of Samarkand. In the district a small bird, known as the *qīl-qūyīrūgh* and resembling the *bāghrī qarā*, is found in such countless numbers that it goes by the name of the Qarshī birdie (*murghak*).[4]

Khozār is another district; Karmīna another, lying between Samarkand and Bukhārā; Qarā-kūl another, 7 *yīghāch*[5] n.w. of Bukhārā and at the furthest limit of the water.

Samarkand has good *tūmāns*. One is Soghd with its dependencies. Its head Yār-yīlāq, its foot Bukhārā, there may be not one single *yīghāch* of earth without its village and its cultivated lands. So famous is it that the saying attributed to Tīmūr Beg, 'I have a garden 30 *yīghāch* long,[6] must have been spoken of Soghd. Another *tūmān* is Shāvdār (var. Shādwār), an excellent one adjoining the town-suburbs. On one side it has the range (Aītmāk Dābān), lying between Samarkand and
Fol. 50. Shahr-i-sabz, on the skirts of which are many of its villages. On the other side is the Kohik Water (*i.e.* the Dar-i-gham canal). There it lies! an excellent *tūmān*, with fine air, full of beauty, abounding in waters, its good things cheap. Observers of Egypt and Syria have not pointed out its match.

1 Abū'l-fidā (Reinaud II, ii, 21) says that Nasaf is the Arabic and Nakhshab the local name for Qarshī. Ibn Haukal (Ouseley p. 260) writes Nakhshab.

2 This word has been translated *burial-place* and *cimetière* but Qarshī means castle, or royal-residence. The Z.N. (i, 111) says that Qarshī is an equivalent for Ar. *qaṣr*, palace, and was so called, from one built there by Qublāī Khān (d. 1294 AD.). Perhaps Bābur's word is connected with Gūrkhān, the title of sovereigns in Khutan, and means great or royal-house, *i.e.* palace.

3 94 m. 6½ fur. via Jām (Kostenko i, 115.)

4 See Appendix B.

5 some 34 m. (Kostenko i, 196). Schuyler mentions that he heard in Qarā-kūl a tradition that the district, in bye-gone days, was fertilized from the Sir.

6 *Cf.* f. 45.

Though Samarkand has other *tūmāns*, none rank with those enumerated; with so much, enough has been said.

Tīmūr Beg gave the government of Samarkand to his eldest son, Jahāngīr Mīrzā (in 776 AH.-1375 AD.); when Jahāngīr Mīrzā died (805 AH.-1403 AD.), he gave it to the Mīrzā's eldest son, Muḥammad Sulṭān-i-jahāngīr; when Muḥammad Sulṭān Mīrzā died, it went to Shāh-rukh Mīrzā, Tīmūr Beg's youngest son. Shāh-rukh Mīrzā gave the whole of Mā warā'u'n-nahr (in 872 AH.-1467 AD.) to his eldest son, Aūlūgh Beg Mīrzā. From him his own son, 'Abdu'l-laṭīf Mīrzā took it, (853 AH.-1449 AD.), for the sake of this five days' fleeting world martyring a father so full of years and knowledge.

The following chronogram gives the date of Aūlūgh Beg Mīrzā's death:—

> Aūlūgh Beg, an ocean of wisdom and science,
> The pillar of realm and religion,
> Sipped from the hand of 'Abbās, the mead of martyrdom,
> And the date of the death is *'Abbās kasht* ('Abbās slew).[1]

Though 'Abdu'l-laṭīf Mīrzā did not rule more than five or six months, the following couplet was current about him:—

> Ill does sovereignty befit the parricide;
> Should he rule, be it for no more than six months.[2]

This chronogram of the death of 'Abdu'l-laṭīf Mīrzā is also well done:—

> 'Abdu'l-laṭīf, in glory a Khusrau and Jamshīd, Fol. 50*b*.
> In his train a Farīdūn and Zardusht,
> Bābā Ḥusain slew on the Friday Eve,
> With an arrow. Write as its date, *Bābā Ḥusain kasht* (Bābā Ḥusain slew).[3]

After 'Abdu'l-laṭīf Mīrzā's death, (Jumāda I, 22, 855 AH.-June 22nd. 1450 AD.), (his cousin) 'Abdu'l-lāh Mīrzā, the grandson of Shāh-rukh Mīrzā through Ibrāhīm Mīrzā, seated him-

[1] By *abjad* the words *'Abbās kasht* yield 853. The date of the murder was Ramẓān 9, 853 AH. (Oct. 27th. 1449 AD.).

[2] This couplet is quoted in the *Rauẓatu'ṣ-ṣafā* (lith. ed. vi. f. 234 foot) and in the Ḥ.S. ii, 44. It is said, in the R.Ṣ. to be by Niẓāmī and to refer to the killing by Shīrūya of his father, Khusrau Parwīz in 7 AH. (628 AD.). The Ḥ.S. says that 'Abdu'l-laṭīf constantly repeated the couplet, after he had murdered his father. [See also Daulat Shāh (Browne p. 356 and p. 366.) H.B.

[3] By *abjad*, *Bābā Ḥusain kasht* yields 854. The death was on Rabī' I, 26, 854 AH. (May 9th. 1450 AD.). See R.Ṣ. vi, 235 for an account of this death.

self on the throne and ruled for 18 months to two years.[1] From him Sl. Abū-sa'īd Mīrzā took it (855 AH.-1451 AD.). He in his life-time gave it to his eldest son, Sl. Aḥmad Mīrzā; Sl. Aḥmad Mīrzā continued to rule it after his father's death (873 AH.-1469 AD.). On his death (899 AH.-1494 AD.) Sl. Maḥmūd Mīrzā was seated on the throne and on his death (900 AH.-1495 AD.) Bāī-sunghar Mīrzā. Bāī-sunghar Mīrzā was made prisoner for a few days, during the Tarkhān rebellion (901 AH.-1496 AD.), and his younger brother, Sl. 'Alī Mīrzā was seated on the throne, but Bāī-sunghar Mīrzā, as has been related in this history, took it again directly. From Bāī-sunghar Mīrzā I took it (903 AH.-1497 AD.). Further details will be learned from the ensuing history.

(*c. Bābur's rule in Samarkand.*)

When I was seated on the throne, I shewed the Samarkand begs precisely the same favour and kindness they had had before. I bestowed rank and favour also on the begs with me, Fol. 51. to each according to his circumstances, the largest share falling to Sl. Aḥmad *Tambal*; he had been in the household begs' circle; I now raised him to that of the great begs.

We had taken the town after a seven months' hard siege. Things of one sort or other fell to our men when we got in. The whole country, with exception of Samarkand itself, had come in earlier either to me or to Sl. 'Alī Mīrzā and consequently had not been over-run. In any case however, what could have been taken from districts so long subjected to raid and rapine? The booty our men had taken, such as it was, came to an end. When we entered the town, it was in such distress that it needed seed-corn and money-advances; what place was this to take anything from? On these accounts our men suffered great privation. We ourselves could give them nothing. Moreover they yearned for their homes and, by ones and twos, set their faces for flight. The first to go was Bayān Qulī's (son) Khān Qulī; Ibrāhīm *Begchīk* was another; all the Mughūls went off and, a little later, Sl. Aḥmad *Tambal*.

Aūzūn Ḥasan counted himself a very sincere and faithful

[1] This overstates the time; dates shew 1 yr. 1 mth. and a few days.

friend of Khwāja-i-qāẓī; we therefore, to put a stop to these desertions, sent the Khwāja to him (in Andijān) so that they, in agreement, might punish some of the deserters and send others back to us. But that very Aūzūn Ḥasan, that traitor to his salt, may have been the stirrer-up of the whole trouble and the spur-to-evil of the deserters from Samarkand. Directly Sl. Aḥmad *Tambal* had gone, all the rest took up a wrong position. Fol. 51*b*.

(*d. Andijān demanded of Bābur by The Khān, and also for Jahāngīr Mīrzā.*)

Although, during the years in which, coveting Samarkand, I had persistently led my army out, Sl. Maḥmūd Khān[1] had provided me with no help whatever, yet, now it had been taken, he wanted Andijān. Moreover, Aūzūn Ḥasan and Sl. Aḥmad *Tambal*, just when soldiers of ours and all the Mughūls had deserted to Andijān and Akhsī, wanted those two districts for Jahāngīr Mīrzā. For several reasons, those districts could not be given to them. One was, that though not promised to The Khān, yet he had asked for them and, as he persisted in asking, an agreement with him was necessary, if they were to be given to Jahāngīr Mīrzā. A further reason was that to ask for them just when deserters from us had fled to them, was very like a command. If the matter had been brought forward earlier, some way of tolerating a command might have been found. At Fol. 52. the moment, as the Mughūls and the Andijān army and several even of my household had gone to Andijān, I had with me in Samarkand, beg for beg, good and bad, somewhere about 1000 men.

When Aūzūn Ḥasan and Sl. Aḥmad *Tambal* did not get what they wanted, they invited all those timid fugitives to join them. Just such a happening, those timid people, for their own sakes, had been asking of God in their terror. Hereupon, Aūzūn Ḥasan and Sl. Aḥmad *Tambal*, becoming openly hostile and rebellious, led their army from Akhsī against Andijān.

Tūlūn Khwāja was a bold, dashing, eager brave of the Bārīn (Mughūls). My father had favoured him and he was still in favour, I myself having raised him to the rank of beg. In

[1] *i.e.* The Khān of the Mughūls, Bābur's uncle.

truth he deserved favour, a wonderfully bold and dashing brave! He, as being the man I favoured amongst the Mughūls, was sent (after them) when they began to desert from Samarkand, to counsel the clans and to chase fear from their hearts so that
Fol. 52b. they might not turn their heads to the wind.[1] Those two traitors however, those false guides, had so wrought on the clans that nothing availed, promise or entreaty, counsel or threat. Tūlūn Khwāja's march lay through Aīkī-sū-ārāsī,[2] known also as Rabāṭik-aūrchīnī. Aūzūn Ḥasan sent a skirmishing party against him; it found him off his guard, seized and killed him. This done, they took Jahāngīr Mīrzā and went to besiege Andijān.

(*e. Bābur loses Andijān.*)

In Andijān when my army rode out for Samarkand, I had left Aūzūn Ḥasan and 'Alī-dost Ṭaghāī (Ramẓān 902AH.-May 1497 AD.). Khwāja-i-qāẓī had gone there later on, and there too were many of my men from Samarkand. During the siege, the Khwāja, out of good-will to me, apportioned 18,000 of his own sheep to the garrison and to the families of the men still with me. While the siege was going on, letters kept coming to me from my mothers[3] and from the Khwāja, saying in effect, 'They are besieging us in this way; if at our cry of distress you do not come, things will go all to ruin. Samarkand was taken
Fol. 53. by the strength of Andijān; if Andijān is in your hands, God willing, Samarkand can be had again.' One after another came letters to this purport. Just then I was recovering from illness but, not having been able to take due care in the days of convalescence, I went all to pieces again and this time, became so very ill that for four days my speech was impeded and they

[1] Elph. MS. *aūrmāghāīlār*, might not turn; Ilai. and Kehr's MSS. (*sar bā bād*) *birmāghāīlār*, might not give. Both metaphors seem drawn from the protective habit of man and beast of turning the back to a storm-wind.

[2] *i.e.* betwixt two waters, the Miyān-i-dū-āb of India. Here, it is the most fertile triangle of land in Turkistān (Réclus, vi, 199), enclosed by the eastern mountains, the Nārīn and the Qarā-sū; Rabāṭik-aūrchīnī, its alternative name, means Small Station sub-district. From the uses of *aūrchīn* I infer that it describes a district in which there is no considerable head-quarters fort.

[3] *i.e.* his own, Qūtlūq-nigār Khānīm and hers, Aīsān-daulat Begīm, with perhaps other widows of his father, probably Shāh Sulṭān Begīm.

used to drop water into my mouth with cotton. Those with me, begs and bare braves alike, despairing of my life, began each to take thought for himself. While I was in this condition, the begs, by an error of judgment, shewed me to a servant of Aūzūn Ḥasan's, a messenger come with wild proposals, and then dismissed him. In four or five days, I became somewhat better but still could not speak, in another few days, was myself again.

Such letters! so anxious, so beseeching, coming from my mothers, that is from my own and hers, Aīsān-daulat Begīm, and from my teacher and spiritual guide, that is, Khwāja-i-maulānā-i-qāẓī, with what heart would a man not move? We left Samarkand for Andijān on a Saturday in Rajab (Feb.-March), when I had ruled 100 days in the town. It was Fol. 53*b*. Saturday again when we reached Khujand and on that day a person brought news from Andijān, that seven days before, that is on the very day we had left Samarkand, 'Alī-dost Ṭaghāī had surrendered Andijān.

These are the particulars;—The servant of Aūzūn Ḥasan who, after seeing me, was allowed to leave, had gone to Andijān and there said, 'The *pādshāh* cannot speak and they are dropping water into his mouth with cotton.' Having gone and made these assertions in the ordinary way, he took oath in 'Alī-dost Ṭaghāī's presence. 'Alī-dost Ṭaghāī was in the Khākān Gate. Becoming without footing through this matter, he invited the opposite party into the fort, made covenant and treaty with them, and surrendered Andijān. Of provisions and of fighting men, there was no lack whatever; the starting point of the surrender was the cowardice of that false and faithless manikin; what was told him, he made a pretext to put himself in the right.

When the enemy, after taking possession of Andijān, heard of my arrival in Khujand, they martyred Khwāja-i-maulānā-i-qāẓī by hanging him, with dishonour, in the Gate of the citadel. Fol. 54. He had come to be known as Khwāja-maulānā-i-qāẓī but his own name was 'Abdu'l-lāh. On his father's side, his line went back to Shaikh Burhānu'd-dīn 'Alī *Qīlīch*, on his mother's to Sl. Aīlīk *Māẓī*. This family had come to be the Religious

Guides (*muqtadā*) and pontiff (*Shaikhu'l-islām*) and Judge (*qāẓī*) in the Farghāna country.[1] He was a disciple of his Highness 'Ubaidu'l-lāh (*Aḥrārī*) and from him had his upbringing. I have no doubt he was a saint (*walī*); what better witnesses to his sanctity than the fact that within a short time, no sign or trace remained of those active for his death? He was a wonderful man; it was not in him to be afraid; in no other man was seen such courage as his. This quality is a further witness to his sanctity. Other men, however bold, have anxieties and tremours; he had none. When they had killed him, they seized and plundered those connected with him, retainers and servants, tribesmen and followers.

In anxiety for Andijān, we had given Samarkand out of our hands; then heard we had lost Andijān. It was like the saying, 'In ignorance, made to leave this place, shut out from that' (*Ghafil az īn jā rānda, az ān jā mānda*). It was very hard and vexing to me; for why? never since I had ruled, had I been cut
Fol. 54*b*. off like this from my retainers and my country; never since I had known myself, had I known such annoyance and such hardship.

(*f. Bābur's action from Khujand as his base.*)

On our arrival in Khujand, certain hypocrites, not enduring to see Khalīfa in my Gate, had so wrought on Muḥammad Ḥusain Mīrzā *Dūghlāt* and others that he was dismissed towards Tāshkīnt. To Tāshkīnt also Qāsim Beg *Qūchīn* had been sent earlier, in order to ask The Khān's help for a move on Andijān. The Khān consented to give it and came himself by way of the Ahangarān Dale,[2] to the foot of the Kīndīrlīk Pass.[3] There I went also, from Khujand, and saw my Khān dādā.[4] We then crossed the pass and halted on the Akhsī side. The enemy for their part, gathered their men and went to Akhsī.

[1] *Cf.* f. 16 for almost verbatim statements.

[2] Blacksmith's Dale. *Ahangarān* appears corrupted in modern maps to *Angren*. *See* H.S. ii, 293 for Khwānd-amir's wording of this episode.

[3] *Cf.* f. 1*b* and Kostenko i, 101.

[4] *i.e.* Khān Uncle (Mother's brother).

Just at that time, the people in Pāp[1] sent me word they had made fast the fort but, owing to something misleading in The Khān's advance, the enemy stormed and took it. Though The Khān had other good qualities and was in other ways businesslike, he was much without merit as a soldier and commander. Just when matters were at the point that if he made one more march, it was most probable the country would be had without fighting, at such a time! he gave ear to what the enemy said with alloy of deceit, spoke of peace and, as his messengers, sent them Khwāja Abū'l-makāram and his own Lord of the Gate, Beg *Tilba* (Fool), *Tambal's* elder brother. To save themselves those others (*i.e.* Ḥasan and Tambal) mixed something true with what they fabled and agreed to give gifts and bribes either to The Khān or to his intermediaries. With this, The Khān retired. Fol. 55.

As the families of most of my begs and household and braves were in Andijān, 7 or 800 of the great and lesser begs and bare braves, left us in despair of our taking the place. Of the begs were 'Alī-darwesh Beg, 'Alī-mazīd *Qūchīn*, Muḥammad Bāqir Beg, Shaikh 'Abdu'l-lāh, Lord of the Gate and Mīrīm *Lāgharī*. Of men choosing exile and hardship with me, there may have been, of good and bad, between 200 and 300. Of begs there were Qāsim *Qūchīn* Beg, Wais *Lāgharī* Beg, Ibrāhīm *Sārū Mīnglīgh* Beg, Shīrīm Ṭaghāī, Sayyidī Qarā Beg; and of my household, Mīr Shāh *Qūchīn*, Sayyid Qāsim *Jalāīr*, Lord of the Gate, Qāsim-'ajab, 'Alī-dost Ṭaghāī's (son) Muḥammad-dost, Muḥammad-'alī *Mubashir*,[2] Khudāī-bīrdī *Tūghchī Mughūl*, Yārīk Ṭaghāī, Bābā 'Alī's (son) Bābā Qulī, Pīr Wais, Shaikh Wais, Yār-'alī *Balāl*,[3] Qāsim *Mīr Akhwūr* (Chief Equerry) and Ḥaidar *Rikābdār* (stirrup-holder). Fol. 55b.

It came very hard on me; I could not help crying a good deal. Back I went to Khujand and thither they sent me my

[1] n.w. of the Sang ferry over the Sīr.

[2] perhaps, messenger of good tidings.

[3] This man's family connections are interesting. He was 'Alī-shukr Beg *Bahārlū's* grandson, nephew therefore of Pāshā Begim; through his son, Saif-'alī Beg, he was the grandfather of Bairām Khān-i-khānān and thus the g.g.f. of 'Abdu'r-raḥīm Mīrzā, the translator of the Second *Wāqi'āt-i-bāburī*. *See* Firishta lith. ed. p. 250.

mother and my grandmother and the families of some of the men with me.

That Ramẓān (April-May) we spent in Khujand, then mounted for Samarkand. We had already sent to ask The Khān's help; he assigned, to act with us against Samarkand, his son, Sl. Muḥammad (Sulṭānīm) Khānika and (his son's guardian) Aḥmad Beg with 4 or 5000 men and rode himself as far as Aūrā-tīpā. There I saw him and from there went on by way of Yār-yīlāq, past the Būrka-yīlāq Fort, the head-quarters of the sub-governor (*dārogha*) of the district. Sl. Muḥammad Sulṭān and Aḥmad Beg, riding light and by another road, got to Yār-yīlāq first but on their hearing that Shaibānī Khān was raiding Shīrāz and thereabouts, turned back. There was no help for it! Back I too had to go. Again I went to Khujand!

As there was in me ambition for rule and desire of conquest, I did not sit at gaze when once or twice an affair had made no progress. Now I myself, thinking to make another move for
Fol. 56. Andijān, went to ask The Khān's help. Over and above this, it was seven or eight years since I had seen Shāh Begīm[1] and other relations; they also were seen under the same pretext. After a few days, The Khān appointed Sayyid Muḥammad Ḥusain (*Dūghlāt*) and Ayūb *Begchīk* and Jān-ḥasan *Bārīn* with 7 or 8000 men to help us. With this help we started, rode light, through Khujand without a halt, left Kand-i-badām on the left and so to Nasūkh, 9 or 10 *yīghāch* of road beyond Khujand and 3 *yīghāch* (12-18 m.) from Kand-i-badām, there set our ladders up and took the fort. It was the melon season; one kind grown here, known as Ismā'īl Shaikhī, has a yellow rind, feels like shagreen leather, has seeds like an apple's and flesh four fingers thick. It is a wonderfully delicate melon; no other such grows thereabout. Next day the Mughūl begs represented to me, 'Our fighting men are few; to what would holding this one fort lead on?' In truth they were right; of what use was it to make that fort fast and stay there? Back once more to Khujand!

[1] Bābur's (step-)grandmother, co-widow with Aīsān-daulat of Yūnas Khān and mother of Aḥmad and Maḥmud *Chaghatāi*.

(*f. Affairs of Khusrau Shāh and the Tīmūrid Mīrzās*).[1]

This year Khusrau Shāh, taking Bāī-sunghar Mīrzā with him, led his army (from Qūndūz) to Chaghānīān and with false and treacherous intent, sent this message to Ḥiṣār for Sl. Mas'ūd Mīrzā, 'Come, betake yourself to Samarkand; if Fol. 56*b*. Samarkand is taken, one Mīrzā may seat himself there, the other in Ḥiṣār.' Just at the time, the Mīrzā's begs and household were displeased with him, because he had shewn excessive favour to his father-in-law, Shaikh 'Abdu'l-lāh *Barlās* who from Bāī-sunghar Mīrzā had gone to him. Small district though Ḥiṣār is, the Mīrzā had made the Shaikh's allowance 1,000 *tūmāns* of *fulūs*[2] and had given him the whole of Khutlān in which were the holdings of many of the Mīrzā's begs and household. All this Shaikh 'Abdu'l-lāh had; he and his sons took also in whole and in part, the control of the Mīrzā's gate. Those angered began, one after the other, to desert to Bāī-sunghar Mīrzā.

By those words of false alloy, having put Sl. Mas'ūd Mīrzā off his guard, Khusrau Shāh and Bāī-sunghar Mīrzā moved light out of Chaghānīān, surrounded Ḥiṣār and, at beat of morning-drum, took possession of it. Sl. Mas'ūd Mīrzā was in Daulat Sarāī, a house his father had built in the suburbs. Not being able to get into the fort, he drew off towards Khutlān with Shaikh 'Abu'l-lāh *Barlās*, parted from him half-way, crossed the river at the Aūbāj ferry and betook himself to Sl. Ḥusain Mīrzā. Khusrau Shāh, having taken Ḥiṣār, set Bāī- Fol. 57. sunghar Mīrzā on the throne, gave Khutlān to his own younger brother, Walī and rode a few days later, to lay siege to Balkh where, with many of his father's begs, was Ibrāhīm Ḥusain Mīrzā (*Bāī-qarā*). He sent Naẓar *Bahādur*, his chief retainer, on in advance with 3 or 400 men to near Balkh, and himself taking Bāī-sunghar Mīrzā with him, followed and laid the siege.

[1] Here the narrative picks up the thread of Khusrau Shāh's affairs, dropped on f. 44.

[2] *ming tūmān fulūs*, *i.e.* a thousand sets-of-ten-thousand small copper coins. Mr. Erskine (Mems. p. 61) here has a note on coins. As here the *tūmān* does not seem to be a coin but a number, I do not reproduce it, valuable as it is *per se*.

Walī he sent off with a large force to besiege Shabarghān and raid and ravage thereabouts. Walī, for his part, not being able to lay close siege, sent his men off to plunder the clans and hordes of the Zardak Chūl, and they took him back over 100,000 sheep and some 3000 camels. He then came, plundering the Sān-chīrīk country on his way, and raiding and making captive the clans fortified in the hills, to join Khusrau Shāh before Balkh.

One day during the siege, Khusrau Shāh sent the Naẓar *Bahādur* already mentioned, to destroy the water-channels[1] of
Fol. 57*b*. Balkh. Out on him sallied Tīngrī-bīrdī *Samānchī*,[2] Sl. Ḥusain Mīrzā's favourite beg, with 70 or 80 men, struck him down, cut off his head, carried it off, and went back into the fort. A very bold sally, and he did a striking deed.

(*g. Affairs of Sl. Ḥusain Mīrzā and Badī'u'z-zamān Mīrzā.*)

This same year, Sl. Ḥusain Mīrzā led his army out to Bast and there encamped,[3] for the purpose of putting down Ẕū'n-nūn *Arghūn* and his son, Shāh Shujā', because they had become Badī'u'z-zamān Mīrzā's retainers, had given him a daughter of Ẕū'n-nūn in marriage and taken up a position hostile to himself. No corn for his army coming in from any quarter, it had begun to be distressed with hunger when the sub-governor of Bast surrendered. By help of the stores of Bast, the Mīrzā got back to Khurāsān.

Since such a great ruler as Sl. Ḥusain Mīrzā had twice led a splendid and well-appointed army out and twice retired, without taking Qūndūz, or Ḥiṣār or Qandahār, his sons and his begs waxed bold in revolt and rebellion. In the spring of this year, he sent a large army under Muḥammad Walī Beg to put down (his son) Muḥammad Ḥusain Mīrzā who, supreme in Astarābād, had taken up a position hostile to himself. While Sl. Ḥusain Mīrzā was still lying in the Nīshīn meadow (near

[1] *āriqlār*; this the annotator of the Elph. MS. has changed to *āshliq*, provisions, corn.

[2] *Samān-chī* may mean Keeper of the Goods. Tīngrī-bīrdī, Theodore, is the purely Turkī form of the Khudāī-bīrdī, already met with several times in the B.N.

[3] Bast (Bost) is on the left bank of the Halmand.

Harāt), he was surprised by Badī'u'z-zamān Mīrzā and Shāh Shujā' Beg (*Arghūn*). By unexpected good-fortune, he had been Fol. 58. joined that very day by Sl. Mas'ūd Mīrzā, a refugee after bringing about the loss of Ḥiṣār,[1] and also rejoined by a force of his own returning from Astarābād. There was no question of fighting. Badī'u'z-zamān Mīrzā and Shāh Beg, brought face to face with these armies, took to flight.

Sl. Ḥusain Mīrzā looked kindly on Sl. Mas'ūd Mīrzā, made him kneel as a son-in-law and gave him a place in his favour and affection. None-the-less Sl. Mas'ūd Mīrzā, at the instigation of Bāqī *Chaghāniānī*, who had come earlier into Sl. Ḥusain Mīrzā's service, started off on some pretext, without asking leave, and went from the presence of Sl. Ḥusain Mīrzā to that of Khusrau Shāh!

Khusrau Shāh had already invited and brought from Ḥiṣār, Bāī-sunghar Mīrzā; to him had gone Aūlūgh Beg Mīrzā's son,[2] Mīrān-shāh Mīrzā who, having gone amongst the Hazāra in rebellion against his father, had been unable to remain amongst them because of his own immoderate acts. Some short-sighted persons were themselves ready to kill these three (Tīmūrid) Mīrzās and to read Khusrau Shāh's name in the *khuṭba* but he himself did not think this combination desirable. The ungrate- Fol. 58*b*. ful manikin however, for the sake of gain in this five days' fleeting world,—it was not true to him nor will it be true to any man soever,—seized that Sl. Mas'ūd Mīrzā whom he had seen grow up in his charge from childhood, whose guardian he had been, and blinded him with the lancet.

Some of the Mīrzā's foster-brethren and friends of affection and old servants took him to Kesh intending to convey him to his (half)-brother Sl. 'Alī Mīrzā in Samarkand but as that party also (*i.e.* 'Alī's) became threatening, they fled with him, crossed the river at the Aūbāj ferry and went to Sl. Ḥusain Mīrzā.

[1] *Cf.* f. 56*b*.

[2] known as *Kābuli*. He was a son of Abū-sa'īd and thus an uncle of Bābur. He ruled Kābul and Ghaznī from a date previous to his father's death in 873 AH. (perhaps from the time 'Umar Shaikh was *not* sent there, in 870 AH. *See* f. 6*b*) to his death in 907 AH. Bābur was his virtual successor in Kābul, in 910 AH.

A hundred thousand curses light on him who planned and did a deed so horrible! Up to the very verge of Resurrection, let him who hears of this act of Khusrau Shāh, curse him; and may he who hearing, curses not, know cursing equally deserved!

This horrid deed done, Khusrau Shāh made Bāī-sunghar Mīrzā ruler in Ḥiṣār and dismissed him; Mīrān-shāh Mīrzā he despatched for Bāmīān with Sayyid Qāsim to help him.

904 AH.—AUG. 19TH. 1498 TO AUG. 8TH. 1499 AD.[1]

(a. Bābur borrows Pashāghar and leaves Khujand.)

Twice we had moved out of Khujand, once for Andijān, once for Samarkand, and twice we had gone back to it because our work was not opened out.[2] Khujand is a poor place; a man with 2 or 300 followers would have a hard time there; with what outlook would an ambitious man set himself down in it? Fol. 59.

As it was our wish to return to Samarkand, we sent people to confer with Muḥammad Ḥusain *Kūrkān Dūghlāt* in Aūrā-tīpā and to ask of him the loan for the winter of Pashāghar where we might sit till it was practicable to make a move on Samarkand. He consenting, I rode out from Khujand for Pashāghar.

(Author's note on Pashāghar.) Pashāghar is one of the villages of Yār-yīlāq; it had belonged to his Highness the Khwāja,[3] but during recent interregna,[4] it had become dependent on Muḥammad Ḥusain Mīrzā.

I had fever when we reached *Zamīn*, but spite of my fever we hurried off by the mountain road till we came over against Rabāṭ-i-khwāja, the head-quarters of the sub-governor of the Shavdār *tūmān*, where we hoped to take the garrison at unawares, set our ladders up and so get into the

[1] Elph. MS. f. 42; W.-i-B. I.O. 215 f. 47*b* and 217 f. 38; Mems. p. 63. Bābur here resumes his own story, interrupted on f. 56.

[2] *aish achilmādī*, a phrase recurring on f. 59*b* foot. It appears to imply, of trust in Providence, what the English "The way was not opened," does. *Cf.* f. 60*b* for another example of trust, there clinching discussion whether to go or not to go to Marghīnān.

[3] *i.e. Aḥrārī*. He had been dead some 10 years. The despoilment of his family is mentioned on f. 23*b*.

[4] *fatratlār*, here those due to the deaths of Aḥmad and Maḥmūd with their sequel of unstable government in Samarkand.

fort. We reached it at dawn, found its men on guard, turned back and rode without halt to Pashāghar. The pains and misery of fever notwithstanding, I had ridden 14 or 15 *yīghāch* (70 to 80 miles).

After a few days in Pashāghar, we appointed Ibrāhīm *Sārū*,
Fol. 59*b*. Wais *Lāgharī*, Sherīm Ṭaghāī and some of the household and braves to make an expedition amongst the Yār-yīlāq forts and get them into our hands. Yār-yīlāq, at that time was Sayyid Yūsuf Beg's,[1] he having remained in Samarkand at the exodus and been much favoured by Sl. 'Ali Mīrzā. To manage the forts, Sayyid Yūsuf had sent his younger brother's son, Aḥmad-i-yūsuf, now[2] Governor of Sialkot, and Aḥmad-i-yūsuf was then in occupation. In the course of that winter, our begs and braves made the round, got possession of some of the forts peacefully, fought and took others, gained some by ruse and craft. In the whole of that district there is perhaps not a single village without its defences because of the Mughūls and the Aūzbegs. Meantime Sl. 'Alī Mīrzā became suspicious of Sayyid Yūsuf and his nephew on my account and dismissed both towards Khurāsān.

The winter passed in this sort of tug-of-war; with the on-coming heats,[3] they sent Khwāja Yaḥya to treat with me, while they, urged on by the (Samarkand) army, marched out to near Shīrāz and Kabud. I may have had 200 or 300 soldiers (*sipāhī*); powerful foes were on my every side; Fortune had
Fol. 60. not favoured me when I turned to Andijān; when I put a hand out for Samarkand, no work was opened out. Of necessity, some sort of terms were made and I went back from Pashāghar.

Khujand is a poor place; one beg would have a hard time in it; there we and our families and following had been for half a

[1] *Aūghlāqchī*, the player of the kid-game, the gray-wolfer. Yār-yīlāq will have gone with the rest of Samarkand into 'Alī's hands in Rajab 903 AH. (March 1498). Contingent terms between him and Bābur will have been made; Yūsuf may have recognized some show of right under them, for allowing Bābur to occupy Yār-yīlāq.

[2] *i.e.* after 933 AH. *Cf.* f. 46*b* and note concerning the Bikramāditya era. See index *s.n.* Aḥmad-i-yūsuf and Ḥ.S. ii, 293.

[3] This plural, unless ironical, cannot be read as honouring 'Alī; Bābur uses the honorific plural most rarely and specially, *e.g.* for saintly persons, for The Khān and for elder women-kinsfolk.

year[1] and during the time the Musalmāns of the place had not been backward in bearing our charges and serving us to the best of their power. With what face could we go there again? and what, for his own part, could a man do there? 'To what home to go? For what gain to stay?'[2]

In the end and with the same anxieties and uncertainty, we went to the summer-pastures in the south of Aūrā-tīpā. There we spent some days in amazement at our position, not knowing where to go or where to stay, our heads in a whirl. On one of those days, Khwāja Abū'l-makāram came to see me, he like me, a wanderer, driven from his home.[3] He questioned us about our goings and stayings, about what had or had not been done and about our whole position. He was touched with compassion for our state and recited the *fātiḥa* for me before he left. I also was much touched; I pitied him.

(b. Bābur recovers Marghīnān.)

Near the Afternoon Prayer of that same day, a horseman appeared at the foot of the valley. He was a man named Yūl-chūq, presumably 'Ali-dost Ṭaghāī's own servant, and had been sent with this written message, 'Although many great misdeeds have had their rise in me, yet, if you will do me the favour and kindness of coming to me, I hope to purge my offences and remove my reproach, by giving you Marghīnān and by my future submission and single-minded service.' Fol. 60*b*.

Such news! coming on such despair and whirl-of-mind! Off we hurried, that very hour,—it was sun-set,—without reflecting, without a moment's delay, just as if for a sudden raid, straight for Marghīnān. From where we were to Marghīnān may have been 24 or 25 *yīghāch* of road.[4] Through that night it was rushed without delaying anywhere, and on

1 *bīr yārīm yīl*. Dates shew this to mean six months. It appears a parallel expression to Pers. *hasht-yak*, one-eighth.

2 Ḥ.S. ii, 293, in place of these two quotations, has a *misra'*,—*Na rāy safar kardan u na rūy iqāmat*, (Nor resolve to march, nor face to stay).

3 *i.e.* in Samarkand.

4 Point to point, some 145 m. but much further by the road. Tang-āb seems likely to be one of the head-waters of Khwāja Bikargān-water. Thence the route would be by unfrequented hill-tracks, each man leading his second horse.

next day till at the Mid-day Prayer, halt was made at Tang-āb (Narrow-water), one of the villages of Khujand. There we cooled down our horses and gave them corn. We rode out again at beat of (twilight-) drum[1] and on through that night till shoot of dawn, and through the next day till sunset, and on through that night till, just before dawn, we were one *yīghāch* from Marghīnān. Here Wais Beg and others represented to me with some anxiety what sort of an evil-doer 'Ali-dost was. 'No-one,' they said, 'has come and gone, time and again, between him and us; no terms and compact have been made; trusting to what are we going?' In truth their fears were just! After waiting awhile to consult, we at last agreed that
Fol. 61. reasonable as anxiety was, it ought to have been earlier; that there we were after coming three nights and two days without rest or halt; in what horse or in what man was any strength left?—from where we were, how could return be made? and, if made, where were we to go?—that, having come so far, on we must, and that nothing happens without God's will. At this we left the matter and moved on, our trust set on Him.

At the Sunnat Prayer[2] we reached Fort Marghīnān. 'Alī-dost Ṭaghāī kept himself behind (*arqa*) the closed gate and asked for terms; these granted, he opened it. He did me obeisance between the (two) gates.[3] After seeing him, we dismounted at a suitable house in the walled-town. With me, great and small, were 240 men.

As Aūzūn Ḥasan and Tambal had been tyrannical and oppressive, all the clans of the country were asking for me. We therefore, after two or three days spent in Marghīnān, joined to Qāsim Beg over a hundred men of the Pashāgharīs, the new retainers of Marghīnān and of 'Alī-dost's following, and sent them to bring over to me, by force or fair words, such

[1] *tūn yārīmī naqāra waqtīdā. Tūn yārīmī* seems to mean half-dark, twilight. Here it cannot mean mid-night since this would imply a halt of twelve hours and Bābur says no halt was made. The drum next following mid-day is the one beaten at sunset.

[2] The voluntary prayer, offered when the sun has well risen, fits the context.

[3] I understand that the obeisance was made in the Gate-house, between the inner and outer doors.

hill-people of the south of Andijān as the Ashpārī, Tūrūqshār, Chīkrāk and others roundabout. Ibrāhīm Sārū and Wais *Lāgharī* and Sayyidī Qarā were also sent out, to cross the Khujand-water and, by whatever means, to induce the people on that side to turn their eyes to me. Fol. 61*b*.

Aūzūn Ḥasan and Tambal, for their parts, gathered together what soldiers and Mughūls they had and called up the men accustomed to serve in the Andijān and Akhsī armies. Then, bringing Jahāngīr Mīrzā with them, they came to Sapān, a village 2m. east of Marghīnān, a few days after our arrival, and dismounted there with the intention of besieging Marghīnān. They advanced a day or two later, formed up to fight, as far as the suburbs. Though after the departure of the Commanders, Qāsim Beg, Ibrāhīm *Sārū* and Wais *Lāgharī*, few men were left with me, those there were formed up, sallied out and prevented the enemy from advancing beyond the suburbs. On that day, Page Khalīl, the turban-twister, went well forward and got his hand into the work. They had come; they could do nothing; on two other days they failed to get near the fort. Fol. 62*a*.

When Qāsim Beg went into the hills on the south of Andijān, all the Ashpārī, Tūrūqshār, Chīkrāk, and the peasants and highland and lowland clans came in for us. When the Commanders, Ibrāhīm *Sārū* and Wais *Lāgharī*, crossed the river to the Akhsī side, Pāp and several other forts came in.

Aūzūn Ḥasan and Tambal being the heathenish and vicious tyrants they were, had inflicted great misery on the peasantry and clansmen. One of the chief men of Akhsī, Ḥasan-dīkcha by name,[1] gathered together his own following and a body of the Akhsī mob and rabble, black-bludgeoned[2] Aūzūn Ḥasan's and Tambal's men in the outer fort and drubbed them into the citadel. They then invited the Commanders, Ibrāhīm *Sārū*, Wais *Lāgharī* and Sayyidī Qarā and admitted them into the fort.

Sl. Maḥmūd Khān had appointed to help us, Ḥaidar *Kūkūldāsh's* (son) Banda-'alī and Ḥājī Ghāzī *Manghīt*,[3] the latter

[1] This seeming sobriquet may be due to eloquence or to good looks.

[2] *qarā tīyāq*. *Cf.* f. 63 where black bludgeons are used by a red rabble.

[3] He was head-man of his clan and again with Shaibānī in 909 AH. (Sh. N. Vambéry, p. 272). Erskine (p. 67) notes that the Manghīts are the modern Nogais.

just then a fugitive from Shaibānī Khān, and also the Bārīn *tūmān* with its begs. They arrived precisely at this time.

Fol. 62b. These news were altogether upsetting to Aūzūn Ḥasan; he at once started off his most favoured retainers and most serviceable braves to help his men in the citadel of Akhsī. His force reached the brow of the river at dawn. Our Commanders and the (Tāshkīnt) Mughūls had heard of its approach and had made some of their men strip their horses and cross the river (to the Andijān side). Aūzūn Ḥasan's men, in their haste, did not draw the ferry-boat up-stream;[1] they consequently went right away from the landing-place, could not cross for the fort and went down stream.[2] Here-upon, our men and the (Tāshkīnt) Mughūls began to ride bare-back into the water from both banks. Those in the boat could make no fight at all. Qārlūghāch (var. Qārbūghāch) *Bakhshī* (Pay-master) called one of Mughūl Beg's sons to him, took him by the hand, chopped at him and killed him. Of what use was it? The affair was past that! His act was the cause why most of those in the boat went to their death. Instantly our men seized them all (*arīq*) and killed all (but a few).[3] Of Aūzūn Ḥasan's confidants escaped Qārlūghāch *Bakhshī* and Khalīl *Dīwān* and Qāẓī *Ghulām*, the last getting off by pretending to be a slave (*ghulām*); and of his trusted braves, Sayyid 'Alī, now in trust in my own service,[4] and Ḥaidar-i-qulī and Qilka *Kāshgharī* escaped. Of his 70 or 80 men, no more than this

Fol. 63. same poor five or six got free.

On hearing of this affair, Aūzūn Ḥasan and Tambal, not being able to remain near Marghīnān, marched in haste and disorder for Andijān. There they had left Nāṣir Beg, the husband of Aūzūn Ḥasan's sister. He, if not Aūzūn Ḥasan's second, what question is there he was his third?[5] He was an

[1] *i.e.* in order to allow for the here very swift current. The H.S. varying a good deal in details from the B.N. gives the useful information that Aūzūn Ḥasan's men knew nothing of the coming of the Tāshkīnt Mughūls.

[2] *Cf.* f. 4*b* and App. A. as to the position of Akhsī.

[3] *bārīnī qirdīlār*. After this statement the five exceptions are unexpected; Bābur's wording is somewhat confused here.

[4] *i.e.* in Hindūstān.

[5] Tambal would be the competitor for the second place.

experienced man, brave too; when he heard particulars, he knew their ground was lost, made Andijān fast and sent a man to me. They broke up in disaccord when they found the fort made fast against them; Aūzūn Ḥasan drew off to his wife in Akhsī, Tambal to his district of Aūsh. A few of Jahāngīr Mīrzā's household and braves fled with him from Aūzūn Ḥasan and joined Tambal before he had reached Aūsh.

(c. Bābur recovers Andijān.)

Directly we heard that Andijān had been made fast against them, I rode out, at sun-rise, from Marghīnān and by mid-day was in Andijān.[1] There I saw Nāṣir Beg and his two sons, that is to say, Dost Beg and Mīrīm Beg, questioned them and uplifted their heads with hope of favour and kindness. In this way, by God's grace, my father's country, lost to me for two years, was regained and re-possessed, in the month Ẕū'l-qa'da of Fol. 63*b*. the date 904 (June 1498).[2]

Sl. Aḥmad Tambal, after being joined by Jahāngīr Mīrzā, drew away for Aūsh. On his entering the town, the red rabble (*qīzīl ayāq*) there, as in Akhsī, black-bludgeoned (*qarā tīyāq qīlīb*) and drubbed his men out, blow upon blow, then kept the fort for me and sent me a man. Jahāngīr and Tambal went off confounded, with a few followers only, and entered Aūzkīnt Fort.

Of Aūzūn Ḥasan news came that after failing to get into Andijān, he had gone to Akhsī and, it was understood, had entered the citadel. He had been head and chief in the rebellion; we therefore, on getting this news, without more than four or five days' delay in Andijān, set out for Akhsī. On our arrival, there was nothing for him to do but ask for peace and terms, and surrender the fort.

We stayed in Akhsī[3] a few days in order to settle its affairs

[1] 47 m. 4½ fur.

[2] Bābur had been about two lunar years absent from Andijān but his loss of rule was of under 16 months.

[3] A scribe's note entered here on the margin of the Ḥai. MS. is to the effect that certain words are not in the noble archetype (*nashka sharīf*); this supports other circumstances which make for the opinion that this Codex is a direct copy of Bābur's own MS. *See* Index s.n. Ḥai. MS. and JRAS 1906, p. 87.

and those of Kāsān and that country-side. We gave the Mughūls who had come in to help us, leave for return (to Tāshkīnt), then went back to Andijān, taking with us Aūzūn Ḥasan and his family and dependants. In Akhsī was left, for a time, Qāsim-i-'ajab (Wonderful Qāsim), formerly one of the household circle, now arrived at beg's rank.

(d. Renewed rebellion of the Mughūls.)

As terms had been made, Aūzūn Ḥasan, without hurt to life
Fol. 64. or goods, was allowed to go by the Qarā-tīgīn road for Ḥiṣār. A few of his retainers went with him, the rest parted from him and stayed behind. These were the men who in the throne-less times had captured and plundered various Musalmān dependants of my own and of the Khwāja. In agreement with several begs, their affair was left at this;—'This very band have been the captors and plunderers of our faithful Musalmān dependants;[1] what loyalty have they shown to their own (Mughūl) begs that they should be loyal to us? If we had them seized and stripped bare, where would be the wrong? and this especially because they might be going about, before our very eyes, riding our horses, wearing our coats, eating our sheep. Who could put up with that? If, out of humanity, they are not imprisoned and not plundered, they certainly ought to take it as a favour if they get off with the order to give back to our companions of the hard guerilla times, whatever goods of theirs are known to be here.'

In truth this seemed reasonable; our men were ordered to take what they knew to be theirs. Reasonable and just though the order was, (I now) understand that it was a little hasty.
Fol. 64b. With a worry like Jahāngīr seated at my side, there was no sense in frightening people in this way. In conquest and government, though many things may have an outside appearance of reason and justice, yet 100,000 reflections are right and necessary as to the bearings of each one of them. From this single incautious order of ours,[2] what troubles! what rebellions

[1] *Musalmān* here seems to indicate mental contrast with Pagan practices or neglect of Musalmān observances amongst Mughūls.

[2] *i.e.* of his advisors and himself.

arose! In the end this same ill-considered order was the cause of our second exile from Andijān. Now, through it, the Mughūls gave way to anxiety and fear, marched through Rabāṭik-aūrchīnī, that is, Aīkī-sū-ārāsī, for Aūzkīnt and sent a man to Taṃbal.

In my mother's service were 1500 to 2000 Mughūls from the horde; as many more had come from Ḥiṣār with Ḥamza Sl. and Mahdī Sl. and Muḥammad *Dūghlāt Ḥiṣārī*.[1] Mischief and devastation must always be expected from the Mughūl horde. Up to now[2] they have rebelled five times against me. It must not be understood that they rebelled through not getting on with me; they have done the same thing with their own Khāns, again and again. Sl. Qulī *Chūnāq*[3] brought me the news. His late father, Khudāī-bīrdī *Būqāq*[4] I had favoured amongst the Mughūls; he was himself with the (rebel) Mughūls Fol. 65.
and he did well in thus leaving the horde and his own family to bring me the news. Well as he did then however, he, as will be told,[5] did a thing so shameful later on that it would hide a hundred such good deeds as this, if he had done them. His later action was the clear product of his Mughūl nature. When this news came, the begs, gathered for counsel, represented to me, 'This is a trifling matter; what need for the pādshāh to ride out? Let Qāsim Beg go with the begs and men assembled here.' So it was settled; they took it lightly; to do so must have been an error of judgment. Qāsim Beg led his force out that same day; Taṃbal meantime must have joined the Mughūls. Our men crossed the Aīlāīsh river[6] early next morning by the Yāsī-kījīt (Broad-crossing) and at once came face to

[1] *Cf.* f. 34.

[2] *circa* 933 AH. All the revolts chronicled by Bābur as made against himself were under Mughūl leadership. Long Ḥasan, Taṃbal and 'Alī-dost were all Mughūls. The worst was that of 914 AH. (1518 AD.) in which Qulī *Chūnāq* disgraced himself (T.R. p. 357).

[3] *Chūnāq* may indicate the loss of one ear.

[4] *Būqāq*, amongst other meanings, has that of *one who lies in ambush*.

[5] This remark has interest because it shews that (as Bābur planned to write more than is now with the B.N. MSS.) the first gap in the book (914 AH. to 925 AH.) is accidental. His own last illness is the probable cause of this gap. *Cf.* JRAS 1905, p. 744. Two other passages referring to unchronicled matters are one about the Bāgh-i-ṣafā (f. 224, and one about Sl. 'Alī Taghāī (f. 242).

[6] I surmise Aīlāīsh to be a local name of the Qarā-daryā affluent of the Sir.

face with the rebels. Well did they chop at one another (*chāpqūlāshūrlār*)! Qāsim Beg himself came face to face with Muḥammad *Arghūn* and did not desist from chopping at him in order to cut off his head.[1] Most of our braves exchanged
Fol. 65*b*. good blows but in the end were beaten. Qāsim Beg, 'Alī-dost Ṭaghāī, Ibrāhīm *Sārū*, Wais *Lāgharī*, Sayyidī Qarā and three or four more of our begs and household got away but most of the rest fell into the hands of the rebels. Amongst them were 'Alī-darwesh Beg and Mīrīm *Lāgharī* and (Sherīm ?) Ṭaghāī Beg's (son) Tūqā[2] and 'Alī-dost's son, Muḥammad-dost and Mīr Shāh *Qūchīn* and Mīrīm Dīwān.

Two braves chopped very well at one another; on our side, Samad, Ibrāhīm *Sārū*'s younger brother, and on their side, Shāh-suwār, one of the Ḥiṣārī Mughūls. Shāh-suwār struck so that his sword drove through Samad's helm and seated itself well in his head; Samad, spite of his wound, struck so that his sword cut off Shāh-suwār's head a piece of bone as large as the palm of a hand. Shāh-suwār must have worn no helm; they trepanned his head and it healed; there was no one to trepan Samad's and in a few days, he departed simply through the wound.[3]

Amazingly unseasonable was this defeat, coming as it did just in the respite from guerilla fighting and just when we had regained the country. One of our great props, Qaṃbar-'alī *Mughūl* (the Skinner) had gone to his district when Andijān
Fol. 66. was occupied and therefore was not with us.

(*e. Taṃbal attempts to take Andijān.*)

Having effected so much, Taṃbal, bringing Jāhāngir Mīrzā with him, came to the east of Andijān and dismounted 2 miles off, in the meadow lying in front of the Hill of Pleasure ('Aīsh).[4]

[1] *aīkī aūch naubat chāpqūlāb bāsh chiqārghalī qūimās.* I cannot feel so sure as Mr. E. and M. de C. were that the man's head held fast, especially as for it to fall would make the better story.

[2] Tūqā appears to have been the son of a Ṭaghāī, perhaps of Sherīm; his name may imply blood-relationship.

[3] For the verb *awimāq*, to trepan, *see* f. 67 note 5.

[4] The Fr. map of 1904 shews a hill suiting Bābur's location of this Hill of Pleasure.

Once or twice he advanced in battle-array, past Chihil-dukhterān[1] to the town side of the hill but, as our braves went out arrayed to fight, beyond the gardens and suburbs, he could not advance further and returned to the other side of the hill. On his first coming to those parts, he killed two of the begs he had captured, Mīrīm *Lāgharī* and Tūqā Beg. For nearly a month he lay round-about without effecting anything; after that he retired, his face set for Aūsh. Aūsh had been given to Ibrāhīm *Sārū* and his man in it now made it fast.

[1] A place near Kābul bears the same name; in both the name is explained by a legend that there Earth opened a refuge for forty menaced daughters.

905 AH. AUG. 8TH. 1499 TO JULY 28TH. 1500 AD.[1]

(*a. Bābur's campaign against Aḥmad Tambal Mughūl.*)

Commissaries were sent gallopping off at once, some to call up the horse and foot of the district-armies, others to urge return on Qambar-'alī and whoever else was away in his own district, while energetic people were told off to get together mantelets (*tūra*), shovels, axes and the what-not of war-material and stores for the men already with us.

As soon as the horse and foot, called up from the various districts to join the army, and the soldiers and retainers who had been scattered to this and that side on their own affairs, were gathered together, I went out, on Muḥarram 18th. (August 25th.), putting my trust in God, to Ḥāfiẓ Beg's Four-
Fol. 66b. gardens and there stayed a few days in order to complete our equipment. This done, we formed up in array of right and left, centre and van, horse and foot, and started direct for Aūsh against our foe.

On approaching Aūsh, news was had that Tambal, unable to make stand in that neighbourhood, had drawn off to the north, to the Rabāṭ-i-sarhang sub-district, it was understood. That night we dismounted in Lāt-kint. Next day as we were passing through Aūsh, news came that Tambal was understood to have gone to Andijān. We, for our part, marched on as for Aūzkīnt, detaching raiders ahead to over-run those parts.[2] Our opponents went to Andijān and at night got into the ditch but being discovered by the garrison when they set their ladders up against the ramparts, could effect no more and retired. Our raiders

[1] Elph. MS. f. 47b; W.-i-B. I.O. 215 f. 53 and 217 f. 43; Mems. p. 70.

[2] From Andijān to Aūsh is a little over 33 miles. Tambal's road was east of Bābur's and placed him between Andijān and Aūzkīnt where was the force protecting his family.

retired also after over-running round about Aūzkīnt without getting into their hands anything worth their trouble.

Tambal had stationed his younger brother, Khalīl, with 200 or 300 men, in Mādū,[1] one of the forts of Aūsh, renowned in that centre (*ārā*) for its strength. We turned back (on the Aūzkīnt road) to assault it. It is exceedingly strong. Its northern face stands very high above the bed of a torrent; arrows shot from the bed might perhaps reach the ramparts. On this side is the water-thief,[2] made like a lane, with ramparts on both sides carried from the fort to the water. Towards the rising ground, on the other sides of the fort, there is a ditch. The torrent being so near, those occupying the fort had carried stones in from it as large as those for large mortars.[3] From no fort of its class we have ever attacked, have stones been thrown so large as those taken into Mādū. They dropped such a large one on 'Abdu'l-qāsim *Kohbur*, Kitta (Little) Beg's elder brother,[4] when he went up under the ramparts, that he spun head over heels and came rolling and rolling, without once getting to his feet, from that great height down to the foot of the glacis (*khāk-rez*). He did not trouble himself about it at all but just got on his horse and rode off. Again, a stone flung from the double water-way, hit Yār-'alī *Balāl* so hard on the head that in the end it had to be trepanned.[5] Many of our men perished by their stones. The assault began at dawn; the water-thief had been taken before breakfast-time;[6] fighting went on till evening; next morning, as they could not hold out after losing the water-thief, they asked for terms and came out. We took 60 or 70 or 80 men of Khalīl's command and sent them to Andijān for safe-keeping; as some of our begs and household were prisoners in their hands, the Mādū affair fell out very well.[7]

Fol. 67.

Fol. 67*b*.

[1] mod. Mazy, on the main Aūsh-Kāshghar road.

[2] *āb-duzd*; de C. i, 144, *prise d'eau*.

[3] This simile seems the fruit of experience in Hindūstān. *See* f. 333, concerning Chānderi.

[4] These two Mughūls rebelled in 914 AH. with Sl. Qulī *Chūnāq* (T.R. *s.n.*).

[5] *awidī*. The head of Captain Dow, fractured at Chunār by a stone flung at it, was trepanned (*Saiyār-i-muta'akhirin*, p. 577 and Irvine l.c. p. 283). Yār-'alī was alive in 910 AH. He seems to be the father of the great Bairām Khān-i-khānān of Akbar's reign.

[6] *chasht-gāh*; midway between sunrise and noon.

[7] *ṭaurī*; because providing prisoners for exchange.

From there we went to Unjū-tūpa, one of the villages of Aūsh, and there dismounted. When Tambal retired from Andijān and went into the Rabāṭ-i-sarhang sub-district, he dismounted in a village called Āb-i-khān. Between him and me may have been one *yīghāch* (5 m.?). At such a time as this, Qambar-'alī (the Skinner) on account of some sickness, went into Aūsh.

It was lain in Unjū-tūpa a month or forty days without a battle, but day after day our foragers and theirs got to grips. All through the time our camp was mightily well watched at night; a ditch was dug; where no ditch was, branches were set close together;[1] we also made our soldiers go out in their mail
Fol. 68. along the ditch. Spite of such watchfulness, a night-alarm was given every two or three days, and the cry to arms went up. One day when Sayyidī Beg Ṭaghāī had gone out with the foragers, the enemy came up suddenly in greater strength and took him prisoner right out of the middle of the fight.

(b. Bāī-sunghar Mīrzā murdered by Khusrau Shāh.)

Khusrau Shāh, having planned to lead an army against Balkh, in this same year invited Bāī-sunghar Mīrzā to go with him, brought him[2] to Qūndūz and rode out with him for Balkh. But when they reached the Aubāj ferry, that ungrateful infidel, Khusrau Shāh, in his aspiration to sovereignty,—and to what sort of sovereignty, pray, could such a no-body attain? a person of no merit, no birth, no lineage, no judgment, no magnanimity, no justice, no legal-mindedness,—laid hands on Bāī-sunghar Mīrzā with his begs, and bowstrung the Mīrzā. It was upon the 10th. of the month of Muḥarram (August 17th.) that he martyred that scion of sovereignty, so accomplished, so sweet-natured and so adorned by birth and lineage. He killed also a few of the Mīrzā's begs and household.

(c. Bāī-sunghar Mīrzā's birth and descent.)

He was born in 882 (1477 AD.), in the Ḥiṣār district. He was Sl. Maḥmūd Mīrzā's second son, younger than Sl. Mas'ud

[1] *shakh tūtūlūr idī*, perhaps a palisade.
[2] *i.e.* from Ḥiṣār where he had placed him in 903 AH.

M. and older than Sl. 'Alī M. and Sl. Ḥusain M. and Sl. Wais M. known as Khān Mīrzā. His mother was Pasha Begīm. Fol. 68b.

(*d. His appearance and characteristics.*)

He had large eyes, a fleshy face[1] and Turkmān features, was of middle height and altogether an elegant young man (*aet.* 22).

(*e. His qualities and manners.*)

He was just, humane, pleasant-natured and a most accomplished scion of sovereignty. His tutor, Sayyid Maḥmūd,[2] presumably was a Shī'a; through this he himself became infected by that heresy. People said that latterly, in Samarkand, he reverted from that evil belief to the pure Faith. He was much addicted to wine but on his non-drinking days, used to go through the Prayers.[3] He was moderate in gifts and liberality. He wrote the *naskh-ta'līq* character very well; in painting also his hand was not bad. He made 'Ādilī his pen-name and composed good verses but not sufficient to form a *dīwān*. Here is the opening couplet (*maṭla'*) of one of them[4];—

> Like a wavering shadow I fall here and there;
> If not propped by a wall, I drop flat on the ground.

In such repute are his odes held in Samarkand, that they are to be found in most houses.

(*f. His battles.*)

He fought two ranged battles. One, fought when he was first seated on the throne (900 AH.-1495 AD.), was with Sl. Maḥmūd Khān[5] who, incited and stirred up by Sl. Junaid *Barlās* and others to desire Samarkand, drew an army out, crossed the Āq-kutal and went to Rabāṭ-i-soghd and Kān-bāī. Fol. 69. Bāī-sunghar Mīrzā went out from Samarkand, fought him near

[1] *qûba yüzlüq* (f. 6b and note 4). The Turkmān features would be a maternal inheritance.

[2] He is "Saifī Maulānā 'Arūzī" of Rieu's Pers. Cat. p. 525. *Cf.* H.S. ii, 341. His book, *'Arūz-i-saifī* has been translated by Blochmann and by Ranking.

[3] *namāz aūtār idi.* I understand some irony from this (de Meynard's Dict. *s.n. aūtmāq*).

[4] The *maṭla'* of poems serve as an index of first lines.

[5] *Cf.* f. 30.

Kān-bāī, beat him and beheaded 3 or 4000 Mughūls. In this fight died Ḥaidar *Kūkūldāsh*, the Khān's looser and binder (*ḥall u'aqdī*). His second battle was fought near Bukhārā with Sl. 'Alī Mīrzā (901 AH.-1496 AD.); in this he was beaten.[1]

(*g. His countries.*)

His father, Sl. Maḥmūd Mīrzā, gave him Bukhārā; when Sl. Maḥmūd M. died, his begs assembled and in agreement made Bāī-sunghar M. ruler in Samarkand. For a time, Bukhārā was included with Samarkand in his jurisdiction but it went out of his hands after the Tarkhān rebellion (901 AH.-1496 AD.). When he left Samarkand to go to Khusrau Shāh and I got possession of it (903 AH.-1497 AD.), Khusrau Shāh took Ḥiṣār and gave it to him.

(*h. Other details concerning him.*)

He left no child. He took a daughter of his paternal uncle, Sl. Khalīl Mīrzā, when he went to Khusrau Shāh; he had no other wife or concubine.

He never ruled with authority so independent that any beg was heard of as promoted by him to be his confidant; his begs
Fol. 69*b*. were just those of his father and his paternal uncle (Aḥmad).

(*i. Resumed account of Bābur's campaign against Tambal.*)

After Bāī-sunghar Mīrzā's death, Sl. Aḥmad *Qarāwal*,[2] the father of Qūch (Qūj) Beg, sent us word (of his intention) and came to us from Ḥiṣār through the Qarā-tīgīn country, together with his brethren, elder and younger, and their families and dependants. From Aūsh too came Qambar-'alī, risen from his sickness. Arriving, as it did, at such a moment, we took the providential help of Sl. Aḥmad and his party for a happy omen. Next day we formed up at dawn and moved direct upon our foe. He made no stand at Āb-i-khān but marched from his

[1] *Cf.* f. 37*b*.

[2] *i.e.* scout and in times of peace, huntsman. On the margin of the Elph. Codex here stands a note, mutilated in rebinding;—*Sl. Aḥmad pidr-i-Qūch Beg ast* * * * *pidr-i-Sher-afgan u Sher-afgan* * * * *u Sl. Ḥusain Khān* * * * *Qūch Beg ast. Hamesha* * * * *dar khāna Shaham Khān* * * *.

ground, leaving many tents and blankets and things of the baggage for our men. We dismounted in his camp.

That evening Tambal, having Jahāngīr with him, turned our left and went to a village called Khūbān (var. Khūnān), some 3 *yīghāch* from us (15 m.?) and between us and Andijān. Next day we moved out against him, formed up with right and left, centre and van, our horses in their mail, our men in theirs, and with foot-soldiers, bearing mantelets, flung to the front. Our right was 'Alī-dost and his dependants, our left Ibrāhīm *Sārū*, Wais *Lāgharī*, Sayyidī Qarā Muḥammad-'alī *Mubashir*, and Khwāja-i-kalān's elder brother, Kīchīk Beg, with several of Fol. 70. the household. In the left were inscribed[1] also Sl. Aḥmad *Qarāwal* and Qūch Beg with their brethren. With me in the centre was Qāsim Beg *Qūchīn*; in the van were Qambar-'alī (the Skinner) and some of the household. When we reached Sāqā, a village two miles east of Khūbān, the enemy came out of Khūbān, arrayed to fight. We, for our part, moved on the faster. At the time of engaging, our foot-soldiers, provided how laboriously with the mantelets! were quite in the rear! By God's grace, there was no need of them; our left had got hands in with their right before they came up. Kīchīk Beg chopped away very well; next to him ranked Muḥammad 'Alī *Mubashir*. Not being able to bring equal zeal to oppose us, the enemy took to flight. The fighting did not reach the front of our van or right. Our men brought in many of their braves; we ordered the heads of all to be struck off. Favouring caution and good generalship, our begs, Qāsim Beg and, especially, 'Alī-dost did not think it advisable to send far in pursuit; for Fol. 70*b*. this reason, many of their men did not fall into our hands. We dismounted right in Khūbān village. This was my first ranged battle; the Most High God, of His own favour and mercy, made it a day of victory and triumph. We accepted the omen.

On the next following day, my father's mother, my grandmother, Shāh Sulṭān Begīm[2] arrived from Andijān, thinking to beg off Jahāngīr Mīrzā if he had been taken.

1 *pītīldī*; W.-i-B. *navishta shud*, words indicating the use by Bābur of a written record.

2 *Cf.* f. 6*b* and note and f. 17 and note.

(j. Bābur goes into winter-quarters in Between-the-two-rivers.)

As it was now almost winter and no grain or fruits[1] remained in the open country, it was not thought desirable to move against (Tambal in) Aūzkīnt but return was made to Andijān. A few days later, it was settled after consultation, that for us to winter in the town would in no way hurt or hamper the enemy, rather that he would wax the stronger by it through raids and guerilla fighting; moreover on our own account, it was necessary that we should winter where our men would not become enfeebled through want of grain and where we could straiten the enemy by some sort of blockade. For these de-
Fol. 71. sirable ends we marched out of Andijān, meaning to winter near Armiyān and Nūsh-āb in the Rabāṭik-aūrchīnī, known also as Between-the-two-rivers. On arriving in the two villages above-mentioned, we prepared winter-quarters.

The hunting-grounds are good in that neighbourhood; in the jungle near the Aīlāīsh river is much *būghū-marāl*[2] and pig; the small scattered clumps of jungle are thick with hare and pheasant; and on the near rising-ground, are many foxes[3] of fine colour and swifter than those of any other place. While we were in those quarters, I used to ride hunting every two or three days; we would beat through the great jungle and hunt *būghū-marāl*, or we would wander about, making a circle round scattered clumps and flying our hawks at the pheasants. The pheasants are unlimited[4] there; pheasant-meat was abundant as long as we were in those quarters.

While we were there, Khudāī-bīrdī *Tūghchī*, then newly-favoured with beg's rank, fell on some of Tambal's raiders and brought in a few heads. Our braves went out also from Aūsh and Andijān and raided untiringly on the enemy, driving in his

[1] *tūlūk*; *i.e.* other food than grain. Fruit, fresh or preserved, being a principal constituent of food in Central Asia, *tūlūk* will include several, but chiefly melons. "Les melons constituent presque seuls vers le fin d'été, la nourriture des classes pauvres (Th. Radloff. l.c. p. 343).

[2] *Cf. f.* 6*b* and note.

[3] *tūlkī* var. *tūlkū*, the yellow fox. Following this word the Ilai. MS. has *u dar kamīn dūr* instead of *u rangīn dūr*.

[4] *bī ḥadd*; with which I.O. 215 agrees but I.O. 217 adds *farbih*, fat, which is right in fact (f. 2*b*) but less pertinent here than an unlimited quantity.

herds of horses and much enfeebling him. If the whole winter had been passed in those quarters, the more probable thing is that he would have broken up simply without a fight. Fol. 71b.

(k. Qambar-'alī again asks leave.)

It was at such a time, just when our foe was growing weak and helpless, that Qambar-'alī asked leave to go to his district. The more he was dissuaded by reminder of the probabilities of the position, the more stupidity he shewed. An amazingly fickle and veering manikin he was! It had to be! Leave for his district was given him. That district had been Khujand formerly but when Andijān was taken this last time, Asfara and Kand-i-badām were given him in addition. Amongst our begs, he was the one with large districts and many followers; no-one's land or following equalled his. We had been 40 or 50 days in those winter-quarters. At his recommendation, leave was given also to some of the clans in the army. We, for our part, went into Andijān.

(l. Sl. Maḥmūd Khān sends Mughūls to help Tambal.)

Both while we were in our winter-quarters and later on in Andijān, Tambal's people came and went unceasingly between him and The Khān in Tāshkīnt. His paternal uncle of the full-blood, Aḥmad Beg, was guardian of The Khān's son, Sl. Muḥammad Sl. and high in favour; his elder brother of the full-blood, Beg Tīlba (Fool), was The Khān's Lord of the Gate. After all the comings and goings, these two brought The Khān to the point of reinforcing Tambal. Beg Tīlba, leaving his wife and domestics and family in Tāshkīnt, came on ahead of the reinforcement and joined his younger brother, Tambal,—Beg Tīlba! who from his birth up had been in Mughūlistān, had grown up amongst Mughūls, had never entered a cultivated country or served the rulers of one, but from first to last had served The Khāns! Fol. 72.

Just then a wonderful ('*ajab*) thing happened;[1] Qāsim-i-'ajab (wonderful Qāsim) when he had been left for a time in Akhsī,

[1] Here a pun on '*ajab* may be read.

went out one day after a few marauders, crossed the Khujand-water by Bachrātā, met in with a few of Taṃbal's men and was made prisoner.

When Taṃbal heard that our army was disbanded and was assured of The Khān's help by the arrival of his brother, Beg Tīlba, who had talked with The Khān, he rode from Aūzkīnt into Between-the-two-rivers. Meantime safe news had come to us from Kāsān that The Khān had appointed his son, Sl. Muḥ. Khānika, commonly known as Sulṭānīm,[1] and Aḥmad Beg, with 5 or 6000 men, to help Taṃbal, that they had crossed by the Archa-kīnt road[2] and were laying siege to Kāsān. Hereupon we, without delay, without a glance at our absent men, just with those there were, in the hard cold of winter, put our
Fol. 72b. trust in God and rode off by the Band-i-sālār road to oppose them. That night we stopped no-where; on we went through the darkness till, at dawn, we dismounted in Akhsī.[3] So mightily bitter was the cold that night that it bit the hands and feet of several men and swelled up the ears of many, each ear like an apple. We made no stay in Akhsī but leaving there Yārak Ṭaghāī, temporarily also, in Qāsim-i-'ajab's place, passed on for Kāsān. Two miles from Kāsān news came that on hearing of our approach, Aḥmad Beg and Sulṭānīm had hurried off in disorder.

(*m. Bābur and Taṃbal again opposed.*)

Taṃbal must have had news of our getting to horse for he had hurried to help his elder brother.[4] Somewhere between the two Prayers of the day,[5] his blackness[6] became visible towards Nū-kīnt. Astonished and perplexed by his elder brother's light departure and by our quick arrival, he stopped short. Said we, 'It is God has brought them in this fashion! here they have come with their horses' necks at full stretch;[7]

[1] *Cf.* f. 15, note to Ṭaghāī.

[2] Apparently not the usual Kīndīr-līk pass but one n.w. of Kāsān.

[3] A ride of at least 40 miles, followed by one of 20 to Kāsān.

[4] *Cf.* f. 72 and f. 72b. Tīlba would seem to have left Taṃbal.

[5] *Taṃbalning qarāsi.*

[6] *i.e.* the Other (Mid-afternoon) Prayer.

[7] *ātining būīnini qātib. Qātmāq* has also the here-appropriate meaning of *to stiffen.*

if we join hands[1] and go out, and if God bring it right, not a man of them will get off.' But Wais *Lāgharī* and some others said, 'It is late in the day; even if we do not go out today, where can they go tomorrow? Wherever it is, we will meet them at dawn.' So they said, not thinking it well to make the joint effort there and then; so too the enemy, come so opportunely, broke up and got away without any hurt whatever. The (Turkī) proverb is, 'Who does not snatch at a chance, will worry himself about it till old age.' Fol. 73*a*.

(*Persian*) *couplet*. Work must be snatched at betimes,
Vain is the slacker's mistimed work.

Seizing the advantage of a respite till the morrow, the enemy slipped away in the night, and without dismounting on the road, went into Fort Archīān. When a morrow's move against a foe was made, we found no foe; after him we went and, not thinking it well to lay close siege to Archīān, dismounted two miles off (one *shar'ī*) in Ghazna-namangān.[2] We were in camp there for 30 or 40 days, Tambal being in Fort Archīān. Every now and then a very few would go from our side and come from theirs, fling themselves on one another midway and return. They made one night-attack, rained arrows in on us and retired. As the camp was encircled by a ditch or by branches close-set, and as watch was kept, they could effect no more.

(n. Qambar-'alī, the Skinner, again gives trouble.)

Two or three times while we lay in that camp, Qambar-'alī, in ill-temper, was for going to his district; once he even had got to horse and started in a fume, but we sent several begs after him who, with much trouble, got him to turn back. Fol. 73*b*.

[1] *ailik qūshmāq, i.e.* Bābur's men with the Kāsān garrison. But the two W.-i-B. write merely *dast burd* and *dast kardan*.

[2] The meaning of *Ghazna* here is uncertain. The Second W.-i-B. renders it by ar. *qaryat* but up to this point Bābur has not used *qaryat* for *village*. Ghazna-namangān cannot be modern Namangān. It was 2 m. from Archīān where Tambal was, and Bābur went to Bīshkhārān to be between Tambal and Machamī, coming from the south. Archīān and Ghazna-namangān seem both to have been n. or n.w. of Bīshkārān (see maps).

It may be mentioned that at Archīān, in 909 AH. the two Chaghatāī Khāns and Bābur were defeated by Shaibānī.

(o. Further action against Taṃbal and an accommodation made.)

Meantime Sayyid Yūsuf of Macham had sent a man to Taṃbal and was looking towards him. He was the head-man of one of the two foot-hills of Andijān, Macham and Awīghūr. Latterly he had become known in my Gate, having outgrown the head-man and put on the beg, though no-one ever had made him a beg. He was a singularly hypocritical manikin, of no standing whatever. From our last taking of Andijān (June 1499) till then (Feb. 1500), he had revolted two or three times from Taṃbal and come to me, and two or three times had revolted from me and gone to Taṃbal. This was his last change of side. With him were many from the (Mughūl) horde and tribesmen and clansmen. 'Don't let him join Taṃbal,' we said and rode in between them. We got to Bīshkhārān with one night's halt. Taṃbal's men must have come earlier and entered the fort. A party of our begs, 'Alī-darwesh Beg and Qūch Beg, with his brothers, went close up to the Gate of
Fol. 74. Bīshkhārān and exchanged good blows with the enemy. Qūch Beg and his brothers did very well there, their hands getting in for most of the work. We dismounted on a height some two miles from Bīshkhārān; Taṃbal, having Jahāngīr with him, dismounted with the fort behind him.

Three or four days later, begs unfriendly to us, that is to say, 'Alī-dost and Qaṃbar-'alī, the Skinner, with their followers and dependants, began to interpose with talk of peace. I and my well-wishers had no knowledge of a peace and we all[1] were utterly averse from the project. Those two manikins however were our two great begs; if we gave no ear to their words and if we did not make peace, other things from them were probable! It had to be! Peace was made in this fashion;—the districts on the Akhsī side of the Khujand-water were to depend on Jahāngīr, those on the Andijān side, on me; Aūzkīnt was to be left in my jurisdiction after they had removed their families from it; when the districts were settled and I and Jahāngīr had

[1] *bizlār*. The double plural is rare with Bābur; he writes *biz*, we, when action is taken in common; he rarely uses *min*, I, with autocratic force; his phrasing is largely impersonal, *e.g.* with rare exceptions, he writes the impersonal passive verb.

made our agreement, we (*bīz*) should march together against Samarkand; and when I was in possession of Samarkand, Andijān was to be given to Jahāngīr. So the affair was settled. Fol. 74*b*. Next day,—it was one of the last of Rajab, (end of Feb. 1500) Jahāngīr Mīrzā and Tambal came and did me obeisance; the terms and conditions were ratified as stated above; leave for Akhsī was given to Jahāngīr and I betook myself to Andijān.

On our arrival, Khalīl-of-Tambal and our whole band of prisoners were released; robes of honour were put on them and leave to go was given. They, in their turn, set free our begs and household, *viz.* the commanders[1] (Sherīm ?) Ṭaghāī Beg, Muḥammad-dost, Mīr Shāh *Qūchīn*, Sayyidī Qarā Beg, Qāsim-i-'ajab, Mīr Wais, Mīrīm *Dīwān*, and those under them.

(*p. The self-aggrandizement of 'Alī-dost Ṭaghāī.*)

After our return to Andijān, 'Alī-dost's manners and behaviour changed entirely. He began to live ill with my companions of the guerilla days and times of hardship. First, he dismissed Khalīfa; next seized and plundered Ibrāhīm *Sārū* and Wais *Lāgharī*, and for no fault or cause deprived them of their districts and dismissed them. He entangled himself with Qāsim Beg and *he* was made to go; he openly declared, 'Khalīfa and Ibrāhīm are in sympathy about Khwāja-i-qāẓī; they will avenge him on me.'[2] His son, Muḥammad-dost set himself up on a regal footing, starting receptions and a public table and a Fol. 75. Court and workshops, after the fashion of sulṭāns. Like father, like son, they set themselves up in this improper way because they had Tambal at their backs. No authority to restrain their unreasonable misdeeds was left to me; for why? Whatever their hearts desired, that they did because such a foe of mine as Tambal was their backer. The position was singularly delicate; not a word was said but many humiliations were endured from that father and that son alike.

[1] *bāshlīghlār.* Teufel was of opinion that this word is not used as a noun in the B.N. In this he is mistaken; it is so used frequently, as here, in apposition. *See* ZDMG, xxxvii, art. Bābur und Abū'l-faẓl.

[2] *Cf.* f. 54 foot.

(*q. Bābur's first marriage.*)

'Āyisha-sulṭān Begīm whom my father and hers, *i.e.* my uncle, Sl. Aḥmad Mīrzā had betrothed to me, came (this year) to Khujand[1] and I took her in the month of Sha'bān. Though I was not ill-disposed towards her, yet, this being my first marriage, out of modesty and bashfulness, I used to see her once in 10, 15 or 20 days. Later on when even my first inclination did not last, my bashfulness increased. Then my mother Khānīm used to send me, once a month or every 40
Fol. 75*b*. days, with driving and driving, dunnings and worryings.

(*r. A personal episode and some verses by Bābur.*)

In those leisurely days I discovered in myself a strange inclination, nay! as the verse says, 'I maddened and afflicted myself' for a boy in the camp-bazar, his very name, Bāburī, fitting in. Up till then I had had no inclination for any-one, indeed of love and desire, either by hear-say or experience, I had not heard, I had not talked. At that time I composed Persian couplets, one or two at a time; this is one of the them:—

May none be as I, humbled and wretched and love-sick;
No beloved as thou art to me, cruel and careless.

From time to time Bāburī used to come to my presence but out of modesty and bashfulness, I could never look straight at him; how then could I make conversation (*ikhtilāṭ*) and recital (*hikāyat*)? In my joy and agitation I could not thank him (for coming); how was it possible for me to reproach him with going away? What power had I to command the duty of service to myself?[2] One day, during that time of desire and passion when I was going with companions along a lane and suddenly met him face to face, I got into such a state of confusion that I almost went right off. To look straight at him
Fol. 76. or to put words together was impossible. With a hundred torments and shames, I went on. A (Persian) couplet of Muḥammad Ṣāliḥ's[3] came into my mind:—

[1] *Cf.* f. 20. She may have come from Samarkand and 'Alī's household or from Kesh and the Tarkhān households.

[2] *Cf.* f. 26 l. 2 for the same phrase.

[3] He is the author of the *Shaibānī-nāma*.

I am abashed with shame when I see my friend ;
My companions look at me, I look the other way.

That couplet suited the case wonderfully well. In that frothing-up of desire and passion, and under that stress of youthful folly, I used to wander, bare-head, bare-foot, through street and lane, orchard and vineyard. I shewed civility neither to friend nor stranger, took no care for myself or others.

(*Turki*) Out of myself desire rushed me, unknowing
That this is so with the lover of a fairy-face.

Sometimes like the madmen, I used to wander alone over hill and plain; sometimes I betook myself to gardens and the suburbs, lane by lane. My wandering was not of my choice, not I decided whether to go or stay.

(*Turki*) Nor power to go was mine, nor power to stay ;
I was just what you made me, o thief of my heart.

(*s. Sl. 'Alī Mīrzā's quarrels with the Tarkhāns.*)

In this same year, Sl. 'Alī Mīrzā fell out with Muḥammad Mazīd Tarkhān for the following reasons ;—The Tarkhāns had risen to over-much predominance and honour ; Bāqī had taken the whole revenue of the Bukhārā Government and gave not a half-penny (*dāng*)[1] to any-one else ; Muḥammad Mazīd, for his part, had control in Samarkand and took all its districts for his sons and dependants ; a small sum only excepted, fixed by them, not a farthing (*fils*) from the town reached the Mīrzā by any channel. Sl. 'Alī Mīrzā was a grown man ; how was he to tolerate such conduct as theirs ? He and some of his household formed a design against Muḥ. Mazīd Tarkhān ; the latter came to know of it and left the town with all his following and with whatever begs and other persons were in sympathy with him,[2] such as Sl. Ḥusain *Arghūn*, Pīr Aḥmad, Aūzūn Ḥasan's younger brother, Khwāja Ḥusain, Qarā *Barlās*, Ṣāliḥ Muḥammad[3] and some other begs and braves. Fol. 76b.

[1] *dāng* and *fils* (*infra*) are small copper coins.
[2] *Cf.* f. 25 l. 1 and note 1.
[3] Probably the poet again ; he had left Harāt and was in Samarkand (Sh. N. Vambéry, p. 34 l. 14).

At the time The Khān had joined to Khān Mīrzā a number of Mughūl begs with Muḥ. Ḥusain *Dūghlāt* and Aḥmad Beg, and had appointed them to act against Samarkand.[1] Khān Mīrzā's guardians were Ḥāfiẓ Beg *Dūldāī* and his son, Ṭāhir Beg; because of relationship to them, (Muḥ. Sīghal's) grandson, Ḥasan and Hindū Beg fled with several braves from Sl. 'Alī
Fol. 77. Mīrzā's presence to Khān Mīrzā's.

Muḥammad Mazīd Tarkhān invited Khān Mīrzā and the Mughūl army, moved to near Shavdār, there saw the Mīrzā and met the begs of the Mughūls. No small useful friendlinesses however, came out of the meeting between his begs and the Mughūls; the latter indeed seem to have thought of making him a prisoner. Of this he and his begs coming to know, separated themselves from the Mughūl army. As without him the Mughūls could make no stand, they retired. Here-upon, Sl. 'Alī Mīrzā hurried light out of Samarkand with a few men and caught them up where they had dismounted in Yār-yīlāq. They could not even fight but were routed and put to flight. This deed, done in his last days, was Sl. 'Alī Mīrzā's one good little affair.

Muḥ. Mazīd Tarkhān and his people, despairing both of the Mughūls and of these Mīrzās, sent Mīr Mughūl, son of 'Abdu'l-wahhāb *Shaghāwal*[2] to invite me (to Samarkand). Mīr Mughūl had already been in my service; he had risked his life in good accord with Khwāja-i-qāẓī during the siege of Andijān (903 AH.-1498 AD.).

This business hurt us also[3] and, as it was for that purpose we had made peace (with Jahāngīr), we resolved to move on Samarkand. We sent Mīr Mughūl off at once to give rendezvous[4]
Fol. 77b. to Jahāngīr Mīrzā and prepared to get to horse. We rode out

[1] From what follows, this Mughūl advance seems a sequel to a Tarkhān invitation.

[2] By omitting the word *Mīr* the Turki text has caused confusion between this father and son (Index *s.nn.*).

[3] *bīz khūd kharāb bū mu'āmla aīdūk.* These words have been understood earlier, as referring to the abnormal state of Bābur's mind described under Sec. r. They better suit the affairs of Samarkand because Bābur is able to resolve on action and also because he here writes *bīz*, we, and not *min*, I as in Sec. r.

[4] For *būlghār*, rendezvous, *see* also f. 78 l. 2 fr. ft.

in the month of Ẕū'l-qa'da (June) and with two halts on the way, came to Qabā and there dismounted.[1] At the mid-afternoon Prayer of that day, news came that Tambal's brother, Khalīl had taken Aūsh by surprise.

The particulars are as follows;—As has been mentioned, Khalīl and those under him were set free when peace was made. Tambal then sent Khalīl to fetch away their wives and families from Aūzkīnt. He had gone and he went into the fort on this pretext. He kept saying untruthfully, 'We will go out today,' or 'We will go out tomorrow,' but he did not go. When we got to horse, he seized the chance of the emptiness of Aūsh to go by night and surprise it. For several reasons it was of no advantage for us to stay and entangle ourselves with him; we went straight on therefore. One reason was that as, for the purpose of making ready military equipment, all my men of name had scattered, heads of houses to their homes, we had no news of them because we had relied on the peace and were by this off our guard against the treachery and falsity of the other party. Another reason was that for some time, as has been said, the misconduct of our great begs, 'Alī-dost and Qambar-'alī had been such that no confidence in them was left. A further reason was that the Samarkand begs, under Muḥ. Mazīd Tarkhān had sent Mīr Mughūl to invite us and, so long as a capital such as Samarkand stood there, what would incline a man to waste his days for a place like Andijān? Fol. 78.

From Qabā we moved on to Marghīnān (20 m.). Marghīnān had been given to Qūch Beg's father, Sl. Aḥmad *Qarāwal*, and he was then in it. As he, owing to various ties and attachments, could not attach himself to me,[2] he stayed behind while his son, Qūch Beg and one or two of his brethren, older and younger, went with me.

Taking the road for Asfara, we dismounted in one of its villages, called Mahan. That night there came and joined us in Mahan, by splendid chance, just as if to a rendezvous, Qāsim Beg *Qūchīn* with his company, 'Alī-dost with his, and Sayyid

[1] 25 m. only; the halts were due probably to belated arrivals.

[2] Some of his ties would be those of old acquaintance in Ḥiṣār with 'Alī's father's begs, now with him in Samarkand.

Qāsim with a large body of braves. We rode from Mahan by the Khasbān (var. Yasān) plain, crossed the Chūpān (Shepherd)-bridge and so to Aūrā-tīpā.[1]

(t. Qaṃbar-'alī punishes himself.)

Trusting to Taṃbal, Qaṃbar-'alī went from his own district (Khujand) to Akhsī in order to discuss army-matters with him.
Fol. 78b. Such an event happening,[2] Taṃbal laid hands on Qaṃbar-'alī, marched against his district and carried him along. Here the (Turkī) proverb fits, 'Distrust your friend! he'll stuff your hide with straw.' While Qaṃbar-'alī was being made to go to Khujand, he escaped on foot and after a hundred difficulties reached Aūrā-tīpā.

News came to us there that Shaibānī Khān had beaten Bāqī Tarkhān in Dabūsī and was moving on Bukhārā. We went on from Aūrā-tīpā, by way of Burka-yīlāq, to Sangzār[3] which the sub-governor surrendered. There we placed Qaṃbar-'alī, as, after effecting his own capture and betrayal, he had come to us. We then passed on.

(u. Affairs of Samarkand and the end of 'Alī-dost.)

On our arrival in Khān-yūrtī, the Samarkand begs under Muḥ. Mazīd Tarkhān came and did me obeisance. Conference was held with them as to details for taking the town; they said, 'Khwāja Yaḥya also is wishing for the *pādshāh*;[4] with his consent the town may be had easily without fighting or disturbance.' The Khwāja did not say decidedly to our messengers that he had resolved to admit us to the town but at the same time, he said nothing likely to lead us to despair.

Leaving Khān-yūrtī, we moved to the bank of the Dar-i-gham (canal) and from there sent our librarian, Khwāja Muḥammad
Fol. 79. 'Alī to Khwāja Yaḥya. He brought word back, 'Let them come; we will give them the town.' Accordingly we rode from the Dar-i-gham straight for the town, at night-fall, but

1 Point to point, some 90 m. but further by road.
2 *Bū waqi' būlghāch*, manifestly ironical.
3 Sangzār to Aūrā-tīpā, by way of the hills, some 50 miles.
4 The Sh. N. Vambéry, p. 60, confirms this.

our plan came to nothing because Sl. Muḥammad *Dūldāī's* father, Sl. Maḥmūd had fled from our camp and given such information to (Sl. 'Alī's party) as put them on their guard. Back we went to the Dar-i-gham bank.

While I had been in Yār-yīlāq, one of my favoured begs, Ibrāhīm *Sārū* who had been plundered and driven off by 'Alī-dost,[1] came and did me obeisance, together with Muḥ. Yūsuf, the elder son of Sayyid Yūsuf (*Aūghlāqchī*). Coming in by ones and twos, old family servants and begs and some of the household gathered back to me there. All were enemies of 'Alī-dost; some he had driven away; others he had plundered; others again he had imprisoned. He became afraid. For why? Because with Tambal's backing, he had harassed and persecuted me and my well-wishers. As for me, my very nature sorted ill with the manikin's! From shame and fear, he could stay no longer with us; he asked leave; I took it as a personal favour; I gave it. On this leave, he and his son, Muḥammad-dost went to Tambal's presence. They became his intimates, Fol. 79b. and from father and son alike, much evil and sedition issued. 'Alī-dost died a few years later from ulceration of the hand. Muḥammad-dost went amongst the Aūzbegs; that was not altogether bad but, after some treachery to his salt, he fled from them and went into the Andijān foot-hills.[2] There he stirred up much revolt and trouble. In the end he fell into the hands of Aūzbeg people and they blinded him. The meaning of 'The salt took his eyes,' is clear in his case.[3]

After giving this pair their leave, we sent Ghūrī *Barlās* toward Bukhārā for news. He brought word that Shaibānī Khān had taken Bukhārā and was on his way to Samarkand. Here-upon, seeing no advantage in staying in that neighbourhood, we set out for Kesh where, moreover, were the families of most of the Samarkand begs.

When we had been a few weeks there, news came that Sl. 'Alī Mīrzā had given Samarkand to Shaibānī Khān. The particulars are these;—The Mīrzā's mother, Zuhra Begī Āghā

[1] *Cf.* f. 74*b*.

[2] Macham and Awighūr, presumably.

[3] *gūzlār tūz tūtī*, *i.e.* he was blinded for some treachery to his hosts.

(*Aūzbeg*), in her ignorance and folly, had secretly written to
Fol. 80. Shaibānī Khān that if he would take her (to wife) her son should give him Samarkand and that when Shaibānī had taken (her son's) father's country, he should give her son a country.[1] Sayyid Yūsuf *Arghūn* must have known of this plan, indeed will have been the traitor inventing it.

[1] Muḥ. Ṣāliḥ's well-informed account of this episode has much interest, filling out and, as by Shaibānī's Boswell, balancing Bābur's. Bābur is obscure about what country was to be given to 'Alī. Pāyanda-ḥasan paraphrases his brief words;—Shaibānī was to be as a father to 'Alī and when he had taken 'Alī's father's *wilāyāt*, he was to give a country to 'Alī. It has been thought that the gift to 'Alī was to follow Shaibānī's recovery of his own ancestral camping-ground (*yūrt*) but this is negatived, I think, by the word, *wilāyat*, cultivated land.

906 AH.—JULY 28TH. 1500 TO JULY 17TH. 1501 AD.[1]

(a. Samarkand in the hands of the Aūzbegs.)

When, acting on that woman's promise, Shaibānī Khān went to Samarkand, he dismounted in the Garden of the Plain. About mid-day Sl. 'Alī Mīrzā went out to him through the Four-roads Gate, without a word to any of his begs or un-mailed braves, without taking counsel with any-one soever and accompanied only by a few men of little consideration from his own close circle. The Khān, for his part, did not receive him very favourably; when they had seen one another, he seated him on his less honourable hand.[2] Khwāja Yaḥya, on hearing of the Mīrzā's departure, became very anxious but as he could find no remedy,[3] went out also. The Khān looked at him with-out rising and said a few words in which blame had part, but when the Khwāja rose to leave, showed him the respect of rising.

As soon as Khwāja 'Alī[4] Bāy's[5] son, Jān-'alī heard in Rabāṭ-

[1] Elp. MS. f. 57*b*; W.-i-B. I.O. 215 f. 63*b* and I.O. 217 f. 52; Mems. p. 82. Two contemporary works here supplement the B.N.; (1) the (*Tawārikh-i-guzīda*) *Naṣrat-nāma*, dated 908 AH. (B.M. Turkī Or. 3222) of which Berezin's *Shaibānī-nāma* is an abridgment; (2) Muḥ. Ṣāliḥ Mīrzā's *Shaibānī-nāma* (Vambéry trs. cap. xix *et seq.*). The Ḥ.S. (Bomb. ed. p. 302, and Tehran ed. p. 384) is also useful.

[2] *i.e.* on his right. The Ḥ.S. ii, 302 represents that 'Alī was well-received. After Shaibāq had had Zuhra's overtures, he sent an envoy to 'Alī and Yaḥya; the first was not won over but the second fell in with his mother's scheme. This difference of view explains why 'Alī slipped away while Yaḥya was engaged in the Friday Mosque. It seems likely that mother and son alike expected their Aūzbeg blood to stand them in good stead with Shaibāq.

[3] He tried vainly to get the town defended. "Would to God Bābur Mīrzā were here!" he is reported as saying, by Muḥ. Ṣāliḥ.

[4] Perhaps it is for the play of words on 'Alī and 'Alī's life (*jān*) that this man makes his sole appearance here.

[5] *i.e.* rich man or merchant, but *Bī* (*infra*) is an equivalent of Beg.

i-khwāja of the Mīrzā's going to Shaibānī Khān, he also went. As for that calamitous woman who, in her folly, gave her son's
Fol. 80*b*. house and possessions to the winds in order to get herself a husband, Shaibānī Khān cared not one atom for her, indeed did not regard her as the equal of a mistress or a concubine.[1]

Confounded by his own act, Sl. 'Alī Mīrzā's repentance was extreme. Some of his close circle, after hearing particulars, planned for him to escape with them but to this he would not agree; his hour had come; he was not to be freed. He had dismounted in Tīmūr Sulṭān's quarters; three or four days later they killed him in Plough-meadow.[2] For a matter of this five-days' mortal life, he died with a bad name; having entered into a woman's affairs, he withdrew himself from the circle of men of good repute. Of such people's doings no more should be written; of acts so shameful, no more should be heard.

The Mīrzā having been killed, Shaibānī Khān sent Jān-'alī after his Mīrzā. He had apprehensions also about Khwāja Yaḥya and therefore dismissed him, with his two sons, Khwāja Muḥ. *Zakarīya* and Khwāja Bāqī, towards Khurāsān.[3] A few Aūzbegs followed them and near Khwāja Kārdzan martyred both the Khwāja and his two young sons. Though Shaibānī's
Fol. 81. words were, 'Not through me the Khwāja's affair! Qambar Bī and Kūpuk Bī did it,' this is worse than that! There is a proverb,[4] 'His excuse is worse than his fault,' for if begs, out of their own heads, start such deeds, unknown to their Khāns or Pādshāhs, what becomes of the authority of khānship and and sovereignty?

(*b. Bābur leaves Kesh and crosses the Mūra pass.*)

Since the Aūzbegs were in possession of Samarkand, we left Kesh and went in the direction of Ḥiṣār. With us started off

[1] Muḥ. Ṣāliḥ, invoking curses on such a mother, mentions that Zuhra was given to a person of her own sort.

[2] The Sh. N. and *Naṣrat-nāma* attempt to lift the blame of 'Alī's death from Shaibāq; the second saying that he fell into the Kohik-water when drunk.

[3] Harāt might be his destination but the H.S. names Makka. Some dismissals towards Khurāsān may imply pilgrimage to Meshhed.

[4] Used also by Bābur's daughter, Gul-badan (l.c. f. 31).

Muḥ. Mazīd Tārkhān and the Samarkand begs under his command, together with their wives and families and people, but when we dismounted in the Chultū meadow of Chaghāniān, they parted from us, went to Khusrau Shāh and became his retainers.

Cut off from our own abiding-town and country,[1] not knowing where (else) to go or where to stay, we were obliged to traverse the very heart of Khusrau Shāh's districts, spite of what measure of misery he had inflicted on the men of our dynasty!

One of our plans had been to go to my younger Khān dādā, *i.e.* Alacha Khān, by way of Qarā-tigīn and the Alāī,[2] but this was not managed. Next we were for going up the valley of the Kām torrent and over the Sara-tāq pass (*dābān*). When we were near Nūndāk, a servant of Khusrau Shāh brought me one set of nine horses[3] and one of nine pieces of cloth. When we dismounted at the mouth of the Kām valley, Sher-'alī, the page, deserted to Khusrau Shāh's brother, Walī and, next day, Qūch Beg parted from us and went to Ḥiṣār.[4] Fol. 81*b*.

We entered the valley and made our way up it. On its steep and narrow roads and at its sharp and precipitous saddles[5] many horses and camels were left. Before we reached the Sara-tāq pass we had (in 25 m.) to make three or four night-halts. A pass! and what a pass! Never was such a steep and narrow pass seen; never were traversed such ravines and precipices. Those dangerous narrows and sudden falls, those perilous heights and knife-edge saddles, we got through with much difficulty and suffering, with countless hardships and miseries. Amongst the Fān mountains is a large lake (Iskandar); it is 2 miles in circumference, a beautiful lake and not devoid of marvels.[6]

[1] Cut off by alien lands and weary travel.

[2] The Pers. annotator of the Elph. Codex has changed Alāī to *wilāyat*, and *dābān* (pass) to *yān*, side. For the difficult route *see* Schuyler, i, 275, Kostenko, i, 129 and Rickmers, JRGS. 1907, art. Fan Valley.

[3] Amongst Turks and Mughūls, gifts were made by nines.

[4] Ḥiṣār was his earlier home.

[5] Many of these will have been climbed in order to get over places impassable at the river's level.

[6] Schuyler quotes a legend of the lake. He and Kostenko make it larger.

News came that Ibrāhīm Tarkhān had strengthened Fort Shīrāz and was seated in it; also that Qambar-'alī (the Skinner) and Abū'l-qāsim *Kohbur*, the latter not being able to stay in Khwāja Dīdār with the Aūzbegs in Samarkand,—had both come into Yār-yīlāq, strengthened its lower forts and occupied them.

Leaving Fān on our right, we moved on for Keshtūd. The head-man of Fān had a reputation for hospitality, generosity,
Fol. 82. serviceableness and kindness. He had given tribute of 70 or 80 horses to Sl. Mas'ūd Mīrzā at the time the Mīrzā, when Sl. Ḥusain Mīrzā made attack on Ḥisār, went through Fān on his way to his younger brother, Bāī-sunghar Mīrzā in Samarkand. He did like service to others. To me he sent one second-rate horse; moreover he did not wait on me himself. So it was! Those renowned for liberality became misers when they had to do with me, and the politeness of the polite was forgotten. Khusrau Shāh was celebrated for liberality and kindness; what service he did Badī'u'z-zamān Mīrzā has been mentioned; to Bāqī Tarkhān and other begs he shewed great generosity also. Twice I happened to pass through his country;[1] not to speak of courtesy shewn to my peers, what he shewed to my lowest servants he did not shew to me, indeed he shewed less regard for us than for them.

(*Turki*) Who, o my heart! has seen goodness from worldlings?
Look not for goodness from him who has none.

Under the impression that the Aūzbegs were in Keshtūd, we made an excursion to it, after passing Fān. Of itself it seemed
Fol. 82*b*. to have gone to ruin; no-one seemed to be occupying it. We went on to the bank of the Kohik-water (Zar-afshān) and there dismounted. From that place we sent a few begs under Qāsim *Qūchīn* to surprise Rabāṭ-i-khwāja; that done, we crossed the river by a bridge from opposite Yārī, went through Yārī and over the Shunqār-khāna (Falcons'-home) range into Yār-yīlāq. Our begs went to Rabāṭ-i-khwāja and had set up ladders when the men within came to know about them and

[1] The second occasion was when he crossed from Sūkh for Kābul in 910 AH. (fol. 120).

forced them to retire. As they could not take the fort, they rejoined us.

(*c. Bābur renews attack on Samarkand.*)

Qambar-'alī (the Skinner) was (still) holding Sangzār; he came and saw us; Abū'l-qāsim *Kohbur* and Ibrāhīm Tarkhān showed loyalty and attachment by sending efficient men for our service. We went into Asfīdik (var. Asfīndik), one of the Yār-yīlāq villages. At that time Shaibāq Khān lay near Khwāja Dīdār with 3 or 4000 Aūzbegs and as many more soldiers gathered in locally. He had given the Government of Samarkand to Jān-wafā, and Jan-wafā was then in the fort with 500 or 600 men. Ḥamza Sl. and Mahdī Sl. were lying near the fort, in the Quail-reserve. Our men, good and bad were 240. Fol. 83.

Having discussed the position with all my begs and unmailed braves, we left it at this;—that as Shaibānī Khān had taken possession of Samarkand so recently, the Samarkandīs would not be attached to him nor he to them; that if we made an effort at once, we might do the thing; that if we set ladders up and took the fort by surprise, the Samarkandīs would be for us; how should they not be? even if they gave us no help, they would not fight us for the Aūzbegs; and that Samarkand once in our hands, whatever was God's will, would happen.

Acting on this decision, we rode out of Yār-yīlāq after the Mid-day Prayer, and on through the dark till mid-night when we reached Khān-yūrtī. Here we had word that the Samarkandīs knew of our coming; for this reason we went no nearer to the town but made straight back from Khān-yūrtī. It was dawn when, after crossing the Kohik-water below Rabāṭ-i-khwāja, we were once more in Yār-yīlāq.

One day in Fort Asfīdik a household party was sitting in my presence; Dost-i-nāṣir and Nuyān[1] *Kūkūldāsh* and Khān-qulī-i-Karīm-dād and Shaikh Darwesh and Mīrīm-i-nāṣir were all there. Words were crossing from all sides when (I said), 'Come now! say when, if God bring it right, we shall take Fol. 83*b*.

[1] This name appears to indicate a Command of 10,000 (Bretschneider's *Mediæval Researches*, i, 112).

Samarkand.' Some said, 'We shall take it in the heats.' It was then late in autumn. Others said, 'In a month,' 'Forty days,' 'Twenty days.' Nuyān *Kūkūldāsh* said, 'We shall take it in 14.' God shewed him right! we did take it in exactly 14 days.

Just at that time I had a wonderful dream;—His Highness Khwāja 'Ubaid'l-lāh (*Aḥrārī*) seemed to come; I seemed to go out to give him honourable meeting; he came in and seated himself; people seemed to lay a table-cloth before him, apparently without sufficient care and, on account of this, something seemed to come into his Highness Khwāja's mind. Mullā Bābā (? *Pashāgharī*) made me a sign; I signed back, 'Not through me! the table-layer is in fault!' The Khwāja understood and accepted the excuse.[1] When he rose, I escorted him out. In the hall of that house he took hold of either my right or left arm and lifted me up till one of my feet was off the ground, saying, in Turkī, 'Shaikh Maṣlaḥat has given (Samarkand.)'[2] I really took Samarkand a few days later.

(*d. Bābur takes Samarkand by surprise.*)

In two or three days move was made from Fort Asfīdik to Fort Wasmand. Although by our first approach, we had let
Fol. 84. our plan be known, we put our trust in God and made another expedition to Samarkand. It was after the Mid-day Prayer that we rode out of Fort Wasmand, Khwāja Abū'l-makāram accompanying us. By mid-night we reached the Deep-fosse-bridge in the Avenue. From there we sent forward a detachment of 70 or 80 good men who were to set up ladders opposite the Lovers'-cave, mount them and get inside, stand up to those in the Turquoise Gate, get possession of it and send a man

[1] It seems likely that the cloth was soiled. *Cf.* f. 25 and Hughes Dict. of Islām *s.n.* Eating.

[2] As, of the quoted speech, one word only, of three, is Turkī, others may have been dreamed. Shaikh Maṣlaḥat's tomb is in Khujand where Bābur had found refuge in 903 AH.; it had been circumambulated by Tīmūr in 790 AH. (1390 AD.) and is still honoured.

This account of a dream compares well for naturalness with that in the seemingly-spurious passage, entered with the Ḥai. MS. on f. 118. For examination of the passage *see* JRAS, Jan. 1911, and App. D.

to me. Those braves went, set their ladders up opposite the Lovers'-cave, got in without making anyone aware, went to the Gate, attacked Fāẓil Tarkhān, chopped at him and his few retainers, killed them, broke the lock with an axe and opened the Gate. At that moment I came up and went in.

(*Author's note on Fāẓil Tarkhān.*) He was not one of those (Samarkand) Tarkhāns; he was a merchant-tarkhān of Turkistān. He had served Shaibānī Khān in Turkistān and had found favour with him.[1]

Abū'l-qāsim *Kohbur* himself had not come with us but had sent 30 or 40 of his retainers under his younger brother, Aḥmad-i-qāsim. No man of Ibrāhīm Tarkhān's was with us; his younger brother, Aḥmad Tarkhān came with a few retainers after I had entered the town and taken post in the Monastery. Fol. 84*b*.

The towns-people were still slumbering; a few traders peeped out of their shops, recognized me and put up prayers. When, a little later, the news spread through the town, there was rare delight and satisfaction for our men and the towns-folk. They killed the Aūzbegs in the lanes and gullies with clubs and stones like mad dogs; four or five hundred were killed in this fashion. Jān-wafā, the then governor, was living in Khwāja Yaḥya's house; he fled and got away to Shaibāq Khān.[2]

On entering the Turquoise Gate I went straight to the College and took post over the arch of the Monastery. There was a hubbub and shouting of 'Down! down!' till day-break. Some of the notables and traders, hearing what was happening, came joyfully to see me, bringing what food was ready and putting up prayers for me. At day-light we had news that the Aūzbegs were fighting in the Iron Gate where they had made themselves fast between the (outer and inner) doors. With 10, 15 or 20 men, I at once set off for the Gate but before I came up, the town-rabble, busy ransacking every corner of the newly-taken town for loot, had driven the Aūzbegs out through

[1] He was made a Tarkhān by diploma of Shaibānī (H.S. ii, 306, l. 2).

[2] Here the Ḥai. MS. begins to use the word *Shaibāq* in place of its previously uniform *Shaibānī*. As has been noted (f. 5*b* n. 2), the Elph. MS. writes *Shaibāq*. It may be therefore that a scribe has changed the earlier part of the Ḥai. MS. and that Bābur wrote *Shaibāq*. From this point my text will follow the double authority of the Elph. and Ḥai. MSS.

Fol. 85. it. Shaibāq Khān, on hearing what was happening, hurried at sun-rise to the Iron Gate with 100 or 140 men. His coming was a wonderful chance but, as has been said, my men were very few. Seeing that he could do nothing, he rode off at once. From the Iron Gate I went to the citadel and there dismounted, at the Bū-stān palace. Men of rank and consequence and various head-men came to me there, saw me and invoked blessings on me.

Samarkand for nearly 140 years had been the capital of our dynasty. An alien, and of what stamp! an Aūzbeg foe, had taken possession of it! It had slipped from our hands; God gave it again! plundered and ravaged, our own returned to us.

Sl. Ḥusain Mīrzā took Harāt[1] as we took Samarkand, by surprise, but to the experienced, and discerning, and just, it will be clear that between his affair and mine there are distinctions and differences, and that his capture and mine are things apart.

Firstly there is this;—He had ruled many years, passed through much experience and seen many affairs.

Secondly;—He had for opponent, Yādgār Muḥ. Nāṣir Mīrzā,
Fol. 85*b*. an inexperienced boy of 17 or 18.

Thirdly;—(Yādgār Mīrzā's) Head-equerry, Mīr 'Alī, a person well-acquainted with the particulars of the whole position, sent a man out from amongst Sl. Ḥusain Mīrzā's opponents to bring him to surprise them.

Fourthly;—His opponent was not in the fort but was in the Ravens'-garden. Moreover Yādgār Muḥ. Nāṣir Mīrzā and his followers are said to have been so prostrate with drink that three men only were in the Gate, they also drunk.

Fifthly;—he surprised and captured Harāt the first time he approached it.

On the other hand: firstly;—I was 19 when I took Samarkand.

Secondly;—I had as my opponent, such a man as Shaibāq Khān, of mature age and an eye-witness of many affairs.

[1] In 875 AH. (1470 AD.). Ḥusain was then 32 years old. Bābur might have compared his taking of Samarkand with Tīmūr's capture of Qarshī, also with 240 followers (Z.N. i, 127). Firishta (lith. ed. p. 196) ascribes his omission to do so to reluctance to rank himself with his great ancestor.

Thirdly;—No-one came out of Samarkand to me; though the heart of its people was towards me, no-one could dream of coming, from dread of Shaibāq Khān.

Fourthly;—My foe was in the fort; not only was the fort taken but he was driven off.

Fifthly;—I had come once already; my opponent was on his guard about me. The second time we came, God brought it right! Samarkand was won.

In saying these things there is no desire to be-little the reputation of any man; the facts were as here stated. In Fol. 86. writing these things, there is no desire to magnify myself; the truth is set down.

The poets composed chronograms on the victory; this one remains in my memory;—Wisdom answered, 'Know that its date is the *Victory* (*Fatḥ*) *of Bābur Bahādur*.'

Samarkand being taken, Shavdār and Soghd and the *tūmāns* and nearer forts began, one after another, to return to us. From some their Aūzbeg commandants fled in fear and escaped; from others the inhabitants drove them and came in to us; in some they made them prisoner, and held the forts for us.

Just then the wives and families of Shaibāq Khān and his Aūzbegs arrived from Turkistān;[1] he was lying near Khwāja Dīdār and 'Alī-ābād but when he saw the forts and people returning to me, marched off towards Bukhārā. By God's grace, all the forts of Soghd and Miyān-kāl returned to me within three or four months. Over and above this, Bāqī Tarkhān seized this opportunity to occupy Qarshī; Khuzār and Qarshī (? Kesh) both went out of Aūzbeg hands; Qarā-kūl Fol. 86b. also was taken from them by people of Abū'l-muḥsin Mīrzā (*Bāī-qarā*), coming up from Merv. My affairs were in a very good way.

(*e. Birth of Bābur's first child.*)

After our departure (last year) from Andījān, my mothers and my wife and relations came, with a hundred difficulties and

[1] This arrival shews that Shaibānī expected to stay in Samarkand. He had been occupying Turkistān under The Chaghatāī Khān.

hardships, to Aūrātīpā. We now sent for them to Samarkand. Within a few days after their arrival, a daughter was born to me by 'Āyisha-sulṭān Begīm, my first wife, the daughter of Sl. Aḥmad Mīrzā. They named the child Fakhru'n-nisā' (Ornament of women); she was my first-born, I was 19. In a month or 40 days, she went to God's mercy.

(f. Bābur in Samarkand.)

On taking Samarkand, envoys and summoners were sent off at once, and sent again and again, with reiterated request for aid and reinforcement, to the khāns and sulṭāns and begs and marchers on every side. Some, though experienced men, made foolish refusal; others whose relations towards our family had been discourteous and unpleasant, were afraid for themselves and took no notice; others again, though they sent help, sent it insufficient. Each such case will be duly mentioned.

When Samarkand was taken the second time, 'Alī-sher Beg
Fol. 87. was alive. We exchanged letters once; on the back of mine to him I wrote one of my Turkī couplets. Before his reply reached me, separations (*tafarqa*) and disturbances (*ghūghā*) had happened.[1] Mullā Binā'ī had been taken iuto Shaibāq Khān's service when the latter took possession of Samarkand; he stayed with him until a few days after I took the place, when he came into the town to me. Qāsim Beg had his suspicions about him and consequently dismissed him towards Shahr-i-sabz but, as he was a man of parts, and as no fault of his came to light, I had him fetched back. He constantly presented me with odes (*qaṣīda u ghazal*). He brought me a song in the Nawā mode composed to my name and at the same time the following quatrain;—[2]

[1] 'Alī-sher died Jan. 3rd. 1501. It is not clear to what disturbances Bābur refers. He himself was at ease till after April 20th. 1502 and his defeat at Sar-i-pul. Possibly the reference is to the quarrels between Binā'ī and 'Alī-sher. *Cf.* Sām Mīrzā's Anthology, trs. S. de Saçy, *Notices et Extraits* iv, 287 *et seq.*

[2] I surmise a double play-of-words in this verse. One is on two rhyming words, *ghala* and *mallah* and is illustrated by rendering them as *oat* and *coat*. The other is on pointed and unpointed letters, *i.e. ghala* and *'ala*. We cannot find however a Persian word *'ala*, meaning garment.

No grain (*ghala*) have I by which I can be fed (*noshid*);
No rhyme of grain (*mallah*, nankeen) wherewith I can be clad (*poshid*);
The man who lacks both food and clothes,
In art or science where can he compete (*koshid*)?

In those days of respite, I had written one or two couplets but had not completed an ode. As an answer to Mullā Binā'ī I made up and set this poor little Turkī quatrain;—[1]

As is the wish of your heart, so shall it be (*būlghūsidūr*);
For gift and stipend both an order shall be made (*buyurūlghūsidūr*);
I know the grain and its rhyme you write of;
The garments, you, your house, the corn shall fill (*tūlghūsidūr*).

The Mullā in return wrote and presented a quatrain to me in which for his refrain, he took a rhyme to (the *tūlghūsidūr* of) my last line and chose another rhyme;— Fol. 87*b*.

Mīrzā-of-mine, the Lord of sea and land shall be (*yīr būlghūsidūr*);
His art and skill, world o'er, the evening tale shall be (*samar būlghūsidūr*);
If gifts like these reward one rhyming (*or* pointless) word;
For words of sense, what guerdon will there be (*nīlār būlghūsidūr*)?

Abū'l-barka, known as *Farāqī* (Parted), who just then had come to Samarkand from Shahr-i-sabz, said Binā'ī ought to have rhymed. He made this verse;—

Into Time's wrong to you quest shall be made (*sūrūlghūsidūr*);
Your wish the Sulṭān's grace from Time shall ask (*qūlghūsidūr*);
O Ganymede! our cups, ne'er filled as yet,
In this new Age, brimmed-up, filled full shall be (*tūlghūsidūr*).

Though this winter our affairs were in a very good way and Shaibāq Khān's were on the wane, one or two occurrences were somewhat of a disservice; (1) the Merv men who had taken Qarā-kūl, could not be persuaded to stay there and it went back into the hands of the Aūzbegs; (2) Shaibāq Khān besieged Ibrāhīm Tarkhān's younger brother, Aḥmad in Dabūsī, stormed the place and made a general massacre of its inhabitants before the army we were collecting was ready to march.

With 240 proved men I had taken Samarkand; in the next five or six months, things so fell out by the favour of the Most High God, that, as will be told, we fought the arrayed battle of Sar-i-pul with a man like Shaibāq Khān. The help those Fol. 88.

[1] Bābur's refrain is *ghūsidūr*, his rhymes *būl*, (*buyur*)*ūl* and *tūl*. Binā'ī makes *būlghūsidūr* his refrain but his rhymes are not true *viz*. *yīr*, (*sa*)*mar* and *lār*.

round-about gave us was as follows;—From The Khān had come, with 4 or 5000 Bārīns, Ayūb *Begchik* and Qashka Maḥmūd; from Jahāngīr Mīrzā had come Khalīl, Tambal's younger brother, with 100 or 200 men; not a man had come from Sl. Ḥusain Mīrzā, that experienced ruler, than whom none knew better the deeds and dealings of Shaibāq Khān; none came from Badī'u'z-zamān Mīrza; none from Khusrau Shāh because he, the author of what evil done,—as has been told,—to our dynasty! feared us more than he feared Shaibāq Khān.

(*g. Bābur defeated at Sar-i-pul.*)

I marched out of Samarkand, with the wish of fighting Shaibāq Khān, in the month of Shawwāl[1] and went to the New-garden where we lay four or five days for the convenience of gathering our men and completing our equipment. We took the precaution of fortifying our camp with ditch and branch. From the New-garden we advanced, march by march, to beyond Sar-i-pul (Bridge-head) and there dismounted.
Fol. 88*b*. Shaibāq Khān came from the opposite direction and dismounted at Khwāja Kārdzan, perhaps one *yighāch* away (? 5 m.). We lay there for four or five days. Every day our people went from our side and his came from theirs and fell on one another. One day when they were in unusual force, there was much fighting but neither side had the advantage. Out of that engagement one of our men went rather hastily back into the entrenchments; he was using a standard; some said it was Sayyidī Qarā Beg's standard who really was a man of strong words but weak sword. Shaibāq Khān made one night-attack on us but could do nothing because the camp was protected by ditch and close-set branches. His men raised their war-cry, rained in arrows from outside the ditch and then retired.

In the work for the coming battle I exerted myself greatly and took all precautions; Qambar-'alī also did much. In Kesh lay Bāqī Tarkhān with 1000 to 2000 men, in a position to join us after a couple of days. In Diyūl, 4 *yighāch* off

[1] Shawwāl 906 AH. began April 20th. 1501.

(? 20 m.), lay Sayyid Muḥ. Mīrzā *Dūghlāt*, bringing me 1000 to 2000 men from my Khān dādā; he would have joined me at Fol. 89. dawn. With matters in this position, we hurried on the fight!

> **Who lays with haste his hand on the sword,**
> **Shall lift to his teeth the back-hand of regret.**[1]

The reason I was so eager to engage was that on the day of battle, the Eight stars[2] were between the two armies; they would have been in the enemy's rear for 13 or 14 days if the fight had been deferred. I now understand that these considerations are worth nothing and that our haste was without reason.

As we wished to fight, we marched from our camp at dawn, we in our mail, our horses in theirs, formed up in array of right and left, centre and van. Our right was Ibrāhīm *Sārū*, Ibrāhīm Jānī, Abū'l-qāsim *Kohbur* and other begs. Our left was Muḥ. Mazīd Tarkhān, Ibrāhīm Tarkhān and other Samarkandī begs, also Sl. Ḥusain *Arghūn*, Qarā (Black) *Barlās*, Pīr Aḥmad and Khwāja Ḥusain. Qāsim Beg was (with me) in the centre and also several of my close circle and household. In the van were inscribed Qambar-'alī the Skinner, Banda-'alī, Khwāja 'Alī, Mīr Shāh *Qūchīn*, Sayyid Qāsim, Lord of the Gate,—Banda-'alī's younger brother Khaldar (mole-marked) and Ḥaidar-i-qāsim's son Qūch, together with all the good braves there were, and the rest of the household.

Thus arrayed, we marched from our camp; the enemy, also in array, marched out from his. His right was Maḥmūd and Jānī and Tīmūr Sulṭāns; his left, Ḥamza and Mahdī and some Fol. 89*b*. other sulṭāns. When our two armies approached one another, he wheeled his right towards our rear. To meet this, I turned; this left our van,—in which had been inscribed what not of our best braves and tried swordsmen!—to our right and bared our front (*i.e.* the front of the centre). None-the-less we fought those who made the front-attack on us, turned them and forced them back on their own centre. So far did we carry it that some of Shaibāq Khān's old chiefs said to him, 'We must move off! It is past a stand.' He however held fast. His right beat our left, then wheeled (again) to our rear.

[1] From the *Bū-stān*, Graf ed. p. 55, l. 245.

[2] Sikīz Yildūz. *See* Chardin's *Voyages*, v, 136 and Table; also Stanley Lane Poole's *Bābur*, p. 56.

(As has been said), the front of our centre was bare through our van's being left to the right. The enemy attacked us front and rear, raining in arrows on us. (Ayūb *Begchīk's*) Mughūl army, come for our help! was of no use in fighting; it set to work forthwith to unhorse and plunder our men. Not this
Fol. 90. once only! This is always the way with those ill-omened Mughūls! If they win, they grab at booty; if they lose, they unhorse and pilfer their own side! We drove back the Aūzbegs who attacked our front by several vigorous assaults, but those who had wheeled to our rear came up and rained arrows on our standard. Falling on us in this way, from the front and from the rear, they made our men hurry off.

This same turning-movement is one of the great merits of Aūzbeg fighting; no battle of theirs is ever without it. Another merit of theirs is that they all, begs and retainers, from their front to their rear, ride, loose-rein at the gallop, shouting as they come and, in retiring, do not scatter but ride off, at the gallop, in a body.

Ten or fifteen men were left with me. The Kohik-water was close by,—the point of our right had rested on it. We made straight for it. It was the season when it comes down in flood. We rode right into it, man and horse in mail. It was just fordable for half-way over; after that it had to be swum. For more than an arrow's flight[1] we, man and mount in mail! made our horses swim and so got across. Once out of the water, we cut off the horse-armour and let it lie. By thus
Fol. 90*b*. passing to the north bank of the river, we were free of our foes, but at once Mughūl wretches were the captors and pillagers of one after another of my friends. Ibrāhīm Tarkhān and some others, excellent braves all, were unhorsed and killed by Mughūls.[2] We moved along the north bank of the Kohik-river,

[1] In 1791 AD. Muḥ. Effendi shot 482 yards from a Turkish bow, before the R. Tox. S.; not a good shot, he declared. Longer ones are on record. *See* Payne-Gallwey's *Cross-bow* and AQR. 1911, H. Beveridge's *Oriental Cross-bows*.

[2] In the margin of the Elph. Codex, here, stands a Persian verse which appears more likely to be Humāyūn's than Bābur's. It is as follows:

Were the Mughūl race angels, they would be bad;
Written in gold, the name Mughūl would be bad;

recrossed it near Qulba, entered the town by the Shaikh-zāda's Gate and reached the citadel in the middle of the afternoon.

Begs of our greatest, braves of our best and many men perished in that fight. There died Ibrāhīm Tarkhān, Ibrāhīm *Sārū* and Ibrāhīm Jānī; oddly enough three great begs named Ibrāhīm perished. There died also Ḥaidar-i-qāsim's eldest son, Abū'l-qāsim *Kohbur*, and Khudāī-bīrdī *Tūghchī* and Khalīl, Tambal's younger brother, spoken of already several times. Many of our men fled in different directions; Muḥ. Mazīd Tarkhān went towards Qūndūz and Ḥiṣār for Khusrau Shāh. Fol. 91.
Some of the household and of the braves, such as Karīm-dad-i-Khudāī-bīrdī *Turkmān* and Jānaka *Kūkūldāsh* and Mullā Bābā of Pashāghar got away to Aūrā-tīpā. Mullā Bābā at that time was not in my service but had gone out with me in a guest's fashion. Others again, did what Sherīm Ṭaghāī and his band did;—though he had come back with me into the town and though when consultation was had, he had agreed with the rest to make the fort fast, looking for life or death within it, yet spite of this, and although my mothers and sisters, elder and younger, stayed on in Samarkand, he sent off their wives and families to Aūrā-tīpā and remained himself with just a few men, all unencumbered. Not this once only! Whenever hard work had to be done, low and double-minded action was the thing to expect from him!

(h. Bābur besieged in Samarkand.)

Next day, I summoned Khwāja Abū'l-makāram, Qāsim and the other begs, the household and such of the braves as were admitted to our counsels, when after consultation, we resolved to make the fort fast and to look for life or death within it. I and Qāsim Beg with my close circle and household were the

---

Pluck not an ear from the Mughūl's corn-land,
What is sown with Mughūl seed will be bad.

This verse is written into the text of the First W.-i-B. (I.O. 215 f. 72) and is introduced by a scribe's statement that it is by *ān Ḥazrat*, much as notes known to be Humāyūn's are elsewhere attested in the Elph. Codex. It is not in the Ḥai. and Kehr's MSS. nor with, at least many, good copies of the Second W.-i-B.

reserve. For convenience in this I took up quarters in the middle of the town, in tents pitched on the roof of Aūlūgh Beg
Fol. 91*b*. Mīrzā's College. To other begs and braves posts were assigned in the Gates or on the ramparts of the walled-town.

Two or three days later, Shaibāq Khān dismounted at some distance from the fort. On this, the town-rabble came out of lanes and wards, in crowds, to the College gate, shouted good wishes for me and went out to fight in mob-fashion. Shaibāq Khān had got to horse but could not so much as approach the town. Several days went by in this fashion. The mob and rabble, knowing nothing of sword and arrow-wounds, never witnesses of the press and carnage of a stricken field, through these incidents, became bold and began to sally further and further out. If warned by the braves against going out so incautiously, they broke into reproach.

One day when Shaibāq Khān had directed his attack towards the Iron Gate, the mob, grown bold, went out, as usual, daringly and far. To cover their retreat, we sent several braves towards the Camel's-neck,[1] foster-brethren and some of the close household-circle, such as Nuyān *Kūkūldāsh*, Qul-naẓar (son of Sherīm ?) Ṭaghāī Beg, and Mazīd. An Aūzbeg or two
Fol. 92. put their horses at them and with Qul-naẓar swords were crossed. The rest of the Aūzbegs dismounted and brought their strength to bear on the rabble, hustled them off and rammed them in through the Iron Gate. Qūch Beg and Mīr Shāh *Qūchīn* had dismounted at the side of Khwāja Khiẓr's Mosque and were making a stand there. While the townsmen were being moved off by those on foot, a party of mounted Aūzbegs rode towards the Mosque. Qūch Beg came out when they drew near and exchanged good blows with them. He did distinguished work; all stood to watch. Our fugitives below were occupied only with their own escape; for them the time to shoot arrows and make a stand had gone by. I was shooting with a slur-bow[2] from above the Gate and some of my circle

[1] This subterranean water-course, issuing in a flowing well (Erskine) gave its name to a bastion (Ḥ.S. ii, 300).

[2] *nāwak*, a diminutive of *nāo*, a tube. It is described, in a MS. of Bābur's time, by Muḥ. Budhā'ī, and, in a second of later date, by Amīnu'd-dīn (AQR 1911, H.B.'s *Oriental Cross-bows*).

were shooting arrows (*aūq*). Our attack from above kept the enemy from advancing beyond the Mosque; from there he retired.

During the siege, the round of the ramparts was made each night; sometimes I went, sometimes Qāsim Beg, sometimes one of the household Begs. Though from the Turquoise to the Shaikh-zāda's Gate may be ridden, the rest of the way must be walked. When some men went the whole round on foot, it was dawn before they had finished.[1] Fol. 92*b*.

One day Shaibāq Khān attacked between the Iron Gate and the Shaikh-zāda's. I, as the reserve, went to the spot, without anxiety about the Bleaching-ground and Needle-makers' Gates. That day, (?) in a shooting wager (*aūq aūchīdā*), I made a good shot with a slur-bow, at a Centurion's horse.[2] It died at once (*aūq bārdī*) with the arrow (*aūq bīla*). They made such a vigorous attack this time that they got close under the ramparts. Busy with the fighting and the stress near the Iron Gate, we were entirely off our guard about the other side of the town. There, opposite the space between the Needle-makers' and Bleaching-ground Gates, the enemy had posted 7 or 800 good men in ambush, having with them 24 or 25 ladders so wide that two or three could mount abreast. These men came from their ambush when the attack near the Iron Gate, by occupying all our men, had left those other posts empty, and quickly set up their ladders between the two Gates, Fol. 93. just where a road leads from the ramparts to Muḥ. Mazīd Tarkhān's houses. That post was Qūch Beg's and Muḥammad-qulī *Qūchīn's*, with their detachment of braves, and they had their quarters in Muḥ. Mazīd's houses. In the Needle-makers' Gate was posted Qarā (Black) *Barlās*, in the Bleaching-ground Gate, Qūtlūq Khwāja *Kūkūldāsh* with Sherīm Ṭaghāī and his brethren, older and younger. As attack was being made on the other side of the town, the men attached to these posts were not on guard but had scattered to their quarters or to the

[1] Kostenko, i, 344, would make the rounds 9 m.

[2] *bir yūz ātlīqning ātīni nāwah aūqī bīla yakhshī atīm.* This has been read by Erskine as though *būz āt*, pale horse, and not *yūz ātlīq*, Centurion, were written. De. C. translates by Centurion and a marginal note of the Elph. Codex explains *yūz ātlīq* by *ṣad aspagī*.

bazar for necessary matters of service and servants' work. Only the begs were at their posts, with one or two of the populace. Qūch Beg and Mūhammad-qulī and Shāh Ṣufī and one other brave did very well and boldly. Some Aūzbegs were on the ramparts, some were coming up, when these four men arrived at a run, dealt them blow upon blow, and, by energetic drubbing, forced them all down and put them to flight. Qūch Beg did best; this was his out-standing and, approved good deed; twice during this siege, he got his hand into the work. Qarā *Barlās* had been left alone in the Needle-makers' Gate; he also held out well to the end. Qūtlūq Khwāja and Qul-naẓar Mīrzā were also at their posts in the Bleaching-ground Gate; they held out well too, and charged the foe in his rear.

Another time Qāsim Beg led his braves out through the
Fol. 93*b*. Needle-makers' Gate, pursued the Aūzbegs as far as Khwāja Kafsher, unhorsed some and returned with a few heads.

It was now the time of ripening rain but no-one brought new corn into the town. The long siege caused great privation to the towns-people;[1] it went so far that the poor and destitute began to eat the flesh of dogs and asses and, as there was little grain for the horses, people fed them on leaves. Experience shewed that the leaves best suiting were those of the mulberry and elm (*qarā-yīghāch*). Some people scraped dry wood and gave the shavings, damped, to their horses.

For three or four months Shaibāq Khān did not come near the fort but had it invested at some distance and himself moved round it from post to post. Once when our men were off their guard, at mid-night, the enemy came near to the Turquoise
Fol. 94. Gate, beat his drums and flung his war-cry out. I was in the College, undressed. There was great trepidation and anxiety. After that they came night after night, disturbing us by drumming and shouting their war-cry.

Although envoys and messengers had been sent repeatedly to all sides and quarters, no help and reinforcement arrived from any-one. No-one had helped or reinforced me when I was in strength and power and had suffered no sort of defeat

[1] The Sh. N. gives the reverse side of the picture, the plenty enjoyed by the besiegers.

or loss; on what score would any-one help me now? No hope in any-one whatever recommended us to prolong the siege. The old saying was that to hold a fort there must be a head, two hands and two legs, that is to say, the Commandant is the head; help and reinforcement coming from two quarters are the two arms and the food and water in the fort are the two legs. While we looked for help from those round about, their thoughts were elsewhere. That brave and experienced ruler, Sl. Ḥusain Mīrzā, gave us not even the help of an encouraging message, but none-the-less he sent Kamālu'd-dīn Ḥusain *Gāzur-gāhī*[1] as an envoy to Shaibāq Khān.

(i. Tambal's proceedings in Farghāna.)[2]

(This year) Tambal marched from Andijān to near Bīsh-kīnt.[3] Aḥmad Beg and his party, thereupon, made The Khān move out against him. The two armies came face to face near Lak-lakān and the Tūrāk Four-gardens but separated without engaging. Sl. Maḥmūd was not a fighting man; now when opposed to Tambal, he shewed want of courage in word and deed. Aḥmad Beg was unpolished[4] but brave and well-meaning. In his very rough way, he said, 'What's the measure of this person, Tambal? that you are so tormented with fear and fright about him. If you are afraid to look at him, bandage your eyes before you go out to face him.' Fol. 94b.

[1] He may have been attached to the tomb of Khwāja 'Abdu'l-lāh *Anṣārī* in Harāt.

[2] The brusque entry here and elsewhere of *e.g.* Tambal's affairs, allows the inference that Bābur was quoting from perhaps a news-writer's, contemporary records. For a different view of Tambal the Sh. N. cap. xxxiii should be read.

[3] Five-villages, on the main Khujand-Tāshkīnt road.

[4] *turk*, as on f. 28 of Khusrau Shāh.

907 AH.—JULY 17TH. 1501 TO JULY 7TH. 1502 AD.[1]

(*a. Surrender of Samarkand to Shaibānī.*)

The siege drew on to great length; no provisions and supplies came in from any quarter, no succour and reinforcement from any side. The soldiers and peasantry became hopeless and, by ones and twos, began to let themselves down outside[2] the walls and flee. On Shaibāq Khān's hearing of the distress in the town, he came and dismounted near the Lovers'-cave. I, in turn, went to Malik-muḥammad Mīrzā's dwellings in Low-lane, over against him. On one of those days, Khwāja Ḥusain's brother, Aūzūn Ḥasan[3] came into the town with 10 or 15 of his men,—he who, as has been told, had been the cause of Jahāngīr Mīrzā's rebellion, of my exodus from Samarkand (903 AH.—March 1498 AD.) and, again! of what an amount of sedition and
Fol. 95. disloyalty! That entry of his was a very bold act.[4]

The soldiery and townspeople became more and more distressed. Trusted men of my close circle began to let themselves down from the ramparts and get away; begs of known name and old family servants were amongst them, such as Pīr Wais, Shaikh Wais and Wais *Lāgharī*.[5] Of help from any side we utterly despaired; no hope was left in any quarter; our

[1] Elph. MS. f. 68*b*; W.-i-B. I.O. 215 f. 78 and 217 f. 61*b*; Mems. p. 97. The Kehr-Ilminsky text shews, in this year, a good example of its Persification and of Dr. Ilminsky's dealings with his difficult archetype by the help of the Memoirs.

[2] *tāshlāb*. The Sh. N. places these desertions as after four months of siege.

[3] It strikes one as strange to find Long Ḥasan described, as here, in terms of his younger brother. The singularity may be due to the fact that Ḥusain was with Bābur and may have invited Ḥasan. It may be noted here that Ḥusain seems likely to be that father-in-law of 'Umar Shaikh mentioned on f. 12*b* and 13*b*.

[4] This laudatory comment I find nowhere but in the Ḥai. Codex.

[5] There is some uncertainty about the names of those who left.

supplies and provisions were wretched, what there was was coming to an end; no more came in. Meantime Shaibāq Khān interjected talk of peace.[1] Little ear would have been given to his talk of peace, if there had been hope or food from any side. It had to be! a sort of peace was made and we took our departure from the town, by the Shaikh-*zāda*'s Gate, somewhere about midnight.

(*b. Bābur leaves Samarkand.*)

I took my mother Khānīm out with me; two other women-folk went too, one was Bīshka (var. Peshka)-i-Khalīfa, the other, Mīnglīk *Kūkūldāsh.*[2] At this exodus, my elder sister, Khān-zāda Begīm fell into Shaibāq Khān's hands.[3] In the darkness of that night we lost our way[4] and wandered about amongst the main irrigation channels of Soghd. At shoot of dawn, after a hundred difficulties, we got past Khwāja Dīdār. At the Sunnat Prayer we scrambled up the rising-ground of Qarā-būgh. Fol. 95*b*.
From the north slope of Qarā-būgh we hurried on past the foot of Judūk village and dropped down into Yīlān-aūtī. On the road I raced with Qāsim Beg and Qambar-'alī (the Skinner); my horse was leading when I, thinking to look at theirs behind, twisted myself round; the girth may have slackened, for my saddle turned and I was thrown on my head to the ground. Although I at once got up and remounted, my brain did not steady till the evening; till then this world and what went on appeared to me like things felt and seen in a dream or fancy. Towards afternoon we dismounted in Yīlān-aūtī, there killed a

[1] The Sh. N. is interesting here as giving an eye-witness' account of the surrender of the town and of the part played in the surrender by Khān-zāda's marriage (cap. xxxix).

[2] The first seems likely to be a relation of Niẓāmu'd-dīn 'Alī Khalīfa; the second was Mole-marked, a foster-sister The party numbered some 100 persons of whom Abū'l-makāram was one (H.S. ii, 310).

[3] Bābur's brevity is misleading; his sister was not captured but married with her own and her mother's consent before attempt to leave the town was made. *Cf.* Gul-badan's H.N. f. 3*b* and Sh. N. Vambéry, p. 145.

[4] The route taken avoided the main road for Dizak; it can be traced by the physical features, mentioned by Bābur, on the Fr. map of 1904. The Sh. N. says the night was extraordinarily dark. Departure in blinding darkness and by unusual ways shews distrust of Shaibāq's safe-conduct suggesting that Yaḥyā's fate was in the minds of the fugitives.

horse, spitted and roasted its flesh, rested our horses awhile and rode on. Very weary, we reached Khalīla-village before the dawn and dismounted. From there it was gone on to Dīzak.

In Dīzak just then was Ḥāfiẓ Muḥ. *Dūldāī's* son, Ṭāhir. There, in Dīzak, were fat meats, loaves of fine flour, plenty of sweet melons and abundance of excellent grapes. From what privation we came to such plenty! From what stress to what repose!

From fear and hunger rest we won (*amānī tāptūq*);
A fresh world's new-born life we won (*jahānī tāptūq*).
Fol. 96. From out our minds, death's dread was chased (*rafa' būldī*);
From our men the hunger-pang kept back (*dafa' būldī*).[1]

Never in all our lives had we felt such relief! never in the whole course of them have we appreciated security and plenty so highly. Joy is best and more delightful when it follows sorrow, ease after toil. I have been transported four or five times from toil to rest and from hardship to ease.[2] This was the first. We were set free from the affliction of such a foe and from the pangs of hunger and had reached the repose of security and the relief of abundance.

(*c. Bābur in Dikh-kat.*)

After three or four days of rest in Dīzak, we set out for Aūrā-tīpā. Pashāghar is a little[3] off the road but, as we had occupied it for some time (904 AH.), we made an excursion to it in passing by. In Pashāghar we chanced on one of Khānīm's old servants, a teacher[4] who had been left behind in Samarkand from want of a mount. We saw one another and on questioning her, I found she had come there on foot.

Khūb-nigār Khānīm, my mother Khānīm's younger sister[5]

[1] The texts differ as to whether the last two lines are prose or verse. All four are in Turkī, but I surmise a clerical error in the refrain of the third, where *būlūb* is written for *būldī*.

[2] The second was in 908 AH. (f. 18*b*); the third in 914 AH. (f. 216 *b*); the fourth is not described in the B.N.; it followed Bābur's defeat at Ghaj-dīwān in 918 AH. (Erskine's *History of India*, i, 325). He had a fifth, but of a different kind, when he survived poison in 933 AH. (f. 305).

[3] Ḥai. MS. *qāqāsrāq*; Elph. MS. *yānasrāq*.

[4] *ātūn*, one who instructs in reading, writing and embroidery. *Cf.* Gulbadan's H.N. f. 26. The distance walked may have been 70 or 80 m.

[5] She was the wife of the then Governor of Aūrā-tīpā, Muḥ. Ḥusain *Dūghlāt*

already must have bidden this transitory world farewell; for they let Khānīm and me know of it in Aūrā-tīpā. My father's mother also must have died in Andijān; this too they let us know in Aūrā-tīpā.[1] Since the death of my grandfather, Yūnas Khān (892 AH.), Khānīm had not seen her (step-)mother or her younger brother and sisters, that is to say, Shāh Begīm, Sl. Maḥmūd Khān, Sulṭān-nīgār Khānīm and Daulat-sulṭān Khānīm. The separation had lasted 13 or 14 years. To see these relations she now started for Tāshkīnt. Fol. 96*b*.

After consulting with Muḥ. Ḥusain Mīrzā, it was settled for us to winter in a place called Dikh-kat[2] one of the Aūrā-tīpā villages. There I deposited my impedimenta (*aūrūq*); then set out myself in order to visit Shāh Begīm and my Khān dādā and various relatives. I spent a few days in Tāshkīnt and waited on Shāh Begīm and my Khān dādā. My mother's elder full-sister, Mihr-nigār Khānīm[3] had come from Samarkand and was in Tāshkīnt. There my mother Kkānīm fell very ill; it was a very bad illness; she passed through mighty risks.

His Highness Khwājaka Khwāja, having managed to get out of Samarkand, had settled down in Far-kat; there I visited him. I had hoped my Khān dādā would shew me affection and kindness and would give me a country or a district (*pargana*). He did promise me Aūrā-tīpā but Muḥ. Ḥusain Mīrzā did not make it over, whether acting on his own account or whether upon a hint from above, is not known. After spending a few days with him (in Aūrā-tīpā), I went on to Dikh-kat. Fol. 97.

Dikh-kat is in the Aūrā-tīpā hill-tracts, below the range on the other side of which is the Macha[4] country. Its people, though Sārt, settled in a village, are, like Turks, herdsmen and

[1] It may be noted here that in speaking of these elder women Bābur uses the honorific plural, a form of rare occurrence except for such women, for saintly persons and exceptionally for The supreme Khān For his father he has never used it.

[2] This name has several variants. The village lies, in a valley-bottom, on the Aq-sū and on a road. *See* Kostenko, i, 119.

[3] She had been divorced from Shaibānī in order to allow him to make legal marriage with her niece, Khān-zāda.

[4] Amongst the variants of this name, I select the modern one Macha is the upper valley of the Zar-afshān.

shepherds. Their sheep are reckoned at 40,000. We dismounted at the houses of the peasants in the village; I stayed in a head-man's house. He was old, 70 or 80, but his mother was still alive. She was a woman on whom much life had been bestowed for she was 111 years old. Some relation of hers may have gone, (as was said), with Tīmūr Beg's army to Hindūstān;[1] she had this in her mind and used to tell the tale. In Dikh-kat alone were 96 of her descendants, hers and her grandchildren, great-grandchildren and grandchildren's grandchildren. Counting in the dead, 200 of her descendants were reckoned up. Her grandchild's grandson was a strong young man of 25 or 26, with full black beard. While in Dikh-kat, I constantly made excursions amongst the mountains round
Fol. 97*b*. about. Generally I went bare-foot and, from doing this so much, my feet became so that rock and stone made no difference to them.[2] Once in one of these wanderings, a cow was seen, between the Afternoon and Evening prayers, going down by a narrow, ill-defined road. Said I, 'I wonder which way that road will be going; keep your eye on that cow; don't lose the cow till you know where the road comes out.' Khwāja Asadu'l-lāh made his joke, 'If the cow loses her way,' he said, 'what becomes of us?'

In the winter several of our soldiers asked for leave to Andijān because they could make no raids with us.[3] Qāsim Beg said, with much insistance, 'As these men are going, send something special of your own wear by them to Jahāngīr Mīrzā.' I sent my ermine cap. Again he urged, 'What harm would there be if you sent something for Taṃbal also?' Though I was very unwilling, yet as he urged it, I sent Taṃbal a large broad-sword which Nuyān *Kūkūldāsh* had had made for himself in Samarkand. This very sword it was which, as will

[1] Tīmūr took Dihlī in 801 AH. (Dec. 1398), *i.e.* 103 solar and 106 lunar years earlier. The ancient dame would then have been under 5 years old. It is not surprising therefore that in repeating her story Bābur should use a tense betokening hear-say matter (*bārib ikān dūr*).

[2] The anecdote here following, has been analysed in JRAS 1908, p. 87, in order to show warrant for the opinion that parts of the Kehr-Ilminsky text are retranslations from the Persian W.-i-B.

[3] Amongst those thus leaving seem to have been Qaṃbar-'alī (f. 99*b*).

be told with the events of next year, came down on my own head![1]

A few days later, my grandmother, Aīsān-daulat Begīm, who, when I left Samarkand, had stayed behind, arrived in Dikh-kat Fol. 98.
with our families and baggage (*aūrūq*) and a few lean and hungry followers.

(*d. Shaibāq Khān raids in The Khān's country.*)

That winter Shaibāq Khān crossed the Khujand river on the ice and plundered near Shāhrukhiya and Bīsh-kīnt. On hearing news of this, we gallopped off, not regarding the smallness of our numbers, and made for the villages below Khujand, opposite Hasht-yak (One-eighth). The cold was mightily bitter,[2] a wind not less than the Hā-darwesh[3] raging violently the whole time. So cold it was that during the two or three days we were in those parts, several men died of it. When, needing to make ablution, I went into an irrigation-channel, frozen along both banks but because of its swift current, not ice-bound in the middle, and bathed, dipping under 16 times, the cold of the water went quite through me. Next day we crossed the river on the ice from opposite Khaṣlār and went on through the dark to Bīsh-kīnt.[4] Shaibāq Khān, however, must have gone straight back after plundering the neighbourhood of Shāhrukhiya.

(*e. Death of Nuyān Kūkūldāsh.*)

Bīsh-kīnt, at that time, was held by Mullā Ḥaidar's son, 'Abdu'l-minān. A younger son, named Mūmin, a worthless and dissipated person, had come to my presence in Samarkand and had received all kindness from me. This sodomite, Mūmin, for what sort of quarrel between them is not known, cherished Fol. 98b.
rancour against Nuyān *Kūkūldāsh*. At the time when we, having heard of the retirement of the Aūzbegs, sent a man to

[1] *Cf.* f. 107 foot.

[2] The Sh. N. speaks of the cold in that winter (Vambéry, p. 160). It was unusual for the Sīr to freeze in this part of its course (Sh. N. p. 172) where it is extremely rapid (Kostenko, i, 213).

[3] *Cf.* f. 4*b*.

[4] Point to point, some 50 miles.

The Khān and marched from Bīsh-kīnt to spend two or three days amongst the villages in the Blacksmith's-dale,[1] Mullā Ḥaidar's son, Mūmin invited Nuyān *Kūkūldāsh* and Aḥmad-i-qāsim and some others in order to return them hospitality received in Samarkand. When I left Bīsh-kīnt, therefore they stayed behind. Mūmin's entertainment to this party was given on the edge of a ravine (*jar*). Next day news was brought to us in Sām-sīrak, a village in the Blacksmith's-dale, that Nuyān was dead through falling when drunk into the ravine. We sent his own mother's brother, Ḥaq-naẓar and others, who searched out where he had fallen. They committed Nuyān to the earth in Bīsh-kīnt, and came back to me. They had found the body at the bottom of the ravine an arrow's flight from the place of the entertainment. Some suspected that Mūmin, nursing his trumpery rancour, had taken Nuyān's life. None knew the truth. His death made me strangely sad; for few men have I felt such grief; I wept unceasingly for a week or
Fol. 99. ten days. The chronogram of his death was found in *Nuyān is dead*.[2]

With the heats came the news that Shaibāq Khān was coming up into Aūrā-tīpā. Hereupon, as the land is level about Dikh-kat, we crossed the Āb-burdan pass into the Macha hill-country.[3] Āb-burdan is the last village of Macha; just below it a spring sends its water down (to the Zar-afshān); above the stream is included in Macha, below it depends on Palghar. There is a tomb at the spring-head. I had a rock at the side of the spring-head shaped (*qātirib*) and these three couplets inscribed on it;—

> I have heard that Jamshid, the magnificent,
> Inscribed on a rock at a fountain-head[4]

---

[1] *Āhangarān-julgasi*, a name narrowed on maps to Angren (valley).

[2] *Faut shūd Nuyān*. The numerical value of these words is 907. Bābur when writing, looks back 26 years to the death of this friend.

[3] Ab-burdan village is on the Zar-afshān; the pass is 11,200 ft. above the sea. Bābur's boundaries still hold good and the spring still flows. *See* Ujfalvy *l.c.* i. 14; Kostenko, i, 119 and 193; Rickmers, JRGS 1907, p. 358.

[4] From the *Bū-stān* (Graf's ed. Vienna 1858, p. 561). The last couplet is also in the *Gulistān* (Platts' ed. p. 72). The Bombay lith. ed. of the *Bū-stān* explains (p. 39) that the "We" of the third couplet means Jamshid and his predecessors who have rested by his fountain.

'Many men like us have taken breath at this fountain,
And have passed away in the twinkling of an eye;
We took the world by courage and might,
But we took it not with us to the tomb.'

There is a custom in that hill-country of cutting verses and things[1] on the rocks.

While we were in Macha, Mullā Hijrī,[2] the poet came from Ḥiṣār and waited on me. At that time I composed the following opening lines;—

Let your portrait flatter you never so much, than it you are more (*āndin artūqsin*);
Men call you their Life (*Jān*), than Life, without doubt, you are more (*jāndin artūqsin*).[3]

After plundering round about in Aūrā-tīpā, Shaibāq Khān retired.[4] While he was up there, we, disregarding the fewness of our men and their lack of arms, left our impedimenta (*aūrūq*) in Macha, crossed the Āb-burdan pass and went to Dikh-kat so that, gathered together close at hand, we might miss no chance on one of the next nights. He, however, retired straightway; we went back to Macha. Fol. 99*b*.

It passed through my mind that to wander from mountain to mountain, homeless and houseless, without country or abiding-place, had nothing to recommend it. 'Go you right off to The Khān,' I said to myself. Qāsim Beg was not willing for this move, apparently being uneasy because, as has been told, he had put Mughūls to death at Qarā-būlāq, by way of example. However much we urged it, it was not to be! He drew off for Ḥiṣār with all his brothers and his whole following. We for our part, crossed the Āb-burdan pass and set forward for The Khān's presence in Tāshkīnt.

1 *nīma.* The First W.-i-B. (I.O. 215 f. 81 l. 8) writes *tawārīkh*, annals.

2 This may be the Khwāja Hijrī of the A.N. (index s.n.); and Badāyūnī's Ḥasan *Hijrī*, Bib. Ind. iii, 385; and Ethé's Pers. Cat. No. 793; and Bod. Cat. No. 189.

3 The Ḥai. MS. points in the last line as though punning on Khān and Jān, but appears to be wrong.

4 For an account of the waste of crops, the Sh. N. should be seen (p. 162 and 180).

(*f. Bābur with The Khān.*)

In the days when Tambal had drawn his army out and gone into the Blacksmith's-dale,[1] men at the top of his army, such as Muḥ. *Dūghlāt*, known as *Ḥiṣārī*, and his younger brother Ḥusain, and also Qambar-'alī, the Skinner conspired to attempt his life. When he discovered this weighty matter, they, unable to remain with him, had gone to The Khān.

The Feast of Sacrifices ('Īd-i-qurbān) fell for us in Shāh-rukhiya (Ẕū'l-ḥijja 10th.—June 16th. 1502).

I had written a quatrain in an ordinary measure but was in some doubt about it, because at that time I had not studied
Fol. 100. poetic idiom so much as I have now done. The Khān was good-natured and also he wrote verses, though ones somewhat deficient in the requisites for odes. I presented my quatrain and I laid my doubts before him but got no reply so clear as to remove them. His study of poetic idiom appeared to have been somewhat scant. Here is the verse;—

> One hears no man recall another in trouble (*miḥnat-ta kīshī*);
> None speak of a man as glad in his exile (*ghurbat-ta kīshī*);
> My own heart has no joy in this exile;
> Called glad is no exile, man though he be (*albatta kīshī*).

Later on I came to know that in Turkī verse, for the purpose of rhyme, *ta* and *da* are interchangeable and also *ghain*, *qāf* and *kāf*.[2]

(*g. The acclaiming of the standards.*)

When, a few days later, The Khān heard that Tambal had gone up into Aūrā-tīpā, he got his army to horse and rode out from Tāshkīnt. Between Bīsh-kīnt and Sām-sīrak he formed up into array of right and left and saw the count[3] of his men.

[1] I think this refers to last year's move (f. 94 foot).

[2] In other words, the T. preposition, meaning E. in, at, *etc.* may be written with t or d, as *ta*(*tā*) or as *da*(*dā*). Also the one meaning E. towards, may be *gha*, *qa*, or *ka* (with long or short vowel).

[3] *dīm*, a word found difficult. It may be a derivative of root *de*, tell, and a noun with the meaning of English tale (number). The First W.-i-B. renders it by *san*, and by *san*, Abū'l-ghāzī expresses what Bābur's *dīm* expresses, the numbering of troops. It occurs thrice in the B.N. (here, on f. 183*b* and on f. 264*b*). In the Elphinstone Codex it has been written-over into *Ivīm*, once resembles *vim* more than *dīm* and once is omitted. The L. and E. *Memoirs*

This done, the standards were acclaimed in Mughūl fashion.[1] The Khān dismounted and nine standards were set up in front of him. A Mughūl tied a long strip of white cloth to the thigh-bone (*aūrta aīlīk*) of a cow and took the other end in his hand. Three other long strips of white cloth were tied to the staves of three of the (nine) standards, just below the yak-tails, and their other ends were brought for The Khān to stand on one and for me and Sl. Muḥ. Khānika to stand each on one of the two others. The Mughūl who had hold of the strip of cloth Fol. 100*b*. fastened to the cow's leg, then said something in Mughūl while he looked at the standards and made signs towards them. The Khān and those present sprinkled *qumīz*[2] in the direction of the standards; hautbois and drums were sounded towards them;[3] the army flung the war-cry out three times towards them, mounted, cried it again and rode at the gallop round them.

Precisely as Chīngīz Khān laid down his rules, so the Mughūls still observe them. Each man has his place, just where his ancestors had it; right, right,—left, left,—centre, centre. The most reliable men go to the extreme points of the right and left. The Chīrās and Begchīk clans always demand to go to the point in the right.[4] At that time the Beg of the Chīrās tūmān was a very bold brave, Qāshka (Mole-marked) Maḥmud and the beg of the renowned Begchīk tūmān was Ayūb *Begchīk*. These two, disputing which should go out to the point, drew swords on one another. At last it seems to have been settled that one should take the highest place in the hunting-circle, the other, in the battle-array.

Next day after making the circle, it was hunted near Sām-

(p. 303) inserts what seems a gloss, saying that a whip or bow is used in the count, presumably held by the teller to 'keep his place' in the march past. The *Siyāsat-nāma* (Schefer, trs. p. 22) names the whip as used in numbering an army.

[1] The acclamation of the standards is depicted in B.M. W.-i-B. Or. 3714 f. 128*b*. One cloth is shewn tied to the off fore-leg of a live cow, above the knee, Bābur's word being *aūrtā aīlīk* (middle-hand).

[2] The libation was of fermented mares'-milk.

[3] *lit*. their one way.

[4] *Cf*. T.R. p. 308.

Fol. 101. sīrak; thence move was made to the Tūrāk Four-gardens. On that day and in that camp, I finished the first ode I ever finished. Its opening couplet is as follows;—

> Except my soul, no friend worth trust found I (*wafādār tāpmādīm*);
> Except my heart, no confidant found I (*asrār tāpmādīm*).

There were six couplets; every ode I finished later was written just on this plan.

The Khān moved, march by march, from Sām-sīrak to the bank of the Khujand-river. One day we crossed the water by way of an excursion, cooked food and made merry with the braves and pages. That day some-one stole the gold clasp of my girdle. Next day Bayān-qulī's Khān-qulī and Sl. Muḥ. Wais fled to Tambal. Every-one suspected them of that bad deed. Though this was not ascertained, Aḥmad-i-qāsim *Kohbur* asked leave and went away to Aūrā-tīpa. From that leave he did not return; he too went to Tambal.

908 AH.—JULY 7TH. 1502 TO JUNE 26TH. 1503 AD.[1]

(*a. Bābur's poverty in Tāshkīnt.*)

This move of The Khān's was rather unprofitable; to take no fort, to beat no foe, he went out and went back.

During my stay in Tāshkīnt, I endured much poverty and humiliation. No country or hope of one! Most of my retainers dispersed, those left, unable to move about with me because of their destitution! If I went to my Khān dādā's Gate,[2] I went sometimes with one man, sometimes with two. It was well he was no stranger but one of my own blood. Fol. 101b. After showing myself[3] in his presence, I used to go to Shāh Begīm's, entering her house, bareheaded and barefoot, just as if it were my own.

This uncertainty and want of house and home drove me at last to despair. Said I, 'It would be better to take my head[4] and go off than live in such misery; better to go as far as my feet can carry me than be seen of men in such poverty and humiliation. Having settled on China to go to, I resolved to take my head and get away. From my childhood up I had wished to visit China but had not been able to manage it because of ruling and attachments. Now sovereignty itself was gone! and my mother, for her part, was re-united to her (step)-mother and her younger brother. The hindrances to my journey had been removed; my anxiety for my mother was dispelled. I represented (to Shāh Begīm and The Khān) through Khwāja Abū'l-makāram that now such a foe as

[1] Elph. MS. f. 74; W.-i-B. I.O. 215 f. 83 and 217 f. 66; Mems. p. 104.

[2] It may be noted that Bābur calls his mother's brothers, not *ṭaghāī* but *dādā* father. I have not met with an instance of his saying 'My ṭaghāī' as he says 'My dādā.' *Cf.* index *s.n. taghāī*.

[3] *kūrūnūsh qilib*, reflective from *kūrmak*, to see.

[4] A rider's metaphor.

Shaibāq Khān had made his appearance, Mughūl and Turk[1] alike must guard against him; that thought about him must be taken while he had not well-mastered the (Aūzbeg) horde or grown very strong, for as they have said;—[2]

> To-day, while thou canst, quench the fire,
> Once ablaze it will burn up the world;
> Let thy foe not fix string to his bow,
> While an arrow of thine can pierce him;

that it was 20 or 25 years[3] since they had seen the Younger Khān (Aḥmad *Alacha*) and that I had never seen him; should I be able, if I went to him, not only to see him myself, but to bring about the meeting between him and them?

Fol. 102. Under this pretext I proposed to get out of those surroundings;[4] once in Mughūlistān and Turfān, my reins would be in my own hands, without check or anxiety. I put no-one in possession of my scheme. Why not? Because it was impossible for me to mention such a scheme to my mother, and also because it was with other expectations that the few of all ranks who had been my companions in exile and privation, had cut themselves off with me and with me suffered change of fortune. To speak to them also of such a scheme would be no pleasure.

The Khwāja, having laid my plan before Shāh Begīm and The Khān, understood them to consent to it but, later, it occurred to them that I might be asking leave a second time,[5] because of not receiving kindness. That touching their reputation, they delayed a little to give the leave.

(*b. The Younger Khān comes to Tāshkīnt.*)

At this crisis a man came from the Younger Khān to say that he was actually on his way. This brought my scheme to

[1] As touching the misnomer, 'Mughūl dynasty' for the Tīmūrid rulers in Hindūstān, it may be noted that here, as Bābur is speaking to a Chaghatāī Mughūl, his 'Turk' is left to apply to himself.

[2] Gulistān, cap. viii, Maxim 12 (Platts' ed. p. 147).

[3] This backward count is to 890 AH. when Aḥmad fled from cultivated lands (T.R. p. 113).

[4] It becomes clear that Aḥmad had already been asked to come to Tāshkīnt.

[5] *Cf.* f. 96*b* for his first departure without help.

naught. When a second man announced his near approach, we all went out to give him honourable meeting, Shāh Begīm and his younger sisters, Sulṭān-nigār Khānīm and Daulat-sulṭān Khānīm, and I and Sl. Muḥ. Khānika and Khān Mīrzā (Wais).

Between Tāshkīnt and Sairām is a village called Yagha (var. Yaghma), with some smaller ones, where are the tombs of Father Abraham and Father Isaac. So far we went out. Knowing nothing exact about his coming,[1] I rode out for an excursion, with an easy mind. All at once, he descended on me, face to face. I went forward; when I stopped, he stopped. He was a good deal perturbed; perhaps he was thinking of dismounting in some fixed spot and there seated, of receiving me ceremoniously. There was no time for this; when we were near each other, I dismounted. He had not time even to dismount;[2] I bent the knee, went forward and saw him. Hurriedly and with agitation, he told Sl. Sa'īd Khān and Bābā Khān Sl. to dismount, bend the knee with (*bīla*) me and make my acquaintance.[3] Just these two of his sons had come with him; they may have been 13 or 14 years old. When I had seen them, we all mounted and went to Shāh Begīm's presence. After he had seen her and his sisters, and had renewed acquaintance, they all sat down and for half the night told one another particulars of their past and gone affairs. Fol. 102*b*.

Next day, my Younger Khān dādā bestowed on me arms of his own and one of his own special horses saddled, and a Mughūl head-to-foot dress,—a Mughūl cap,[4] a long coat of Chinese satin, with broidering of stitchery,[5] and Chinese

[1] Yagha (Yaghma) is not on the Fr. map of 1904, but suitably located is Turbat (Tomb) to which roads converge.

[2] Elph. MS. *tüshkücha*; Ḥai. MS. *yūkūnchā*. The importance Aḥmad attached to ceremony can be inferred by the details given (f. 103) of his meeting with Maḥmūd.

[3] *kūrūshkhāilār*. *Cf.* Redhouse who gives no support for reading the verb *kūrmak* as meaning *to embrace*.

[4] *būrk*, a tall felt cap (Redhouse). In the adjective applied to the cap there are several variants. The Ḥai. MS. writes *muftūl*, solid or twisted. The Elph. MS. has *muftūn-lūq* which has been understood by Mr. Erskine to mean, gold-embroidered.

[5] The wording suggests that the decoration is in chain-stitch, pricked up and down through the stuff.

armour; in the old fashion, they had hung, on the left side, a haversack (*chantāī*) and an outer bag,[1] and three or four things such as women usually hang on their collars, perfume-holders and various receptacles;[2] in the same way, three or four things hung on the right side also.

Fol. 103. From there we went to Tāshkīnt. My Elder Khān dādā also had come out for the meeting, some 3 or 4 *yīghāch* (12 to 15 m.) along the road. He had had an awning set up in a chosen spot and was seated there. The Younger Khān went up directly in front of him; on getting near, fetched a circle, from right to left, round him; then dismounted before him. After advancing to the place of interview (*kūrūshūr yīr*), he nine times bent the knee; that done, went close and saw (his brother). The Elder Khān, in his turn, had risen when the Younger Khān drew near. They looked long at one another (*kūrūshtīlār*) and long stood in close embrace (*qūchūshūb*). The Younger Khān again bent the knee nine times when retiring, many times also on offering his gift; after that, he went and sat down.

All his men had adorned themselves in Mughūl fashion. There they were in Mughūl caps (*būrk*); long coats of Chinese satin, broidered with stitchery, Mughūl quivers and saddles of green shagreen-leather, and Mughūl horses adorned in a unique fashion. He had brought rather few men, over 1000 and under 2000 may-be. He was a man of singular manners, a mighty master of the sword, and brave. Amongst arms he preferred to trust to the sword. He used to say that of arms there are, the *shash-par*[3] (six-flanged mace), the *piyāzī* (rugged mace), the *kīstin*,[4] the *tabar-zīn* (saddle-hatchet) and the *bāltū* (battle-axe),

[1] *tāsh chantāī*. These words have been taken to mean whet-stone (*bilgū-tāsh*). I have found no authority for reading *tāsh* as whet-stone. Moreover to allow 'bag of the stone' to be read would require *tāsh* (*nīng*) *chantāī-sī* in the text.

[2] lit. bag-like things. Some will have held spare bow-strings and archers' rings, and other articles of 'repairing kit.' With the gifts, it seems probable that the *gosha-gīr* (f. 107) was given.

[3] Vullers, *clava sex foliis*.

[4] Zenker, *casse-tête*. *Kistin* would seem to be formed from the root, *kis*, cutting, but M. de C. describes it as a ball attached by a strap or chain to a handle. *Sanglākh*, a sort of mace (*gurz*).

all, if they strike, work only with what of them first touches, but the sword, if it touch, works from point to hilt. He never parted with his keen-edged sword; it was either at his waist or to his hand. He was a little rustic and rough-of- Fol. 103*b*.
speech, through having grown up in an out-of-the-way place.

When, adorned in the way described, I went with him to The Khān, Khwāja Abū'l-makāram asked, 'Who is this honoured sulṭān?' and till I spoke, did not recognize me.

(*c. The Khāns march into Farghāna against Tambal.*)

Soon after returning to Tāshkīnt, The Khān led out an army for Andikān (Andijān) direct against Sl. Aḥmad *Tambal*.[1] He took the road over the Kīndīrlīk-pass and from Blacksmiths'-dale (Āhangarān-julgasī) sent the Younger Khān and me on in advance. After the pass had been crossed, we all met again near *Z*arqān (var. *Z*abarqān) of Karnān.

One day, near Karnān, they numbered their men[2] and reckoned them up to be 30,000. From ahead news began to come that Tambal also was collecting a force and going to Akhsī. After having consulted together, The Khāns decided to join some of their men to me, in order that I might cross the Khujand-water, and, marching by way of Aūsh and Aūzkīnt, turn Tambal's rear. Having so settled, they joined to me Ayūb *Begchīk* with his *tūmān*, Jān-ḥasan Bārīn (var. Nārīn) with his Bārīns, Muḥ. *Ḥiṣārī Dūghlāt*, Sl. Ḥusain *Dūghlāt* and Sl. Aḥmad Mīrzā *Dūghlāt*, not in command of the Dūghlāt *tūmān*,—and Qambar-'alī Beg (the Skinner). The commandant (*darogha*) of their force was Sārīgh-bāsh (Yellow-head) Mīrza *Itārchī*.[3]

Leaving The Khāns in Karnān, we crossed the river on rafts near Sakan, traversed the Khūqān sub-district (*aūrchīn*), crushed Fol. 104.

1 The *Rauzatu'ṣ-ṣafā* states that The Khāns left Tāshkīnt on Muḥarram 15th (July 21st. 1502), in order to restore Bābur and expel Tambal (Erskine).

2 lit. saw the count (*dīm*). *Cf.* f. 10*c* and note concerning the count. Using a Persian substitute, the Kehr-Ilminsky text writes *san* (*kūrdīlār*).

3 Elph. MS. *ambārchī*, steward, for Itārchī, a tribal-name. The 'Mīrzā' and the rank of the army-begs are against supposing a steward in command. Here and just above, the texts write Mīrzā-i-Itārchī and Mīrzā-i-Dūghlāt, thus suggesting that in names not ending with a vowel, the *iẓāfat* is required for exact transliteration, *e.g.* Muḥammad-i-dūghlāt.

Qabā and by way of the Alāī sub-districts[1] descended suddenly on Aūsh. We reached it at dawn, unexpected; those in it could but surrender. Naturally the country-folk were wishing much for us, but they had not been able to find their means, both through dread of Taṃbal and through our remoteness. After we entered Aūsh, the hordes and the highland and lowland tribes of southern and eastern Andijān came in to us. The Aūzkīnt people also, willing to serve us, sent me a man and came in.

(*Author's note on Aūzkīnt.*) Aūzkīnt formerly must have been a capital of Farghāna;[2] it has an excellent fort and is situated on the boundary (of Farghāna).

The Marghīnānīs also came in after two or three days, having beaten and chased their commandant (*darogha*). Except Andijān, every fort south of the Khujand-water had now come in to us. Spite of the return in those days of so many forts, and spite of risings and revolt against him, Taṃbal did not yet come to his senses but sat down with an army of horse and foot, fortified with ditch and branch, to face The Khāns, between Karnān and Akhsī. Several times over there was a little fighting and pell-mell but without decided success to either side.

In the Andijān country (*wilāyat*), most of the tribes and
Fol. 104*b*. hordes and the forts and all the districts had come in to me; naturally the Andijānīs also were wishing for me. They however could not find their means.

(*d. Bābur's attempt to enter Andijān frustrated by a mistake.*)

It occurred to me that if we went one night close to the town and sent a man in to discuss with the Khwāja[3] and notables, they might perhaps let us in somewhere. With this idea we rode out from Aūsh. By midnight we were opposite Forty-daughters (Chihil-dukhterān) 2 miles (one *kuroh*) from Andijān. From that place we sent Qaṃbar-'alī Beg forward,

[1] *Alāī-līq aūrchīnī*. I understand the march to have been along the northern slope of the Little Alāī, south of Aūsh.

[2] As of Ālmālīgh and Ālmātū (fol. 2*b*) Bābur reports a tradition with caution. The name Aūz-kint may be read to mean 'Own village,' independent, as *Aūz-beg*, Own-beg.

[3] He would be one of the hereditary Khwājas of Andijān (f. 16).

with some other begs, who were to discuss matters with the Khwāja after by some means or other getting a man into the fort. While waiting for their return, we sat on our horses, some of us patiently humped up, some wrapt away in dream, when suddenly, at about the third watch, there rose a war-cry[1] and a sound of drums. Sleepy and startled, ignorant whether the foe was many or few, my men, without looking to one another, took each his own road and turned for flight. There was no time for me to get at them; I went straight for the enemy. Only Mīr Shāh *Qūchīn* and Bābā Sher-zād (Tiger-whelp) and Nāṣir's Dost sprang forward; we four excepted, every man set his face for flight. I had gone a little way forward, when the enemy rode rapidly up, flung out his war-cry and poured arrows on us. One man, on a horse with a starred forehead,[2] came close to me; I shot at it; it rolled over and died. They made a little as if to retire. The three Fol. 105.
with me said, 'In this darkness it is not certain whether they are many or few; all our men have gone off; what harm could we four do them? Fighting must be when we have overtaken our run-aways and rallied them.' Off we hurried, got up with our men and beat and horse-whipped some of them, but, do what we would, they would not make a stand. Back the four of us went to shoot arrows at the foe. They drew a little back but when, after a discharge or two, they saw we were not more than three or four, they busied themselves in chasing and unhorsing my men. I went three or four times to try to rally my men but all in vain! They were not to be brought to order. Back I went with my three and kept the foe in check with our arrows. They pursued us two or three *kuroh* (4-6 m.), as far as the rising ground opposite Kharābūk and Pashāmūn. There we met Muḥ. 'Alī *Mubashir*. Said I, 'They are only few; let us stop and put our horses at them.' So we did. When we got up to them, they stood still.[3]

Our scattered braves gathered in from this side and that, but

[1] For several battle-cries *see* Th. Radloff's *Réceuils* etc. p. 322.

[2] *qāshqa ātliq kishī*. For a parallel phrase *see* f. 92*b*.

[3] Bābur does not explain how the imbroglio was cleared up; there must have been a dramatic moment when this happened.

several very serviceable men, scattering in this attack, went right away to Aūsh.

The explanation of the affair seemed to be that some of Ayūb *Begchīk's* Mughūls had slipped away from Aūsh to raid near Andijān and, hearing the noise of our troop, came somewhat stealthily towards us; then there seems to have been confusion about the pass-word. The pass-words settled on for use during this movement of ours were Tāshkīnt and Sairām. If

Fol. 105*b*. (*Author's note on pass-words.*) Pass-words are of two kinds;—in each tribe there is one for use in the tribe, such as *Darwāna* or *Tūqqāī* or *Lūlū*;[1] and there is one for the use of the whole army. For a battle, two words are settled on as pass-words so that of two men meeting in the fight, one may give the one, the other give back the second, in order to distinguish friends from foes, own men from strangers.

Tāshkīnt were said, Sairām would be answered; if Sairām, Tāshkīnt. In this muddled affair, Khwāja Muḥ. 'Ali seems to have been somewhat in advance of our party and to have got bewildered,—he was a Sārt person,[2]—when the Mughūls came up saying, 'Tāshkīnt, Tāshkīnt,' for he gave them 'Tāshkīnt, Tāshkīnt,' as the counter-sign. Through this they took him for an enemy, raised their war-cry, beat their saddle-drums and poured arrows on us. It was through this we gave way, and through this false alarm were scattered! We went back to Aūsh.

(*e. Bābur again attempts Andijān.*)

Through the return to me of the forts and the highland and lowland clans, Tambal and his adherents lost heart and footing. His army and people in the next five or six days began to desert him and to flee to retired places and the open country.[3] Of his household some came and said, 'His affairs are nearly ruined; he will break up in three or four days, utterly ruined.' On hearing this, we rode for Andijān.

[1] *Darwāna* (a trap-door in a roof) has the variant *dur-dāna*, a single pearl; *tūqqāī* perhaps implies relationship; *lūlū* is a pearl, a wild cow etc.

[2] Ḥai. MS. *sāirt kīshī*. Muḥ. 'Alī is likely to be the librarian (*cf.* index *s.n.*).

[3] Elph. MS. *ramāqgha u tūr-gā*; Ḥai. MS. *tārtātgha u tūr-gā*. Ilminsky gives no help, varying much here from the true text. The archetype of both MSS. must have been difficult to read.

Sl. Muḥ. *Galpuk*[1] was in Andijān,—the younger of Taṃbal's cadet brothers. We took the Mulberry-road and at the Mid-day Prayer came to the Khākān (canal), south of the town. A foraging-party was arranged; I followed it along Khākān to the skirt of 'Aīsh-hill. When our scouts brought word that Sl. Muḥ *Galpuk* had come out, with what men he had, beyond the suburbs and gardens to the skirt of 'Aīsh, I hurried to meet him, although our foragers were still scattered. He may have had over 500 men; we had more but many had scattered to forage. When we were face to face, his men and ours may have been in equal number. Without caring about order or array, down we rode on them, loose rein, at the gallop. When we got near, they could not stand; there was not so much fighting as the crossing of a few swords. My men followed them almost to the Khākān Gate, unhorsing one after another. Fol. 106.

It was at the Evening Prayer that, our foe outmastered, we reached Khwāja Kitta, on the outskirts of the suburbs. My idea was to go quickly right up to the Gate but Dost Beg's father, Nāṣir Beg and Qaṃbar-'alī Beg, old and experienced begs both, represented to me, 'It is almost night; it would be ill-judged to go in a body into the fort in the dark; let us withdraw a little and dismount. What can they do to-morrow but surrender the place?' Yielding at once to the opinion of these experienced persons, we forthwith retired to the outskirts of the suburbs. If we had gone to the Gate, undoubtedly, Andijān Fol. 106*b*. would have come into our hands.

(*f. Bābur surprised by Taṃbal.*)

After crossing the Khākān-canal, we dismounted, near the Bed-time prayer, at the side of the village of Rabāṭ-i-zauraq (var. rūzaq). Although we knew that Taṃbal had broken camp and was on his way to Andijān, yet, with the negligence of inexperience, we dismounted on level ground close to the village, instead of where the defensive canal would have protected us.[2] There we lay down carelessly, without scouts or rear-ward.

[1] The Ḥai. MS.'s pointing allows the sobriquet to mean 'Butterfly.' His family lent itself to nick-names; in it three brothers were known respectively as Fat or Lubberly, Fool and, perhaps, Butterfly.

[2] *birk ārigh*, doubly strong by its trench and its current.

At the top (*bāsh*) of the morning, just when men are in sweet sleep, Qambar-'alī Beg hurried past, shouting, 'Up with you! the enemy is here!' So much he said and went off without a moment's stay. It was my habit to lie down, even in times of peace, in my tunic; up I got instanter, put on sword and quiver and mounted. My standard-bearer had no time to adjust my standard,[1] he just mounted with it in his hand. There were ten or fifteen men with me when we started toward the enemy; after riding an arrow's flight, when we came up with his scouts, there may have been ten. Going rapidly forward, we overtook him, poured in arrows on him, over-mastered his foremost men and hurried them off. We followed them for another arrow's flight and came up with his centre where Sl. Aḥmad *Tambal* himself was, with as many as
Fol. 107. 100 men. He and another were standing in front of his array, as if keeping a Gate,[2] and were shouting, 'Strike, strike!' but his men, mostly, were sidling, as if asking themselves, 'Shall we run away? Shall we not?' By this time three were left with me; one was Nāṣir's Dost, another, Mīrzā Qulī *Kūkūldāsh*, the third, Khudāī-bīrdī *Turkmān's* Karīm-dād.[3] I shot off the arrow on my thumb,[4] aiming at Tambal's helm. When I put my hand into my quiver, there came out a quite new *gosha-gīr*[5]

[1] I understand that time failed to set the standard in its usual rest. E. and de C. have understood that the yak-tail (*qūtās tūghī* f. 100) was apart from the staff and that time failed to adjust the two parts. The *tūgh* however is the whole standard; moreover if the tail were ever taken off at night from the staff, it would hardly be so treated in a mere bivouac.

[2] *aīshiklik tūrlūq*, as on f. 113. I understand this to mean that the two men were as far from their followers as sentries at a Gate are posted outside the Gate.

[3] So too 'Piero of Cosimo' and 'Lorenzo of Piero of the Medici.' *Cf.* the names of five men on f. 114.

[4] *shashtīm*. The *shasht* (thumb) in archery is the thumb-shield used on the left hand, as the *zih-gīr* (string-grip), the archer's ring, is on the right-hand thumb.

It is useful to remember, when reading accounts of shooting with the Turkī (Turkish) bow, that the arrows (*aūq*) had notches so gripping the string that they kept in place until released with the string.

[5] *sar-i-sabz gosha gīr*. The *gosha-gīr* is an implement for remedying the warp of a bow-tip and string-notch. For further particulars *see* Appendix C.

The term *sar-i-sabz*, lit. green-head, occurs in the sense of 'quite young' or 'new,' in the proverb, 'The red tongue loses the green head,' quoted in the *Tabaqāt-i-akbarī* account of Bābur's death. Applied here, it points to the *gosha-gīr* as part of the recent gift made by Aḥmad to Bābur.

given me by my Younger Khān dādā. It would have been vexing to throw it away but before I got it back into the quiver, there had been time to shoot, maybe, two or three arrows. When once more I had an arrow on the string, I went forward, my three men even holding back. One of those two in advance, Tambal seemingly,[1] moved forward also. The high-road was between us; I from my side, he, from his, got upon it and came face to face, in such a way that his right hand was towards me, mine towards him. His horse's mail excepted, he was fully accoutred; but for sword and quiver, I was unprotected. I shot off the arrow in my hand, adjusting for the attachment of his shield. With matters in this position, they shot my right leg through. I had on the cap of my helm;[2] Tambal chopped Fol. 107b. so violently at my head that it lost all feeling under the blow. A large wound was made on my head, though not a thread of the cap was cut.[3] I had not bared[4] my sword; it was in the scabbard and I had no chance to draw it. Single-handed, I was alone amongst many foes. It was not a time to stand still; I turned rein. Down came a sword again; this time on my arrows. When I had gone 7 or 8 paces, those same three men rejoined me.[5] After using his sword on me, Tambal seems to have used it on Nāṣir's Dost. As far as an arrrow flies to the butt, the enemy followed us.

The Khākān-canal is a great main-channel, flowing in a deep cutting, not everywhere to be crossed. God brought it right! we came exactly opposite a low place where there was a passage over. Directly we had crossed, the horse Nāṣir's Dost was on, being somewhat weakly, fell down. We stopped and re-mounted him, then drew off for Aūsh, over the rising-ground

[1] *Tambal aikāndūr.* By this tense I understand that Bābur was not at first sure of the identity of the pseudo-sentries, partly because of their distance, partly, it may be presumed, because of concealment of identity by armour.

[2] *dūwulgha būrkī*; *i.e.* the soft cap worn under the iron helm.

[3] Nūyān's sword dealt the blow (f. 97*b*). Gul-badan also tells the story (f. 77) à propos of a similar incident in Humāyūn's career. Bābur repeats the story on f. 234.

[4] *yāldāghlāmāi dūr aīdīm.* The Second W.-i-B. has taken this as from *yāltūrmāq*, to cause to glisten, and adds the gloss that the sword was rusty (I.O. 217 f. 70*b*).

[5] The text here seems to say that the three men were on foot, but this is negatived by the context.

between Farāghīna and Khirābūk. Out on the rise, Mazīd Ṭaghāī came up and joined us. An arrow had pierced his right leg also and though it had not gone through and come out again, he got to Aūsh with difficulty. The enemy unhorsed (*tūshūrdīlār*) good men of mine; Nāṣir Beg, Muḥ. 'Alī *Mubashir*, Khwāja Muḥ. 'Alī, Khusrau *Kūkūldāsh*, Na'man the page, all fell (to them, *tūshtīlār*), and also many unmailed braves.[1]

(*g. The Khāns move from Kāsān to Andijān.*)

The Khāns, closely following on Tambal, dismounted near Andijān,—the Elder at the side of the Reserve (*qūrūq*) in the
Fol. 108. garden, known as Birds'-mill (*Qūsh-tīgīrmān*), belonging to my grandmother, Aīsān-daulat Begīm,—the Younger, near Bābā Tawakkul's Alms-house. Two days later I went from Aūsh and saw the Elder Khān in Birds'-mill. At that interview, he simply gave over to the Younger Khān the places which had come in to me. He made some such excuse as that for our advantage, he had brought the Younger Khān, how far! because such a foe as Shaibāq Khān had taken Samarkand and was waxing greater; that the Younger Khān had there no lands whatever, his own being far away; and that the country under Andijān, on the south of the Khujand-water, must be given him to encamp in. He promised me the country under Akhsī, on the north of the Khujand-water. He said that after taking a firm grip of that country (Farghāna), they would move, take Samarkand, give it to me and then the whole of the Farghāna country was to be the Younger Khān's. These words seem to have been meant to deceive me, since there is no knowing what they would have done when they had attained their object. It had to be however! willy-nilly, I agreed.

When, leaving him, I was on my way to the Younger Khān's presence, Qambar-'alī, known as the Skinner, joined me in a friendly way and said, 'Do you see? They have taken the whole of the country just become yours. There is no opening

[1] Amongst the various uses of the verb *tūshmak*, to descend in any way, the B.N. does not allow of 'falling (death) in battle.' When I made the index of the Ilai. MS. facsimile, this was not known to me; I therefore erroneously entered the men enumerated here as killed at this time.

for you through them. You have in your hands Aūsh, Marghīnān, Aūzkīnt and the cultivated land and the tribes and the hordes; go you to Aūsh; make that fort fast; send a man to Tambal, make peace with him, then strike at the Mughūl and drive him out. After that, divide the districts into an elder and a younger brother's shares.' 'Would that be right?' said I. 'The Khāns are my blood relations; better serve them than rule for Tambal.' He saw that his words had made no impression, so turned back, sorry he had spoken. I went on to see my Younger Khān Dādā. At our first interview, I had come upon him without announcement and he had no time to dismount, so it was all rather unceremonious. This time I got even nearer perhaps, and he ran out as far as the end of the tent-ropes. I was walking with some difficulty because of the wound in my leg. We met and renewed acquaintance; then he said, 'You are talked about as a hero, my young brother!' took my arm and led me into his tent. The tents pitched were rather small and through his having grown up in an out-of-the-way place, he let the one he sat in be neglected; it was like a raider's, melons, grapes, saddlery, every sort of thing, in his sitting-tent. I went from his presence straight back to my own camp and there he sent his Mughūl surgeon to examine my wound. Mughūls call a surgeon also a *bakhshī;* this one was called Ātākā Bakhshī.[1] Fol. 108*b*.

He was a very skilful surgeon; if a man's brains had come out, he would cure it, and any sort of wound in an artery he easily healed. For some wounds his remedy was in form of a plaister, for some medicines had to be taken. He ordered a bandage tied on[2] the wound in my leg and put no seton in; once he made me eat something like a fibrous root (*yīldīz*). He told me himself, 'A certain man had his leg broken in the slender part and the bone was shattered for the breadth of the hand. I cut the flesh open and took the bits of bone out. Where they had been, I put a remedy in powder-form. That Fol. 109.

[1] Elph. MS. *yakhshī*. Zenker explains *bakhshi* (pay-master) as meaning also a Court-physician.

[2] The Ḥai. Elph. and Kehr's MS. all have *pūchqāq tāqmāq* or it may be *pūhqāq tāqmāq*. T. *būkhāq* means bandage, *pūchāq*, rind of fruit, but the word clear in the three Turkī MSS. means, skin of a fox's leg.

remedy simply became bone where there had been bone before.' He told many strange and marvellous things such as surgeons in cultivated lands cannot match.

Three or four days later, Qaṃbar-'alī, afraid on account of what he had said to me, fled (to Taṃbal) in Andijān. A few days later, The Khāns joined to me Ayūb *Begchīk* with his *tūmān*, and Jān-ḥasan *Bārīn* with the Bārīn *tūmān* and, as their army-beg, Sārīgh-bāsh Mīrzā,—1000 to 2000 men in all, and sent us towards Akhsī.

(*h. Bābur's expedition to Akhsī.*)

Shaikh Bāyazīd, a younger brother of Taṃbal, was in Akhsī; Shahbāz *Qārlūq* was in Kāsān. At the time, Shahbāz was lying before Nū-kīnt fort; crossing the Khujand-water opposite Bīkhrātā, we hurried to fall upon him there. When, a little Fol. 109*b*. before dawn, we were nearing the place, the begs represented to me that as the man would have had news of us, it was advisable not to go on in broken array. We moved on therefore with less speed. Shahbāz may have been really unaware of us until we were quite close; then getting to know of it, he fled into the fort. It often happens so! Once having said, 'The enemy is on guard!' it is easily fancied true and the chance of action is lost. In short, the experience of such things is that no effort or exertion must be omitted, once the chance for action comes. After-repentance is useless. There was a little fighting round the fort at dawn but we delivered no serious attack.

For the convenience of foraging, we moved from Nū-kīnt towards the hills in the direction of Bīshkhārān. Seizing his opportunity, Shahbāz *Qārlūq* abandoned Nū-kīnt and returned to Kāsān. We went back and occupied Nū-kīnt. During those days, the army several times went out and over-ran all sides and quarters. Once they over-ran the villages of Akhsī, once those of Kāsān. Shahbāz and Long Ḥasan's adopted son, Mīrīm came out of Kāsān to fight; they fought, were beaten, and there Mīrīm died.

(l. Bābur attempts to defend Akhsī.)

Early one morning, when I was in the Hot-bath, Jahāngīr Mīrzā came into Akhsī, from Marghīnān, a fugitive from Tambal. We saw one another, Shaikh Bāyazīd also being present, agitated and afraid. The Mīrzā and Ibrāhīm Beg said, 'Shaikh Bāyazīd must be made prisoner and we must get the citadel into our hands.' In good sooth, the proposal was wise. Said I, 'Promise has been made; how can we break it?' Shaikh Bāyazīd went into the citadel. Men ought to have been posted on the bridge; not even there did we post any-one! These blunders were the fruit of inexperience. At the top of the morning came Tambal himself with 2 or 3000 men in mail, crossed the bridge and went into the citadel. To begin with I had had rather few men; when I first went into Akhsī some had been sent to other forts and some had been made commandants and summoners all round. Left with me in Akhsī may have been something over 100 men. We had got to horse with these and were posting braves at the top of one lane after another and making ready for the fight, when Shaikh Bāyazīd and Qambar-'alī (the Skinner), and Muhammad-dost[1] came gallopping from Tambal with talk of peace. Fol. 111b.

After posting those told off for the fight, each in his appointed place, I dismounted at my father's tomb for a conference, in which I invited Jahāngīr Mīrzā to join. Muhammad-dost went back to Tambal but Qambar-'alī and Shaikh Bāyazīd were present. We sat in the south porch of the tomb and were in consultation when the Mīrzā, who must have settled beforehand with Ibrāhīm *Chāpūk* to lay hands on those other two, said in my ear, 'They must be made prisoner.' Said I, 'Don't hurry! matters are past making prisoners. See here! with terms made, the affair might be coaxed into something. For why? Not only are they many and we few, but they with their strength are in the citadel, we with our weakness, in the outer fort.' Shaikh Bāyazīd and Qambar-'alī both being present, Jahāngīr Mīrzā looked at Ibrāhīm Beg and made him a sign to refrain. Whether he misunderstood to the contrary

[1] 'Alī-dost's son (f. 79b).

or whether he pretended to misunderstand, is not known; suddenly he did the ill-deed of seizing Shaikh Bāyazīd. Braves
Fol. 112. closing in from all sides, flung those two to the ground. Through this the affair was taken past adjustment; we gave them into charge and got to horse for the coming fight.

One side of the town was put into Jahāngīr Mīrzā's charge; as his men were few, I told off some of mine to reinforce him. I went first to his side and posted men for the fight, then to other parts of the town. There is a somewhat level, open space in the middle of Akhsī; I had posted a party of braves there and gone on when a large body of the enemy, mounted and on foot, bore down upon them, drove them from their post and forced them into a narrow lane. Just then I came up (the lane), gallopped my horse at them, and scattered them in flight. While I was thus driving them out from the lane into the flat, and had got my sword to work, they shot my horse in the leg; it stumbled and threw me there amongst them. I got up quickly and shot one arrow off. My squire, Kahil (lazy) had a weakly pony; he got off and led it to me. Mounting this, I started for another lane-head. Sl. Muḥ. Wais noticed the weakness of my mount, dismounted and led me his own. I mounted that horse. Just then, Qāsim Beg's son, Qambar-'alī came, wounded, from Jahāngīr Mīrzā and said the Mīrzā had
Fol. 112*b*. been attacked some time before, driven off in panic, and had gone right away. We were thunderstruck! At the same moment arrived Sayyid Qāsim, the commandant of Pāp! His was a most unseasonable visit, since at such a crisis it was well to have such a strong fort in our hands. Said I to Ibrāhīm Beg, 'What's to be done now?' He was slightly wounded; whether because of this or because of stupefaction, he could give no useful answer. My idea was to get across the bridge, destroy it and make for Andijān. Bābā Sher-zād did very well here. 'We will storm out at the gate and get away at once,' he said. At his word, we set off for the Gate. Khwāja Mīr Mīrān also spoke boldly at that crisis. In one of the lanes, Sayyid Qāsim and Nāṣir's Dost chopped away at Bāqī *Khīz*,[1] I being in front with Ibrāhīm Beg and Mīrzā Qulī *Kūkūldāsh*.

[1] The sobriquet *Khīz* may mean Leaper, or Impetuous.

(*i. The affairs of Pāp.*)

Pāp is a strong fort belonging to Akhsī. The Pāpīs made it fast and sent a man to me. We accordingly sent Sayyid Qāsim with a few braves to occupy it. They crossed the river Fol. 110. (*daryā*) opposite the upper villages of Akhsī and went into Pāp.[1] A few days later, Sayyid Qāsim did an astonishing thing. There were at the time with Shaikh Bāyazīd in Akhsi, Ibrāhīm *Chāpūk* (Slash-face) Ṭaghāī,[2] Aḥmad-of-qāsim *Kohbur*, and Qāsim Khitika (?) *Arghūn*. To these Shaikh Bāyazīd joins 200 serviceable braves and one night sends them to surprise Pāp. Sayyid Qāsim must have lain down carelessly to sleep, without setting a watch. They reach the fort, set ladders up, get up on the Gate, let the drawbridge down and, when 70 or 80 good men in mail are inside, goes the news to Sayyid Qāsim! Drowsy with sleep, he gets into his vest (*kūnglāk*), goes out, with five or six of his men, charges the enemy and drives them out with blow upon blow. He cut off a few heads and sent to me. Though such a careless lying down was bad leadership, yet, with so few, just by force of drubbing, to chase off such a mass of men in mail was very brave indeed.

Meantime The Khāns were busy with the siege of Andijān but the garrison would not let them get near it. The Andijān braves used to make sallies and blows would be exchanged.

(*j. Bābur invited into Akhsī.*)

Shaikh Bāyazīd now began to send persons to us from Akhsī to testify to well-wishing and pressingly invite us to Akhsī. His object was to separate me from The Khāns, by any artifice, because without me, they had no standing-ground. Fol. 110*b* His invitation may have been given after agreeing with his elder brother, Taṃbal that if I were separated from The Khāns, it might be possible, in my presence, to come to some arrange-

[1] The *daryā* here mentioned seems to be the Kāsān-water ; the route taken from Bīshkhārān to Pāp is shewn on the Fr. map to lead past modern Tūpa-qūrghān. Pāp is not marked, but was, I think, at the cross-roads east of Touss (Karnān).

[2] Presumably Jahāngīr's.

ment with them. We gave The Khāns a hint of the invitation. They said, 'Go! and by whatever means, lay hands on Shaikh Bāyazīd.' It was not my habit to cheat and play false; here above all places, when promises would have been made, how was I to break them? It occurred to me however, that if we could get into Akhsī, we might be able, by using all available means, to detach Shaikh Bāyazīd from Taṃbal, when he might take my side or something might turn up to favour my fortunes. We, in our turn, sent a man to him; compact was made, he invited us into Akhsī and when we went, came out to meet us, bringing my younger brother, Nāṣir Mīrzā with him. Then he took us into the town, gave us ground to camp in (*yūrt*) and to me one of my father's houses in the outer fort[1] where I dismounted.

(*k. Taṃbal asks help of Shaibāq Khān.*)

Taṃbal had sent his elder brother, Beg Tīlba, to Shaibāq Khān with proffer of service and invitation to enter Farghāna. At this very time Shaibāq Khān's answer arrived; 'I will come,' he wrote. On hearing this, The Khāns were all upset; they could sit no longer before Andijān and rose from before it.

The Younger Khān himself had a reputation for justice and orthodoxy, but his Mughūls, stationed, contrary to the expectations of the towns-people, in Aūsh, Marghīnān and other places,—places that had come in to me,—began to behave ill

Fol. 111. and oppressively. When The Khāns had broken up from before Andijān, the Aūshīs and Marghīnānīs, rising in tumult, seized the Mughūls in their forts, plundered and beat them, drove them out and pursued them.

The Khāns did not cross the Khujand-water (for the Kīndīrlīk-pass) but left the country by way of Marghīnān and Kand-i-badām and crossed it at Khujand, Taṃbal pursuing them as far as Marghīnān. We had had much uncertainty; we had not had much confidence in their making any stand, yet for us to go away, without clear reason, and leave them, would not have looked well.

[1] Here his father was killed (f. 6*b*). *Cf.* App. A.

passed it by and turned straight up its water. In this position of our affairs there were eight men of us;—Nāṣir's Dost, Qāsim Beg's Qambar-'alī, Bayān-qulī's Khān-qulī, Mīrzā Qulī *Kūkūldāsh*, Nāṣir's Shāham, Sayyidī Qarā's 'Abdu'l-qadūs, Khwāja Ḥusainī and myself, the eighth. Turning up the stream, we found, in the broad valley, a good little road, far from the beaten track. We made straight up the valley, leaving the stream on the right, reached its waterless part and, near the Afternoon Prayer, got up out of it to level land. When we looked across the plain, we saw a blackness on it, far away. I made my party take cover and myself had gone to look out from higher ground, when a number of men came at a gallop up the hill behind us. Without waiting to know whether they were many or few, we mounted and rode off. There were 20 or 25; we, as has been said, were eight. If we had known their number at first, we should have made a good stand against them but we thought they would not be pursuing us, unless they had good support behind. A fleeing foe, even if he be many, cannot face a few pursuers, for as the saying is, '*Hāī* is enough for the beaten ranks.'[1] Fol. 114*b*.

Khān-qulī said, 'This will never do! They will take us all. From amongst the horses there are, you take two good ones and go quickly on with Mīrzā Qulī *Kūkūldāsh*, each with a led horse. May-be you will get away.' He did not speak ill; as there was no fighting to hand, there was a chance of safety in doing as he said, but it really would not have looked well to leave any man alone, without a horse, amongst his foes. In the end they all dropped off, one by one, of themselves. My horse was a little tired; Khān-qulī dismounted and gave me his; I jumped off at once and mounted his, he mine. Just then they unhorsed Sayyidī Qarā's 'Abdu'l-qadūs and Nāṣir's Shāham who had fallen behind. Khān-qulī also was left. It was no time to profer help or defence; on it was gone, at the full speed of our mounts. The horses began to flag; Dost Beg's failed and stopped. Mine began to tire; Qambar-'alī got off

[1] In the Turkī text this saying is in Persian; in the Kehr-Ilminsky, in Turkī, as though it had gone over with its Persian context of the W.-i-B. from which the K.-I. text here is believed to be a translation.

and gave me his; I mounted his, he mine. He was left. Khwāja Ḥusainī was a lame man; he turned aside to the higher ground. I was left with Mīrzā Qulī *Kūkūldāsh*. Our
Fol. 115. horses could not possibly gallop, they trotted. His began to flag. Said I, 'What will become of me, if you fall behind? Come along! let's live or die together.' Several times I looked back at him; at last he said, 'My horse is done! It can't go on. Never mind me! You go on, perhaps you will get away.' It was a miserable position for me; he remained behind, I was alone.

Two of the enemy were in sight, one Bābā of Sairām, the other Banda-'alī. They gained on me; my horse was done; the mountains were still 2 miles (1 *kuroh*) off. A pile of rock was in my path. Thought I to myself, 'My horse is worn out and the hills are still somewhat far away; which way should I go? In my quiver are at least 20 arrows; should I dismount and shoot them off from this pile of rock?' Then again, I thought I might reach the hills and once there, stick a few arrows in my belt and scramble up. I had a good deal of confidence in my feet and went on, with this plan in mind. My horse could not possibly trot; the two men came within arrow's reach.
Fol. 115*b*. For my own sake sparing my arrows, I did not shoot; they, out of caution, came no nearer. By sunset I was near the hills. Suddenly they called out, 'Where are you going in this fashion? Jahāngīr Mīrzā has been brought in a prisoner; Nāṣir Mīrzā also is in their hands.' I made no reply and went on towards the hills. When a good distance further had been gone, they spoke again, this time more respectfully, dismounting to speak. I gave no ear to them but went on up a glen till, at the Bed-time prayer, I reached a rock as big as a house. Going behind it, I saw there were places to be jumped, where no horse could go. They dismounted again and began to speak like servants and courteously. Said they, 'Where are you going in this fashion, without a road and in the dark? Sl. Aḥmad Tambal will make you *pādshāh*.' They swore this. Said I, 'My mind is not easy as to that. I cannot go to him.
Fol 116. If you think to do me timely service, years may pass before you have such another chance. Guide me to a road by which

As we came opposite the Gate, we saw Shaikh Bāyazīd, wearing his pull-over shirt[1] above his vest, coming in with three or four horsemen. He must have been put into the charge of Jahāngīr's men in the morning when, against my will, he was made prisoner, and they must have carried him off when they got away. They had thought it would be well to kill him; they set him free alive. He had been released just when I chanced upon him in the Gate. I drew and shot off the arrow on my thumb; it grazed his neck, a good shot! He came confusedly in at the Gate, turned to the right and fled down a lane. We followed him instantly. Mīrzā Qulī *Kūkūldāsh* got at one man with his rugged-mace and went on. Another man took Fol. 113.
aim at Ibrāhīm Beg, but when the Beg shouted 'Hāī! Hāī!' let him pass and shot me in the arm-pit, from as near as a man on guard at a Gate. Two plates of my Qālmāq mail were cut; he took to flight and I shot after him. Next I shot at a man running away along the ramparts, adjusting for his cap against the battlements; he left his cap nailed on the wall and went off, gathering his turban-sash together in his hand. Then again,—a man was in flight alongside me in the lane down which Shaikh Bāyazīd had gone. I pricked the back of his head with my sword; he bent over from his horse till he leaned against the wall of the lane, but he kept his seat and with some trouble, made good his flight. When we had driven all the enemy's men from the Gate, we took possession of it but the affair was past discussion because they, in the citadel, were 2000 or 3000, we, in the outer fort, 100 or 200. Moreover they had chased off Jahāngīr Mīrzā, as long before as it takes milk to boil, and with him had gone half my men. This notwithstanding, we sent a man, while we were in the Gate, to say to him, 'If you are near at hand, come, let us attack again.' But the matter had gone past that! Ibrāhīm Beg, either because his horse was really weak or because of his wound, said, 'My horse is done.' On this, Sulaimān, one of Muḥ. 'Alī's *Mubashir's* servants, did a plucky thing, for with matters Fol. 113*b*.
as they were and none constraining him, while we were wait-

[1] *kūilāk*, syn. *kūnglāk*, a shirt not opening at the breast. It will have been a short garment since the under-vest was visible.

ing in the Gate, he dismounted and gave his horse to Ibrāhīm Beg. Kīchīk (little) 'Alī, now the Governor of Koel,[1] also shewed courage while we were in the Gate; he was a retainer of Sl. Muḥ. Wais and twice did well, here and in Aūsh. We delayed in the Gate till those sent to Jahāngīr Mīrzā came back and said he had gone off long before. It was too late to stay there; off we flung; it was ill-judged to have stayed as long as we did. Twenty or thirty men were with me. Just as we hustled out of the Gate, a number of armed men[2] came right down upon us, reaching the town-side of the drawbridge just as we had crossed. Banda-'alī, the maternal grandfather of Qāsim Beg's son, Ḥamza, called out to Ibrāhīm Beg, 'You are always boasting of your *zeal*! Let's take to our swords!' 'What hinders? Come along!' said Ibrāhīm Beg, from beside me. The senseless fellows were for displaying their *zeal* at a time of such disaster! Ill-timed *zeal*! That was no time to make stand or delay! We went off quickly, the enemy following and unhorsing our men.

(m. Bābur a fugitive before Taṃbal's men.)

When we were passing Meadow-dome (Guṃbaz-i-chaman), two miles out of Akhsī, Ibrāhīm Beg called out to me. Looking
Fol. 114. back, I saw a page of Shaikh Bāyazīd's striking at him and turned rein, but Bayān-qulī's Khān-qulī, said at my side, 'This is a bad time for going back,' seized my rein and pushed ahead. Many of our men had been unhorsed before we reached Sang, 4 miles (2 *shar'ī*) out of Akhsī.[3] Seeing no pursuers at Sang, we

[1] *i.e.* when Bābur was writing in Hindūstān. Exactly at what date he made this entry is not sure. 'Alī was in Koel in 933 AH. (f. 315) and then taken prisoner, but Bābur does not say he was killed,—as he well might say of a marked man, and, as the captor was himself taken shortly after, 'Alī may have been released, and may have been in Koel again. So that the statement 'now in Koel' may refer to a time later than his capture. The interest of the point is in its relation to the date of composition of the *Bābur-nāma*.

No record of 'Alī's bravery in Aūsh has been preserved. The reference here made to it may indicate something attempted in 908 AH. after Bābur's adventure in Karnān (f. 118*b*) or in 909 AH. from Sūkh. *Cf.* Translator's note f. 118*b*.

[2] *aūpchīnlīk*. Vambéry, *gepanzert*; Shaw, four horse-shoes and their nails; Steingass, *aūpcha-khāna*, a guard-house.

[3] Sang is a ferry-station (Kostenko, i, 213). Pāp may well have been regretted (f. 109*b* and f. 112*b*)! The well-marked features of the French map of 1904 allows Bābur's flight to be followed.

Near the Evening Prayer, a horseman passed from the direction of Karnān for Ghawā. 'Who are you?' we asked. He made some reply. He must have been Muḥ. Bāqir Beg himself, on his way from where we had seen him earlier, going at night-fall to some other hiding-place, but he so changed his voice that, though he had been years with me, I did not know it. It would have been well if I had recognized him and he had joined me. His passing caused much anxiety and alarm; tryst could not be kept with Qādīr-bīrdī of Ghawā. Banda-'alī said, 'There are retired gardens in the suburbs of Karnān where no one will suspect us of being; let us go there and send to Qādīr-bīrdī and have him brought there.' With this idea, we mounted and went to the Karnān suburbs. It was winter and very cold. They found a worn, coarse sheepskin coat and brought it to me; I put it on. They brought me a bowl of millet-porridge; I ate it and was wonderfully refreshed. 'Have you sent off the man to Qādīr-bīrdī?' said I to Banda-'alī. 'I have sent,' he said. But those luckless, clownish mannikins seem to have agreed together to send the man to Tambal in Akhsī!

We went into a house and for awhile my eyes closed in sleep. Those mannikins artfully said to me, 'You must not bestir yourself to leave Karnān till there is news of Qādīr-bīrdī but this house is right amongst the suburbs; on the outskirts the orchards are empty; no-one will suspect if we go there.' Fol. 118. Accordingly we mounted at mid-night and went to a distant orchard. Bābā Sairāmī kept watch from the roof of a house. Near mid-day he came down and said, 'Commandant Yūsuf is coming.' Great fear fell upon me! 'Find out,' I said, 'whether he comes because he knows about me.' He went and after some exchange of words, came back and said, 'He says he met a foot-soldier in the Gate of Akhsī who said to him, "The pādshāh is in such a place," that he told no-one, put the man with Walī the Treasurer whom he had made prisoner in the fight, and then gallopped off here.' Said I, 'How does it strike you?' 'They are all your servants,' he said, 'you must go. What else can you do? They will make you their ruler.' Said I, 'After such rebellion and fighting,

with what confidence could I go?' We were saying this, when Yūsuf knelt before me, saying, 'Why should it be hidden? Sl. Aḥmad Tambal has no news of you, but Shaikh Bāyazīd has and he sent me here.' On hearing this, my state of mind was miserable indeed, for well is it understood that nothing in the world is worse than fear for one's life. 'Tell the truth!' I said, 'if the affair is likely to go on to worse, I will make
Fol. 118*b*. ablution.' Yūsuf swore oaths, but who would trust them? I knew the helplessness of my position. I rose and went to a corner of the garden, saying to myself, 'If a man live a hundred years or a thousand years, at the last nothing . . .'[1]

TRANSLATOR'S NOTE.

Friends are likely to have rescued Bābur from his dangerous isolation. His presence in Karnān was known both in Ghawā and in Akhsī; Muḥ. Bāqir Beg was at hand (f. 117); some of those he had dropped in his flight would follow him when their horses had had rest; Jahāngīr was somewhere north of the river with the half of Bābur's former force (f. 112); The Khāns, with their long-extended line of march, may have been on the main road through or near Karnān. If Yūsuf took Bābur as a prisoner along the Akhsī road, there were these various chances of his meeting friends.

His danger was evaded; he joined his uncles and was with them, leading 1000 men (Sh. N. p. 268), when they were defeated at Archīān just before or in the season of Cancer, *i.e. circa* June (T. R. p. 164). What he was doing between the winter cold of Karnān (f. 117*b*) and June might have been

[1] Here the Turkī text breaks off, as it might through loss of pages, causing a blank of narrative extending over some 16 months. *Cf.* App. D. for a passage, supposedly spurious, found with the Ḥaidarābād Codex and the Kehr-Ilminsky text, purporting to tell how Bābur was rescued from the risk in which the lacuna here leaves him.

I can go to The Khān's presence. If you will do this, I will shew you favour and kindness greater than your heart's-desire. If you will not do it, go back the way you came; that also would be to serve me well.' Said they, 'Would to God we had never come! But since we are here, after following you in the way we have done, how can we go back from you? If you will not go with us, we are at your service, wherever you go.' Said I, 'Swear that you speak the truth.' They, for their part, made solemn oath upon the Holy Book.

I at once confided in them and said, 'People have shewn me a road through a broad valley, somewhere near this glen; take me to it.' Spite of their oath, my trust in them was not so complete but that I gave them the lead and followed. After 2 to 4 miles (1-2 *kuroh*), we came to the bed of a torrent. 'This will not be the road for the broad valley,' I said. They drew back, saying, 'That road is a long way ahead,' but it really must have been the one we were on and they have been concealing the fact, in order to deceive me. About half through the night, we reached another stream. This time they said, 'We have been negligent; it now seems to us that the road through the broad valley is behind.' Said I, 'What is to be done?' Said they, 'The Ghawā road is certainly in front; by it people cross for Far-kat.[1] They guided me for that and we went on till in Fol. 116*b*. the third watch of the night we reached the Karnān gully which comes down from Ghawā. Here Bābā Sairāmī said, 'Stay here a little while I look along the Ghawā road.' He came back after a time and said, 'Some men have gone along that road, led by one wearing a Mughūl cap; there is no going that way.' I took alarm at these words. There I was, at dawn, in the middle of the cultivated land, far from the road I wanted to take. Said I, 'Guide me to where I can hide to-day, and tonight when you will have laid hands on something for the horses, lead me to cross the Khujand-water and along its further bank.' Said they, 'Over there, on the upland, there might be hiding.'

Banda-'alī was Commandant in Karnān. 'There is no doing without food for ourselves or our horses;' he said, 'let me go

[1] *Cf.* f. 96*b* and Fr. Map for route over the Kindīr-tau.

into Karnān and bring what I can find.' We stopped 2 miles (1 *kuroh*) out of Karnān; he went on. He was a long time away; near dawn there was no sign of him. The day had shot when he hurried up, bringing three loaves of bread but no corn for the horses. Each of us putting a loaf into the breast of his tunic, we went quickly up the rise, tethered our horses there in the open valley and went to higher ground, each to keep watch.
Fol. 117. Near mid-day, Aḥmad the Falconer went along the Ghawā road for Akhsī. I thought of calling to him and of saying, with promise and fair word, 'You take those horses,' for they had had a day and a night's strain and struggle, without corn, and were utterly done. But then again, we were a little uneasy as we did not entirely trust him. We decided that, as the men Babā Sairāmī had seen on the road would be in Karnān that night, the two with me should fetch one of their horses for each of us, and that then we should go each his own way.

At mid-day, a something glittering was seen on a horse, as far away as eye can reach. We were not able to make out at all what it was. It must have been Muḥ. Bāqir Beg himself; he had been with us in Akhsī and when we got out and scattered, he must have come this way and have been moving then to a hiding-place.[1]

Banda-'alī and Bābā Sairāmī said, 'The horses have had no corn for two days and two nights; let us go down into the dale and put them there to graze.' Accordingly we rode down and put them to the grass. At the Afternoon Prayer, a horseman passed along the rising-ground where we had been. We recognized him for Qādīr-bīrdī, the head-man of Ghawā. 'Call him,' I said. They called; he came. After questioning him, and speaking to him of favour and kindness, and giving him promise and fair word, I sent him to bring rope, and a grass-hook, and an axe, and material for crossing water,[2] and corn
Fol. 117*b*. for the horses, and food and, if it were possible, other horses. We made tryst with him for that same spot at the Bed-time Prayer.

[1] This account of Muḥ. Bāqir reads like one given later to Bābur; he may have had some part in Bābur's rescue (*cf.* Translator's Note to f. 118*b*).

[2] Perhaps reeds for a raft. Sh. N. p. 258, *Sāl aūchūn bār qāmīsh*, reeds are there also for rafts.

the sport of older men's intrigues, he had been tempered by failure, privation and dangers.

He left Sūkh intending to go to Sl. Ḥusain Mīrzā in Khurāsān but he changed this plan for one taking him to Kābul where a Tīmūrid might claim to dispossess the Arghūns, then holding it since the death, in 907 AH. of his uncle, Aūlūgh Beg Mīrzā *Kābulī*.

known from his lost pages. Muḥ. Ṣāliḥ writes at length of one affair falling within the time,—Jahāngīr's occupation of Khujand, its siege and its capture by Shaibānī. This capture will have occurred considerably more than a month before the defeat of The Khāns (Sh. N. p. 230).

It is not easy to decide in what month of 908 AH. they went into Farghāna or how long their campaign lasted. Bābur chronicles a series of occurrences, previous to the march of the army, which must have filled some time. The road over the Kīndīrlīk-pass was taken, one closed in Bābur's time (f. 1*b*) though now open through the winter. Looking at the rapidity of his own movements in Farghāna, it seems likely that the pass was crossed after and not before its closed time. If so, the campaign may have covered 4 or 5 months. Muḥ. Ṣāliḥ's account of Shaibāq's operations strengthens this view. News that Aḥmad had joined Maḥmūd in Tāshkīnt (f. 102) went to Shaibānī in Khusrau Shāh's territories; he saw his interests in Samarkand threatened by this combination of the Chaghatāī brothers to restore Bābur in Farghāna, came north therefore in order to help Tambal. He then waited a month in Samarkand (Sh. N. p. 230), besieged Jahāngīr, went back and stayed in Samarkand long enough to give his retainers time to equip for a year's campaigning (l. c. p. 244) then went to Akhsī and so to Archīān.

Bābur's statement (f. 110*b*) that The Khāns went from Andijān to the Khujand-crossing over the Sīr attracts attention because this they might have done if they had meant to leave Farghāna by Mīrzā-rabāṭ but they are next heard of as at Akhsī. Why did they make that great détour? Why not have crossed opposite Akhsī or at Sang? Or if they had thought of retiring, what turned them east again? Did they place Jahāngīr in Khujand? Bābur's missing pages would have answered these questions no doubt. It was useful for them to encamp where they did, east of Akhsī, because they there had near them a road by which reinforcement could come from Kāshghar or retreat be made. The Akhsī people told Shaibānī that he could easily overcome The Khāns if he went without warning, and if they had not withdrawn by the Kulja road (Sh. N. p. 262). By that road the few men who went with Aḥmad to Tāshkīnt (f. 103) may have been augmented to the force, enumerated as his in the battle by Muḥ. Ṣāliḥ (Sh. N. cap. LIII.).

When The Khāns were captured, Bābur escaped and made 'for Mughūlistān,' a vague direction seeming here to mean Tāshkīnt, but, finding his road blocked, in obedience to orders from Shaibāq that he and Abū'l-makāram were to be captured, he turned back and, by unfrequented ways, went into the hill-country of Sūkh and Hushīār. There he spent about a year in great misery (f. 14 and Ḥ. S. ii, 318). Of the wretchedness of the time Ḥaidar also writes. If anything was attempted in Farghāna in the course of those months, record of it has been lost with Bābur's missing pages. He was not only homeless and poor, but shut in by enemies. Only the loyalty or kindness of the hill-tribes can have saved him and his few followers. His mother was with him; so also were the families of his men. How Qūtlūq-nigār contrived to join him from Tāshkīnt, though historically a small matter, is one he would chronicle. What had happened there after the Mughūl defeat, was that the horde had marched away for Kāshghar while Shāh Begīm remained in charge of her daughters with whom the Aūzbeg chiefs intended to contract alliance. Shaibānī's orders for her stay and for the general exodus were communicated to her by her son, The Khān, in what Muḥ. Ṣāliḥ, quoting its purport, describes as a right beautiful letter (p. 296).

By some means Qūtlūq-nigār joined Bābur, perhaps helped by the circumstance that her daughter, Khān-zāda was Shaibāq's wife. She spent at least some part of those hard months with him, when his fortunes were at their lowest ebb. A move becoming imperative, the ragged and destitute company started in mid-June 1504 (Muḥ. 910 AH.) on that perilous mountain journey to which Ḥaidar applies the Prophet's dictum, 'Travel is a foretaste of Hell,' but of which the end was the establishment of a Tīmūrid dynasty in Hindūstān. To look down the years from the destitute Bābur to Akbar, Shāh-jahān and Aurangzīb is to see a great stream of human life flow from its source in his resolve to win upward, his quenchless courage and his abounding vitality. Not yet 22,

APPENDICES.

A.—THE SITE AND DISAPPEARANCE OF OLD AKHSI.

SOME modern writers, amongst whom are Dr. Schuyler, General Nalivkine and Mr. Pumpelly, have inferred from the Bābur-nāma account of Akhsī, (in its translations?) that the landslip through which Bābur's father died and the disappearance of old Akhsī were brought about by erosion. Seen by the light of modern information, this erosion theory does not seem to cover the whole ground and some other cause seems necessary in explanation of both events.

For convenience of reference, the Bābur-nāma passages required, are quoted here, with their translations.

Ḥai. MS. f. 4*b*. *Saiḥūn daryā-sī qūrghānī astīdin āqār. Qūrghānī baland jar austīdā wāqi' būlūb tūr. Khandaqī-nīng aūrunīgha 'umīq jārlār dūr. 'Umar Shaikh M. kīm mūnī pāy-takht qildī, bir īkī martaba tāshrāq-dīn yana jarlār sāldi.*

Of this the translations are as follows:—

(*a*) Pers. trans. (I.O. 217, f. 3*b*): *Daryā-i Saiḥūn az pāyhā qila'-i o mīrezad u qila'-i o bar jar balandī wāqi' shuda ba jāy khandaq jarhā-i 'umīq uftāda. ' U. Sh. M. kah ānrā pāy-takht sākhta, yak du martaba az bīrūn ham bāz jarhā andākht.*

(*b*) Erskine (p. 5, translating from the Persian): ' The river Saiḥūn flows under the walls of the castle. The castle is situated on a high precipice, and the steep ravines around serve instead of a moat. When U. Sh. M. made it his capital he, in one or two instances, scarped the ravines outside the fort.'

(*c*) De Courteille (i, 8, translating from Ilminsky's imprint, p. 6): ' Le Seihoun coule au pied de la fortresse qui se dresse sur le sommet d'un ravin, dont les profondeurs lui tiennent lieu d'un fossé. 'U. Sh. M. à l'époque où il en avait fait son capitale, avait augmenté à une ou deux réprises, les escarpements qui la ceignent naturellement.'

Concerning 'Umar Shaikh's death, the words needed are (f. 6*b*);—

Maẓhūr būlūb aīdī kīm Akhsī qūrghānī buland jar austīdā wāqi' būlūb tūr. 'Imāratlār jar yāqāsīdā aīrdī. . . . Mīrzā jardīn kabūtar u kabūlar-khāna bīla aūchūb shunqār būldī;—'It has been mentioned that the walled-town of Akhsī is situated above ravine(s). The royal dwellings are along a ravine. The Mīrzā, having flown with his pigeons and their house from the ravine, became a falcon (*i.e.* died).'

A few particulars about Akhsī will shew that, in the translations just quoted, certain small changes of wording are dictated by what, amongst other writers, Kostenko and von Schwarz have written about the oases of Turkistān.

The name Akhsī, as used by Ibn Haukal, Yāqūt and Bābur, describes an oasis township, *i.e.* a walled-town with its adjacent cultivated lands. In Yāqūt's time Akhsī had a second circumvallation, presumably less for defence than for the protection of crops against wild animals. The oasis was created by the Kāsān-water,[1] upon the riverain loess of the right and higher bank of the Saiḥūn (Sīr), on level ground west of the junction of the Nārīn and the Qarā-daryā, west too of spurs from the northern hills which now abut upon the river. Yāqūt locates it in the 12th century, at one *farsākh* (*circa* 4 m.) north of the river.[2] Depending as it did solely on the Kāsān-water, nothing dictated its location close to the Sīr, along which there is now, and there seems to have been in the 12th century, a strip of waste land. Bābur says of Akhsī what Kostenko says (i, 321) of modern Tāshkīnt, that it stood above ravines (*jarlār*). These were natural or artificial channels of the Kāsān-water.[3]

To turn now to the translations;—Mr. Erskine imaged Akhsī as a castle, high on a precipice in process of erosion by the Sīr. But Bābur's word, *qūrghān* means the walled-town; his for a castle is *ark*, citadel; and his *jar*, a cleft, is not rendered by 'precipice.' Again;—it is no more necessary to understand that

[1] Until the Yāngī-ārīq was taken off the Sīr, late in the last century, for Namangān, the oasis land of Farghāna was fertilized, not from the river but by its intercepted tributaries.

[2] Ujfalvy's translation ot Yāqūt (ii, 179) reads one *farsākh* from the mountains instead of 'north of the river.'

[3] Kostenko describes a division of Tāshkint, one in which is Ravine-lane (*jar-kucha*), as divided by a deep ravine; of another he says that it is cut by deep ravines (Bābur's *'umīq jarlār*).

the Sīr flowed close to the walls than it is to understand, when one says the Thames flows past below Richmond, that it washes the houses on the hill.

The key to the difficulties in the Turkī passage is provided by a special use of the word *jar* for not only natural ravines but artificial water-cuts for irrigation. This use of it makes clear that what 'Umar Shaikh did at Akhsī was not to make escarpments but to cut new water-channels. Presumably he joined those 'further out' on the deltaic fan, on the east and west of the town, so as to secure a continuous defensive cleft round the town[1] or it may be, in order to bring it more water.

Concerning the historic pigeon-house (f. 6*b*), it can be said safely that it did not fall into the Sīr; it fell from a *jar*, and in this part of its course, the river flows in a broad bed, with a low left bank. Moreover the Mīrzā's residence was in the walled-town (f. 110*b*) and there his son stayed 9 years after the accident. The slip did not affect the safety of the residence therefore; it may have been local to the birds' house. It will have been due to some ordinary circumstance since no cause for it is mentioned by Bābur, Ḥaidar or Abū'l-faẓl. If it had marked the crisis of the Sīr's approach, Akhsī could hardly have been described, 25 years later, as a strong fort.

Something is known of Akhsī, in the 10th, the 12th, the 15th and the 19th centuries, which testifies to sæcular decadence. Ibn Haukal and Yāqūt give the township an extent of 3 *farsākh* (12 miles), which may mean from one side to an opposite one. Yāqūt's description of it mentions four gates, each opening into well-watered lands extending a whole *farsākh*, in other words it had a ring of garden-suburb four miles wide.

Two meanings have been given to Bābur's words indicating the status of the oasis in the 15th century. They are,

[1] Bābur writes as though Akhsī had one Gate only (f. 112*b*). It is unlikely that the town had come down to having a single exit; the Gate by which he got out of Akhsī was the one of military importance because served by a draw-bridge, presumably over the ravine-moat, and perhaps not close to that bridge.

mahallāti qūrghān-dīn bīr shar'ī yurāqrāq tūshūb tūr. They have been understood as saying that the suburbs were two miles from their *urbs*. This may be right but I hesitate to accept it without pointing out that the words may mean, 'Its suburbs extend two miles farther than the walled-town.' Whichever verbal reading is correct, reveals a decayed oasis.

In the 19th century, Nalivkine and Ujfalvy describe the place then bearing the name Akhsī, as a small village, a mere winter-station, at some distance from the river's bank, that bank then protected from denudation by a sand-bank.

Three distinctly-marked stages of decadence in the oasis township are thus indicated by Yāqūt, Bābur and the two modern travellers.

It is necessary to say something further about the position of the suburbs in the 15th century. Bābur quotes as especially suitable to Akhsī, the proverbial questions, 'Where is the village?'[1] (qy. Akhsī-kīnt.) 'Where are the trees?' and these might be asked by some-one in the suburbs unable to see Akhsī or *vice versá*. But granting that there were no suburbs within two miles of the town, why had the whole inner circle, two miles of Yāqūt's four, gone out of cultivation? Erosion would have affected only land between the river and the town.

Again;—if the Sīr only were working in the 15th century to destroy a town standing on the Kāsān-water, how is it that this stream does not yet reach the Sīr?

Various ingatherings of information create the impression that failure of Kāsān-water has been the dominant factor in the loss of the Akhsī township. Such failure might be due to the general desiccation of Central Asia and also to increase of cultivation in the Kāsān-valley itself. There may have been erosion, and social and military change may have had its part, but for the loss of the oasis lands and for, as a sequel, the decay of the town, desiccation seems a sufficient cause.

[1] For mention of upper villages *see* f. 110 and note 1.

The Kāsān-water still supports an oasis on its riverain slope, the large Aūzbeg town of Tūpa-qūrghān (Town-of-the-hill), from the modern castle of which a superb view is had up the Kāsān-valley, now thickly studded with villages.[1]

B.—THE BIRDS, *QĪL QŪYIRŪGH* AND *BAGHRĪ QARĀ*.

DESCRIBING a small bird (*qūsh-qīna*), abundant in the Qarshī district (f. 49*b*), Bābur names it the *qīl-qūyirūgh*, horse-tail, and says it resembles the *bāghrī qarā*.

Later on he writes (f. 280) that the *bāghrī qarā* of India is smaller and more slender than 'those' *i.e.* of Transoxiana (f. 49*b*, n. 1), the blackness of its breast less deep, and its cry less piercing.

We have had difficulty in identifying the birds but at length conclude that the *bāghrī qarā* of Transoxiana is *Pterocles arenarius*, Pallas's black-bellied sand-grouse and that the Indian one is a smaller sand-grouse, perhaps a *Syrrhaptes*. As the *qīl qūyirūgh* resembles the other two, it may be a yet smaller *Syrrhaptes*.

Muḥ. Ṣāliḥ, writing of sport Shaibāq Khān had in Qarshī (*Shaibānī-nāma*, Vambéry, p. 192) mentions the 'Little bird (*murghak*) of Qarshī,' as on all sides making lament. The Sang-lākh[2] gives its Persian name as *khar-bala*, ass-hair, says it

[1] *Cf.* f. 114 for distances which would be useful in locating Akhsī if Bābur's *yīghāch* were not variable; Ritter, vii, 3 and 733; Réclus, vi, index *s.n.* Farghāna; Ujfalvy ii, 168, his quotation from Yāqūt and his authorities; Nalivkine's *Histoire du Khanat de Kokand*, p. 14 and p. 53; Schuyler, i, 324; Kostenko, Tables of Contents for cognate general information and i, 320, for Tāshkint; von Schwarz, index under related names, and especially p. 345 and plates; Pumpelly, p. 18 and p. 115.

[2] This Turkī-Persian Dictionary was compiled by Mīrzā Mahdī Khān, Nādir Shāh's secretary and historian, whose life of his master Sir William Jones translated into French (Rieu's Turkī Cat. p. 264*b*).

flies in large flocks and resembles the *bāghrī qarā*. Of the latter he writes as abundant in the open country and as making noise (*bāghīr*).

The Sang-lākh (f. 119) gives the earliest and most informing account we have found of the *bāghrī qarā*. Its says the bird is larger than a pigeon, marked with various colours, yellow especially, black-breasted and a dweller in the stony and waterless desert. These details are followed by a quotation from 'Alī-sher *Nawā'ī*, in which he likens his own heart to that of the bird of the desert, presumably referring to the gloom of the bird's plumage. Three synonyms are then given; Ar. *qiṭā*, one due to its cry (Meninsky); Pers. *sang-shikan*, stone-eating, (Steingass, *sang-khwāra*, stone-eating); and Turkī *bāghīr-tīlāq* which refers, I think, to its cry.

Morier (Ḥājī Bābā) in his *Second journey through Persia* (Lond. 1818, p. 181), mentions that a bird he calls the black-breasted partridge, (*i.e. Francolinus vulgaris*) is known in Turkish as *bokara kara* and in Persian as *siyāh-sīna*, both names, (he says), meaning black-breast; that it has a horse-shoe of black feathers round the forepart of the trunk, more strongly marked in the female than in the male; that they fly in flocks of which he saw immense numbers near Tabrīz (p. 283), have a soft note, inhabit the plains, and, once settled, do not run. Cock and hen alike have a small spur,—a characteristic, it may be said, identifying rather with *Francolinus vulgaris* than with *Pterocles arenarius*. Against this identification, however, is Mr. Blandford's statement that *siyāh-sīna* (Morier's *bokara kara*) is *Pterocles arenarius* (Report of the Persian Boundary Commission, ii, 271).

In Afghānistān and Bikanir, the sand-grouse is called *tūtūrak* and *boora kurra* (Jerdon, ii, 498). Scully explains *baghītāq* as *Pterocles arenarius*.

Perhaps I may mention something making me doubt whether it is correct to translate *baghrī qarā* by *black-liver* and *gorge-noir* or other names in which the same meaning is expressed. To translate thus, is to understand a Turkī noun and adjective in

Persian construction, and to make exception to the rule, amply exemplified in lists of birds, that Turkī names of birds are commonly in Turkī construction, *e.g.* *qarā bāsh* (black-head), *āq-bāsh* (white-head), *sārīgh-sūndūk* (yellow-headed wagtail). *Bāghīr* may refer to the cry of the bird. We learn from Mr. Ogilvie Grant that the Mongol name for the sand-grouse *njūpterjūn*, is derived from its cry in flight, *truck*, *truck*, and its Arabic name *qiṭā* is said by Meninsky to be derived from its cry *kaetha*, *kaetha*. Though the dissimilarity of the two cries is against taking the *njūpterjūn* and the *qiṭā* to be of one class of sand-grouse, the significance of the derivation of the names remains, and shows that there are examples in support of thinking that when a sand-grouse is known as *bāghrī qarā*, it may be so known because of its cry (*bāghir*).

The word *qarā* finds suggestive interpretation in a B. N. phrase (f. 72*b*) *Tambal-nīng qarā-sī*, Tambal's blackness, *i.e.* the dark mass of his moving men, seen at a distance. It is used also for an indefinite number, *e.g.* 'family, servants, retainers, followers, *qarā*,' and I think it may imply a massed flock.

Bābur's words (f. 280) *bāghrī-nīng qarā-sī ham kam dūr*, [its belly (lit. liver) also is less black], do not necessarily contradict the view that the word *bāghrī* in the bird's name means crying. The root *bāgh* has many and pliable derivatives; I suspect both Bābur (here) and Muḥ. Ṣāliḥ (l. c.) of ringing changes on words.

We are indebted for kind reply to our questions to Mr. Douglas Carruthers, Mr. Ogilvie Grant and to our friend, Mr. R. S. Whiteway.

C.—ON THE *GOSHA-GĪR*.

I AM indebted to my husband's examination of two Persian MSS. on archery for an explanation of the word *gosha-gīr*, in its technical sense in archery. The works consulted are the Cyclopædia of Archery (*Kulliyatu'r-rāmī* I. O. 2771) and the Archer's Guide (*Hidāyatu'r-rāmī* I. O. 2768).

It should be premised that in archery, the word *gosha* describes, in the arrow, the notch by which it grips and can be carried on the string, and, in the bow, both the tip (horn) and the notch near the tip in which the string catches. It is explained by Vullers as *cornu et crena arcûs cui immititur nervus.*

Two passages in the Cyclopædia of Archery (f. 9 and f. 36*b*) shew *gosha* as the bow-tip. One says that to bend the bow, two men must grasp the two *gosha*; the other reports a tradition that the Archangel Gabriel brought a bow having its two *gosha* (tips) made of ruby. The same book directs that the *gosha* be made of seasoned ivory, the Archer's Guide prescribing seasoned mulberry wood.

The C. of A. (f. 125*b*) says that a bowman should never be without two things, his arrows and his *gosha-gīr*. The *gosha-gīr* may be called an item of the repairing kit; it is an implement (f. 53) for making good a warped bow-tip and for holding the string into a displaced notch. It is known also as the *chaprās*, brooch or buckle, and the *kardāng*; and is said to bear these names because it fastens in the string. Its shape is that of the upper part of the Ar. letter *jīm*, two converging lines of which the lower curves slightly outward. It serves to make good a warped bow, without the use of fire and it should be kept upon the bow-tip till this has reverted to its original state. Until the warp has been straightened by the *gosha-gīr*, the bow must be kept from the action of fire because it, (composite of sinew and glutinous substance,) is of the nature of wax.

The same implement can be used to straighten the middle of the bow, the *kamān khāna*. It is then called *kar-dāng*. It can be used there on condition that there are not two *daur* (curves) in the bow. If there are two the bow cannot be repaired without fire. The *halāl daur* is said to be characteristic of the Turkish bow. There are three *daur*. I am indebted to Mr. Inigo Simon for the suggestions that *daur* in this connection means *warp* and that the three twists (*daur*) may be those of one horn (*gosha*), of the whole bow warped in one curve, and of the two horns warped in opposite directions.

Of repair to the *kamān-khāna* it is said further that if no *kardāng* be available, its work can be done by means of a stick and string, and if the damage be slight only, the bow and the string can be tightly tied together till the bow comes straight. 'And the cure is with God!'

Both manuscripts named contain much technical information. Some parts of this are included in my husband's article, *Oriental Crossbows* (A.Q.R. 1911, p. 1). Sir Ralph Payne-Gallwey's interesting book on the Cross-bow allows insight into the fine handicraft of Turkish bow-making.

D.—ON THE RESCUE PASSAGE.

I HAVE omitted from my translation an account of Bābur's rescue from expected death, although it is with the Haidarābād Codex, because closer acquaintance with its details has led both my husband and myself to judge it spurious. We had welcomed it because, being with the true Bābur-nāma text, it accredited the same account found in the Kehr-Ilminsky text, and also because, however inefficiently, it did something towards filling the gap found elsewhere within 908 AH.

It is in the Haidarābād MS. (f. 118*b*), in Kehr's MS. (p. 385), in Ilminsky's imprint (p. 144), in *Les Mémoires de Bābour* (i, 255) and with the St. P. University Codex, which is a copy of Kehr's.

On the other hand, it is not with the Elphinstone Codex (f. 89*b*); that it was not with the archetype of that codex the scribe's note shews (f. 90); it is with neither of the *Wāqi'āt-i-bāburī* (Pers. translations) nor with Leyden and Erskine's *Memoirs* (p. 122).[1]

Before giving our grounds for rejecting what has been offered to fill the gap of 908 AH. a few words must be said about the lacuna itself. Nothing indicates that Bābur left it and, since both in the Elphinstone Codex and its archetype, the sentence preceding it lacks the terminal verb, it seems due merely to loss of pages. That the loss, if any, was of early date is clear,—the Elph. MS. itself being copied not later than 1567 AD. (JRAS. 1907, p. 137).

Two known circumstances, both of earlier date than that of the Elphinstone Codex, might have led to the loss,—the first is the storm which in 935 AH. scattered Bābur's papers (f. 376*b*), the second, the vicissitudes to which Humāyūn's library was exposed in his exile.[2] Of the two the first seems the more probable cause.

The rupture of a story at a point so critical as that of Bābur's danger in Karnān would tempt to its completion; so too would wish to make good the composed part of the Bābur-nāma. Humāyūn annotated the archetype of the Elphinstone Codex a good deal but he cannot have written the Rescue passage if only because he was in a position to avoid some of its inaccuracies.

CONTEXT AND TRANSLATION OF THE RESCUE PASSAGE.

To facilitate reference, I quote the last words preceding the gap purported to be filled by the Rescue passage, from several texts;—

[1] The *Pādshāh-nāma* whose author, 'Abdu'l-hamīd, the biographer of Shāh-jahān, died in 1065 AH. (1655 AD.) mentions the existence of lacunæ in a copy of the Bābur-nāma, in the Imperial Library and allowed by his wording to be Bābur's autograph MS. (i, 42 and ii, 703).

[2] *Akbar-nāma*, Bib. Ind. ed. i, 305; H.B. i, 571.

(*a*) Elphinstone MS. f. 89*b*,—*Qūptūm. Bāgh gosha-sī-gha īrdīm. Aūzūm bīla andesha qīldīm. Dīdīm kīm kīshī agar yūz u agar mīng yāshāsā, ākhir hech* . . .

(*b*) The Ḥai. MS. (f. 118*b*) varies from the Elphinstone by omitting the word *hech* and adding *aūlmāk kīrāk*, he must die.

(*c*) Pāyanda-ḥasan's *Wāqi'āt-i-bāburī* (I. O. 215, f. 96*b*),—*Barkhwāstam u dar gosha-i bāgh raftam. Ba khūd andesha karda, guftam kah agar kase ṣad sāl yā hazār sāl 'umr dāshta bāshad, ākhir hech ast.* (It will be seen that this text has the *hech* of the Elph. MS.)

(*d*) 'Abdu'r-raḥīm's *Wāqi'āt-i-bāburī* (I. O. 217, f. 79),—*Barkhwāstam u ba gosha-i-bāgh raftam. Ba khūd andeshīdam u guftam kah agar kase ṣad sāl u agar hazār sāl 'umr bayābad ākhir* . . .

(*e*) Muḥ. *Shīrāzī*'s lith. ed. (p. 75) finishes the sentence with *ākhir khūd bāyad murd*, at last one must die,—varying as it frequently does, from both of the *Wāqi'āt*.

(*f*) Kehr's MS. (p. 383-454), Ilminsky, p. 144.—*Qūpūb bāghnīng bīr būrjī-ghā bārīb, khāṭirīm-ghā kīltūrdīm kīm agar adam yūz yīl u agar mīng yīl tīrīk būlsā, ākhir aūlmāk dīn aūzkā chāra yūq tūr.* (I rose. Having gone to a tower of the garden, I brought it to my mind that if a person be alive 100 years or a thousand years, at last he has no help other than to die.)

The Rescue passage is introduced by a Persian couplet, identified by my husband as from Niẓāmī's *Khusrau u Shīrīn*, which is as follows;—

> If you stay a hundred years, and if one year,
> Forth you must go from this heart-delighting palace.

I steadied myself for death (*qarār bīrdīm*). In that garden a stream came flowing;[1] I made ablution; I recited the prayer of two inclinations (*ra'hat*); having raised my head for silent prayer, I was making earnest petition when my eyes closed in sleep.[2] I am seeing[3] that Khwāja Yaq'ūb, the son of

---

[1] Ḥai. MS. f. 118*b*; *aūshāl bāghdā sū āqīb kīld dūr aīdī*. *Bābur-nāma*, *sū āqīb*, water flowed and *aūshal* is rare, but in the R.P. occurs 7 times.

[2] *gūzūm āwīqī-ghā bārīb tūr.* B.N. f. 117*b*, *gūzūm āwīqū-ghā bārdī.*

[3] *kūrā dūr min*, B.N. f. 83, *tūsh kūrdūm* and *tūsh kūrār min*.

Khwāja Yaḥyā and grandson of His Highness Khwāja 'Ubaidu'l-lāh, came facing me, mounted on a piebald horse, with a large company of piebald horsemen (*sic*).[1] He said: 'Lay sorrow aside! Khwāja *Aḥrār* (*i.e.* 'Ubaidu'l-lāh) has sent me to you; he said, "We, having asked help for him (*i.e.* Bābur), will seat him on the royal throne;[2] wherever difficulty befalls him, let him look towards us (lit. bring us to sight) and call us to mind; there will we be present." Now, in this hour, victory and success are on your side; lift up your head! awake!'

At that time I awoke happy, when Yūsuf and those with him[3] were giving one another advice. 'We will make a pretext to deceive; to seize and bind[4] is necessary.' Hearing these words, I said, 'Your words are of this sort, but I will see which of you will come to my presence to take me.' I was saying this when outside the garden wall[5] came the noise of approaching horsemen. Yūsuf *darogha* said, 'If we had taken you to Tambal our affairs would have gone forward. Now he has sent again many persons to seize you.' He was certain that this noise might be the footfall of the horses of those sent by Tambal. On hearing those words anxiety grew upon me; what to do I did not know. At this time those horsemen, not happening to find the garden gate, broke down the wall where it was old (and) came in. I saw (*kūrsām*, lit. might see) that Qutluq Muh. *Barlās* and Bābā-i *Parghari*, my life-devoted servants, having arrived [with], it may be, ten, fifteen, twenty persons, were approaching. Having flung themselves from their horses,[6] bent the knee from afar and showed respect, they fell at my feet. In that state (*ḥal*) such ecstasy (*ḥāl*) came over me that you might say (*goyā*) God gave me life from a new source (*bāsh*). I said, 'Seize and bind that Yūsuf *darogha* and these here (*tūrghān*) hireling mannikins.' These same mannikins had taken to flight. They (*i.e.* the rescuers), having taken them, one by one, here and there, brought them bound. I said, 'Where do you come from? How did you get news?' Qutluq Muh. *Barlās* said: 'When, having fled from Akhsī, we were separated from you in the flight, we went to Andijān when the Khāns also came to Andijān. I saw a vision that Khwāja 'Ubaidu'l-lāh said, "Bābur *pādshāh*[7] is in a village called Karnān; go and bring him, since the royal seat (*masnad*) has become his possession (*ta'alluq*)." I having seen this vision and become happy, represented (the matter) to the Elder Khān (and) the Younger Khān. I said to the Khāns, "I have five or six younger brothers (and) sons; do you add a few soldiers. I will go through the Karnān side and bring news." The Khāns said, "It occurs to our minds also that (he) may have gone that same road (?)." They appointed ten persons; they said, "Having gone in that direction (*sārī*) and made very sure, bring news. Would to God you might get true news!" We were saying this when Bābā-i *Parghārī* said, "I too will go and seek." He also having agreed with two young men, (his) younger brothers, we rode out. It is three days

---

[1] *ablaq suwār bilān*; P. *suwār* for T. *ātliq* or *ātlīq kishi*; *bilān* for B.N. *bila*, and an odd use of piebald (*ablaq*).

[2] *masnad*, B.N. *takht*, throne. *Masnad* betrays Hindūstān.

[3] *Hamrā'ilārī* (*sic*) *bir bir gā* (*sic*) *maṣlaḥat qilā dūrlār*. *Maṣlaḥat* for B.N. *kingāsh* or *kingāīsh*; *hamrāh*, companion, for *mining bila bār*, etc.

[4] *bāghlāmāq* and f. 119*b* *bāghlāghānlār*; B.N. *ālmāk* or *tūtmāq* to seize or take prisoner.

[5] *dīwār* for *tām*.

[6] f. 119, *āt-tin aūzlār-ni tāshlāb*; B.N. *tūshmāk*, dismount. *Tāshlāmaq* is not used in the sense of dismount by B.

[7] *pādshāh* so used is an anachronism (f. 215); Bābur Mīrzā would be correct.

to-day that we are on the road. Thank God! we have found you.' They said (*dīdīlār*, for *dib*). They spoke (*aitīlār*), 'Make a move! Ride off! Take these bound ones with you! To stay here is not well; Tambal has had news of your coming here; go, in whatever way, and join yourself to the Khāns!' At that time we having ridden out, moved towards Andijān. It was two days that we had eaten no food; the evening prayer had come when we found a sheep, went on, dismounted, killed, and roasted. Of that same roast we ate as much as a feast. After that we rode on, hurried forward, made a five days' journey in a day and two nights, came and entered Andijān. I saluted my uncle the Elder Khān (and) my uncle the Younger Khān, and made recital of past days. With the Khāns I spent four months. My servants, who had gone looking in every place, gathered themselves together; there were more than 300 persons. It came to my mind (*kīm*), 'How long must I wander, a vagabond (*sar-gardān*),[1] in this Farghāna country? I will make search (*ṭalab*) on every side (*dib*).' Having said, I rode out in the month of Muḥarram to seek Khurāsān, and I went out from the country of Farghāna.[2]

REASONS AGAINST THE REJECTION OF THE RESCUE PASSAGE.

Two circumstances have weight against rejecting the passage, its presence with the Ḥaidarābād Codex and its acceptance by Dr. Ilminsky and M. de Courteille.

That it is with the Codex is a matter needing consideration and this the more that it is the only extra matter there found. Not being with the Persian translations, it cannot be of early date. It seems likely to owe its place of honour to distinguished authorship and may well be one of the four portions (*juzwe*) mentioned by Jahāngīr in the Tuzūk-i-jahāngīrī,[3] as added by himself to his ancestor's book. If so, it may be mentioned, it will have been with Bābur's autograph MS. [now not to be found], from which the Ḥaidarābād Codex shews signs of being a direct copy.[4]

[The incongruity of the Rescue passage with the true text has

[1] *ẓāhirān*; B.N. *yāqin*.

[2] Ilminsky's imprint stops at *dib*; he may have taken *kim-dib* for signs of quotation merely. (This I did earlier, JRAS 1902, p. 749.)

[3] Aligarh ed. p. 52; Rogers' trs. i, 109.

[4] *Cf.* f. 63*b*, n. 3.

been indicated by foot-notes to the translation of it already given. What condemns it on historic and other grounds will follow.]

On linguistic grounds it is a strong argument in its favour that Dr. Ilminsky and M. de Courteille should have accepted it but the argument loses weight when some of the circumstances of their work are taken into account.

In the first place, it is not strictly accurate to regard Dr. Ilminsky as accepting it unquestioned, because it is covered by his depreciatory remarks, made in his preface, on Kehr's text. He, like M. de Courteille, worked with a single Turkī MS. and neither of the two ever saw a complete true text. When their source (the Kehr-Ilminsky) was able to be collated with the Elph. and Ḥai. MSS. much and singular divergence was discovered.

I venture to suggest what appears to me to explain M. de Courteille's acceptance of the Rescue passage. Down to its insertion, the Kehr-Ilminsky text is so continuously and so curiously corrupt that it seems necessary to regard it as being a re-translation into Turkī from one of the Persian translations of the *Bābur-nāma*. There being these textual defects in it, it would create on the mind of a reader initiated through it, only, in the book, an incorrect impression of Bābur's style and vocabulary, and such a reader would feel no transition when passing on from it to the Rescue passage.

In opposition to this explanation, it might be said that a wrong standard set up by the corrupt text, would or could be changed by the excellence of later parts of the Kehr-Ilminsky one. In words, this is sound, no doubt, and such reflex criticism is now easy, but more than the one defective MS. was wanted even to suggest the need of such reflex criticism. The *Bābur-nāma* is lengthy, ponderous to poise and grasp, and work on it is still tentative, even with the literary gains since the Seventies.

Few of the grounds which weigh with us for the rejection of the Rescue passage were known to Dr. Ilminsky or M. de Courteille;—the two good Codices bring each its own and varied help; Teufel's critique on the 'Fragments,' though made without acquaintance with those adjuncts as they stand in Kehr's own volume, is of much collateral value; several useful oriental histories seem not to have been available for M. de Courteille's use. I may add, for my own part, that I have the great advantage of my husband's companionship and the guidance of his wide acquaintance with related oriental books. In truth, looking at the drawbacks now removed, an earlier acceptance of the passage appears as natural as does today's rejection.

GROUNDS FOR REJECTING THE RESCUE PASSAGE.

The grounds for rejecting the passage need here little more than recapitulation from my husband's article in the JASB. 1910, p. 221, and are as follows;—

i. The passage is in neither of the *Wāqi'āt-i-bāburī.*

ii. The dreams detailed are too à propos and marvellous for credence.

iii. Khwāja Yaḥyā is not known to have had a son, named Ya'qūb.

iv. The *Bābur-nāma* does not contain the names assigned to the rescuers.

v. The Khāns were not in Andijān and Bābur did not go there.

vi. He did not set out for Khurāsān after spending 4 months with The Khāns but after Aḥmad's death (end of 909 AH.), while Maḥmud was still in Eastern Turkistān and after about a year's stay in Sūkh.

vii. The followers who gathered to him were not 'more than 300' but between 2 and 300.

viii. The '3 days,' and the 'day and two nights,' and the '5 days' journey was one of some 70 miles, and one recorded as made in far less time.

ix. The passage is singularly inadequate to fill a gap of 14 to 16 months, during which events of the first importance occurred to Bābur and to the Chaghatāī dynasty.

x. Khwāja *Aḥrārī's* promises did nothing to fulfil Bābur's wishes for 908 AH. while those of Ya'qūb for immediate victory were closely followed by defeat and exile. Bābur knew the facts; the passage cannot be his. It looks as though the writer saw Bābur in Karnān across Tīmūrid success in Hindūstān.

xi. The style and wording of the passage are not in harmony with those of the true text.

Other reasons for rejection are marked change in choice of the details chosen for commemoration, *e.g.* when Bābur mentions prayer, he does so simply; when he tells a dream, it seems a real one. The passage leaves the impression that the writer did not think in Turkī, composed in it with difficulty, and looked at life from another view-point than Bābur's.

On these various grounds, we have come to the conclusion that it is no part of the *Bābur-nāma*.